DENMARK IN PRINT AND PICTURES

WOMEN IN DENMARK
YESTERDAY AND TODAY

by Inga Dahlsgård

DET DANSKE SELSKAB

The Danish Institute for Information about Denmark
and Cultural Cooperation with other Nations
Kultorvet 2, DK–1175 Copenhagen K.

1980

Translated by
Geoffrey French

Printed in Denmark by
Krohns Bogtrykkeri, Copenhagen

Acknowledgement
The author wishes to thank professor Fridlev
Skrubbeltrang for valuable collaboration on
the chapter Country Women.

Front cover
From the Festival of Women held at the *Fælled* Park,
Copenhagen, in 1974. (Photo: Politiken)

ISBN 87-7429-036-3

Contents

Foreword

It is nearly 40 years since the Danish Institute published its first book on the status of women in Danish life, written by one of the champions of women's rights in Denmark, Aagot Lading (1909–63). When the Institute, acting jointly with the Danish Women's National Council, commissioned Inga Dahlsgård to write a new book on the same topic, reforms were in progress but the basic principles were broadly the same as those referred to in Aagot Lading's book.

However, profound changes have occurred since Inga Dahlsgård began work on the new book, and it will undoubtedly have been an exciting experience for the author to find the subject-matter of her book shifting its character continually during the course of her labours. Not only has a stream of epochmaking events and reforms, many of them of far-reaching practical effect, been flowing while Inga Dahlsgård has been at her desk: invisible changes have also been going on in the basic attitudes involved in the relationship between the sexes in Denmark.

Thus there is virtue in the misfortune that the book has taken so long in the writing, since it is now able to reflect a number of positive results stemming from the toil and struggle of generations for women's equal rights and status in the Danish community. As chairman of the Danish Government Home Economics Council and a member of numerous commissions and boards involved in the feminist cause, including the Prime Minister's Commission on Women, the Ministry of Trade's Consumers' Commission and the Monopolies Council, the author has made a notable contribution to the Danish feminist and consumer movements.

The author would be the last to declare herself satisfied with the ground won so far. She points out that women in Denmark are still not equal in practice. A smaller proportion of women than men have had real vocational training. There are still too few women in senior posts, and women are less prominent than men in public life, in politics, in business life, in science and the arts.

However, to register progress and catalogue unsolved problems is a positive and fruitful activity, for it is the prerequisite of all social advance.

Karen Ytting
President of the Danish Women's
National Council

Earliest Times: Recent Finds Yield More Knowledge

The earliest archaeological finds from the Stone Age made in the Nordic region tell us nothing about the status of women, and it is probable that the situation was not dissimilar to that prevailing among people at the food-gathering and hunting stage in later times under the same sort of climatic and geographical conditions. But there are cairns of various types from the earliest peasant culture of the New Stone Age (i.e., about 5,000 years ago) comprising either a single burial chamber or, more frequently, several. A man's grave will contain at least a flint axe, while women had their amber ornaments with them.

Passage graves replaced cairns as graves of Stone-Age farmers, and these were surrounded by a grave mound fringed in some cases with large stones at the edge of the mound. Pictures of a goddess of fertility are found on earthenware vessels and potsherds in passage graves. She is called "the great goddess" by P. V. *Glob* (b. 1911), Keeper of National Antiquities, and is characterised by a distinctive ornamentation of the eyes. She probably came to Denmark with people from regions around the Mediterranean, who also brought gold, copper and bronze. Women's ornaments predominated in passage graves, and Glob says: "In certain passage graves there is nothing else at all, which may be a sign that it was a woman who headed the clan that built the passage grave."

In Jutland there are fairly shallow barrows along the river valleys and lake shores that feature another burial custom. These are the graves of the battleaxe people, and they date from the time of the most recent passage-grave people about 4,000 years ago. The barrows generally show traces of only a

9

single interment, but in some of the later ones there is more than one body. Where simultaneity of interment can be shown, the remains found are almost always of one man and one woman, and this may possibly signify that the battleaxe people were monogamous. They were nomads, wandering about with their herds, but the cultivation of corn was not unknown to them. The battleaxe people are thought to have come from Asia as conquerors. Men's graves almost always contain a handsome battleaxe with shaft-hole, generally not of flint. Such flint axes as are found are produced by a technique quite different from that employed by the passage-grave people, and the grave goods found can include, in the case of the high-born, two circular discs of amber with convex faces, probably having symbolic and/or religious significance. The grave goods of women consist almost exclusively of amber beads which will have been worn as necklaces or hung from the ears. The battleaxe people are also called single-grave people, and Glob says of them that "a patriarchal situation therefore probably prevailed in their society, perhaps in contrast to the matriarchal situation of the passage-grave people".

The Bronze Age lasted about 1,000 years, and from this period there are graves in which solid oak coffins and special soil conditions have preserved the corpse and its apparel, the household utensils deposited, ornaments of gold and bronze, horn combs, pails of drink brewed from wheat with honey, cowberries and cranberries etc. added. At the National Museum in Copenhagen there are female remains from 3,000 years ago, and the accompanying grave goods do not suggest these women to have been less highly regarded in life than men who were buried at the same time. These are probably graves of the ruling classes, and the costly adornments and rich attire of the women may be a reflection of the prominent status of their menfolk.

10

The best known of these finds is the Maid of Egtved, sent to the National Museum in her unopened oak coffin in 1921. The well-preserved garb of this young woman raised a sensation. It consists of a short jacket with half-length sleeves and a skirt made of cords which was wound twice round the body and did not reach the knees. When these garments were exhibited in the Museum they provoked great scandal, some people believing them to be a fake because they could not imagine any young woman being clothed thus in the Bronze Age! Skirts that did not reach the knees were totally outrageous in the Denmark of the 1920s.

Numerous votive offerings from the era of the Maid of Egtved, at holy wells, in bogs and in fields, show how a goddess gradually supplanted a god. The Bronze Age can be divided into six periods according to the burial finds, and while male goods prevail exclusively in the first of these, in the next they form only 40 % and in the last period about 10 % of the whole. Moreover, in the last two periods small female figures in bronze have been found representing a naked goddess of fertility with a double collar and earrings. Her hands are positioned below the breasts and the sex is strongly indicated. There are finds from the Celtic Iron Age (i.e., from about 400 B.C.), and this goddess, *Nerthus*, testifies that women played an important role as in other primitive agricultural societies. One of the earliest written sources of Denmark's past, the "Germania" of the Roman historian *Tacitus* (98 A.D.), relates that a common characteristic of seven wild tribes is their worship of Nerthus, "that is to say, Mother Earth, and they believe that she intervenes in human affairs and comes driving round to the various tribes". The find of the magnificent Dejbjerg chariot points towards the driving goddess in the same way as other votive offerings of chariots in bogs. She is also seen, for example, driving with her team of oxen on a large bronze kettle found in North Funen and in rock carvings. A shift of religion away from Nerthus to the male god

Njord is thought to have begun in the more recent period of the Bronze Age, and this view is supported by place-name studies and rock carvings.

From the Bronze Age too come the *skåltegn*, or cup-shaped marks, consisting of rounded indentations about 2–8 cm deep and 4–6 cm wide cut into rock. Many interpretations of their meaning have been suggested, and they are found all over the world. They are known in India, for instance, where they are considered – in the northern regions even today – to be the sign of the female sex and a symbol of fertility. In Denmark they are to be seen on some of the erratic blocks of the Ice Age, on the Bornholm cliffs, on the upper sides of cairns and passage graves, and in some cases inside burial chambers where they may have been carved when new interments were being made in the Bronze Age.

The turbulent Iron Age down to the Viking era (about 800–1000 A.D.) was characterised by war, migrations and trading expeditions. The finds of male and female bog-corpses, often clad in costly and artificially-fabricated raiment, date from the earlier periods of the Iron Age – i. e., up to about 400 A.D. Some of these corpses have a noose around the neck, which may possibly signify consecration to the fertility goddess with the necklet, and the noose may have strangled a sacrificial victim. Bog-finds of pairs of necklets and in one case of no fewer than 300 bronze rings on a single victim date from the same period.

Just as in the most recent period of the Bronze Age, cremation supplanted burial at certain times in the Iron Age, so that grave finds are less common. Nevertheless there are some Iron-Age graves of both men and women with sumptuous grave goods such as imported glass and vessels, and ornaments of bronze or gold for men and women of rank. The celebrated golden horns, on one of which the name of a man is carved in runic characters, date from the late Iron Age. A gold necklet with the woman's name Lethro is from the same time. With every passing year new finds let us catch glimpses of Denmark's past. Yet archaeology has obvious limitations, and it is through written chronicles or documents that posterity is granted an insight into the life and ideas of the people.

Tacitus' account says a great deal on the subject of women and tells us that when the Germans fight, it is the family and their kinsmen, not a random mob, who form the cavalry squadron or infantry troop. "Moreover they bring their loved ones to the vicinity, and from them one hears the howling of the women and the whimpering of infants. Every man finds among the women his most precious witnesses, and it is their praise that he values most highly; for it is to the wives that they come with their wounds." And then: "There are stories to the effect that armies which had begun to waver and were about to collapse were rallied by the earnest entreaties of women, who bared their breasts to remind their menfolk of the threat of captivity – a fate which the Germans consider far more terrible and unendurable when it concerns their womenfolk. Indeed, so great is the fear they nourish that one has a better hold on tribes which have been ordered to include young women of noble birth among their hostages. They believe that women are even possessed of visionary powers of a sacred kind. Therefore they neither reject their advice nor ignore their prophecies."

On the subject of marriage Tacitus relates that it is regarded with strictness and gravity, and that nothing in the Germans' (i.e., the men's) way of life is more deserving of praise. Unlike almost all other peoples, they are content with one wife. However, there are few who have more than one, but this is attributed not to any particular amorousness but to their noble birth having caused them to receive an exceptional number of offers of marriage. It is not the woman who gives the man a dowry but the other way round; however, she does bring him a weapon. The dowry consists of oxen, a bridled horse, shield and sword. This means that she is to be the man's companion in war and danger, and she is reminded of it in this way during the wedding celebrations themselves. What the wife receives, she must later hand on to her children; eventually her daughters-in-law will receive it and pass it to the grandchildren. Tacitus also relates that sons of a sister receive as much consideration from their uncle as from their father, but also that it is a father's own sons who inherit from and succeed him, so that the matriarchal features do have their limits.

As far as the women are concerned, marriage is strictly monogamous, and if a wife is unfaithful to her husband punishment is immediate. The husband cuts his wife's hair short and strips her naked in the presence of the family, then expels her from the home and drives her through the village with a whip. Tacitus esteems the sexual morality of the Germans highly and makes allusions to the situation in Rome with regard for example to titillating plays and erotic festivals. Of young people he says: "The young men do not have any love-life until late, so that their manly vigour is not depleted. Neither is there any hurry to marry off the young girls. They possess the same youthful strength as the young men and their figures are just as erect; equals in birth and in vigour, they unite with one another, and the children inherit the rude strength of the parents."

As regards reliability we may say that archaeological finds show a considerable consistency with the text of the "Germania". There are no other sources with which to compare Tacitus' opinions, but the "Germania" is considered by scholars to be an extremely valuable written source of social history. Tacitus himself had never been in Northern Europe, but his other works are based upon primary sources. So the question is the extent to which we can take the "Germania" as applying not only to what is now north Germany but also to Denmark. A number of prominent historians believe it does, for in their accounts of the history of Denmark they cite Tacitus.

Although Tacitus generally presents the Germans in a sympathetic light, he has criticisms to offer as well. He emphasises their bellicose spirit, but this is probably in order that the Romans should not underestimate them. He speaks of their indolence too, and says that the bravest and most warlike of them do nothing at all; the supervision of house, home and land is left to the womenfolk, the aged and the weakest members of the household. He notes that the Germans keep slaves, though to a Roman this would be self-evident. His attitude to the female sex is betrayed by a remark concerning certain tribes called the Sitones who have a female ruler. "So low have they sunk," says Tacitus, "not only beneath free men but beneath the existence of slaves."

Peasants, Chieftains and Vikings

Major unified settlements did not really exist in Denmark prior to the beginning of the Christian epoch. People lived far apart from one onother and cultivated small clearings, while large areas consisted of forest, scrub or marshland. But, says the historian *Erik Arup* (1875–1951), a new technique of cultivation, probably the introduction of the wheel plough used by the Celts for centuries, made it necessary for farmers to cooperate, since several oxen – certainly eight – were required to draw a wheel plough, or any similar plough, and one man alone could not steer it. At all events there is no doubt that a large number of villages still existing were founded in the course of the centuries leading up to the Viking era.

The cooperation required included at least some element of joint cultivation of the soil, and the men of the village accordingly had to reach agreement on a variety of practical matters such as the time of ploughing, sowing, harvesting and so forth. It became necessary also to resolve differences and disputes between the inhabitants. By degrees there evolved distinctive local rules for settling such questions, and those who did not abide by the agreements had to pay fines to the rest of the village community. Disputes with the family, on the other hand, were settled as far as possible between the kinsmen, and only exceptionally did outsiders involve themselves in such affairs.

Dissension between neighbouring villages over such matters as the right to use woodland led to the division of the country into *herreder* (hundreds). Every *herred* had its *thing* or moot, where the men assembled on fixed days, heard complaints, and negotiated and determined disputes. The *thing* also became the place where important legal transactions such as transfers of landed property were effected. In addition, anyone wanting a matter brought before the *herred* could submit it via the *thing*. A man wanting to acknowledge paternity of a child born out of wedlock would do so by a legitimacy declaration. The *thing* only intervened in matters where it was strictly necessary, so that disputes over inheritance, for example, had to be settled by the family itself as far as possible. The killing by the husband of a wife and lover caught *in flagrante delicto* could only be legitimised by placing the bloody bedclothes before the *thing*.

It is not clear whether the peasants were all free proprietors, but there did exist an upper class of chiefs who became rich, possibly through trade and war, although the crucial factor in their power was the ownership of land.

Chieftains' farms were situated on river estuaries or fjords, and in contrast to the villages they each formed only a single household, with both housecarls and thralls, or slaves. Some authorities believe the slaves to have been descended from the original inhabitants from the land: at all events prisoners of war became slaves, both men and women, and it is possible that poor folk voluntarily placed themselves in bondage in order to secure their subsistence. Slaves have no rights, were attached to the land, and could be sold in the same way as cattle.

In the summertime the chief would sail away on expeditions with his housecarls in order to trade and also, especially during Viking times, to plunder and ravage. In the meantime the chief's wife was responsible for running the farm, with the slaves to help her. Her duties were wide-ranging, for she had to superintend the farming operations, with cattle, pigs, sheep and poultry, as well as managing the household, stocking up for winter, baking, brewing, spinning and weaving. She carried a vital share of the responsibility for the well-being of the vast concourse of folk assembled, in winter at least, at the chief's farm. She enjoyed a position of great esteem, and a runic stone praising a chieftain because he "was most generous with food" might more justly have honoured the wife.

It was the chieftains leading the Viking excursions who spread the Nordic people far and wide and transformed Western Europe. The earliest expeditions took place towards the close of the eighth century, and they continued for over 300 years.

Some chiefs simply sailed off in the ships to loot and plunder; several of them might join together to form larger expeditions in order to seize territory, to colonise and to settle, as occurred both in Normandy and in England. Some of the kings assembled entire fleets for warlike expeditions and territorial conquest. Trade, of course, played a part in the vigorous activities of the Nordic people during this period.

Historians in northern France already chronicled the background to all this as early as the 10th and 11th centuries. Some of these writers believed that there was overpopulation in the homelands of these Norsemen, or Normans. How far this alleged overpopulation was due to polygamy cannot be documented, and for economic reasons the latter was probably limited in scope. But that one man could have more than one wife is fully acknowledged in the Jutlandic Law of 1241, which was put into effect with the highest ecclesiastical collaboration (see page 24). Church historians found polygamy in Normandy most reprehensible. They described marriages not blessed by the church as being "according to Danish custom", and they were particularly outraged by the fact that such a marriage could be dissolved on application by the male or female partner equally. It is probable that polygamy was specially widespread among the Danes. One of the first written sources of Danish history, the writings of *Adam of Bremen*, tells us this of Svend Estridsøn and the Danes at the end of the 11th century: "The much-renowned Danish king

(1047–c. 1074) was given to excess with regard to women, which I believe was not exclusive to him, however, but characteristic of the whole nation." Moreover it was not unusual for Norsemen to have wives both abroad and at home.

There are some indications that women participated actively in the Viking expeditions. Danish legends, for example, contain accounts of a number of "shield-maids" who attired themselves in male armour to conceal their sex and performed deeds of valour. The well-preserved Viking vessel known as the Oseberg ship was found in the vicinity of Oslo Fiord in 1903 and can now be seen in a museum near Oslo. It contained the interred bodies of a woman – possibly a queen – aged about 25–30 years and an older bondswoman who had followed her mistress in death. Despite the traces of graverobbers the women were surrounded by costly grave goods: a sumptuous four-wheeled carriage, sledges, ship's equipment, household utensils, beds and bedding, horses and dogs. Of course, this does not prove that the young woman took part in expeditions, but one of the Icelandic sagas does tell of a woman who seized territory in Iceland like the "landnamsmen", or settlers. When Harald Fairhair had subjugated the whole of Norway at the end of the ninth century, she betook herself to Scotland with her father and son and all her kindred. There her father and son died, whereupon she sailed with her kindred to the Orkney Isles and there gave a granddaughter in marriage, who became the first ancestor of the earls of Orkney. She continued her travels to the Faroes, where she gave another granddaughter in marriage. Finally she sailed to Iceland, where she appropriated so much territory that the remaining granddaughters were able to marry in a manner consistent with their station as well as being able to give land to her housecarls and freedmen.

Other Icelandic legends too tell stories of selfreliant and capable women. Njal's Saga relates how a man came to Njal's farm in search of work. Njal was not at home, and the man spoke to his wife Bergthora. "Have you any say here?" he asked. "I am Njal's wife," she replied, "and I have as much say in hiring servants as he." When Njal returned home he asked who the man was. "He is one of your servants," replied Bergthora, "I engaged him." It was also Bergthora who, when Njal's enemies had set fire to the farmstead, wanted to remain and allow herself to be burned with her husband. "I was given to Njal in marriage when young, and I have promised him that we would share the same fate."

The brief texts on runic stones likewise tell us something about women. Wives set up stones for their husbands, husbands for their wives, sons for their mothers as well as their fathers, mothers for their sons. Inscriptions such as the following occur: "Tore, brother of Enråde, raised this stone to his mother and sister, two good women, his mother's death is the worst of misfortunes for the son", "Asfrid made this in remembrance of king Sigtrygg, son of herself and Gnupa", "Ragnhild, sister of Ulv, set this stone and made this mound and stone–setting to Gunnulv, her husband . . .", "Asser the *landhyrd* (i. e., the steward of a chieftain's farm), son of Fogger, raised these runes to his queen (i. e., wife) Gryd".

There have been differences of opinion over the inscription on the smaller of the two celebrated runic stones of Jelling. It says: "*Gorm*, king (c. 940) made this in remembrance of *Tyra* his wife, Denmark's Ornament." The question is whether "Denmark's Ornament" refers to Gorm or to Tyra, and the religious chronicler *Saxo*, who wrote his great work on "The Exploits of the Danes" a couple of hundred years later, says that it was Tyra who strengthened the southern frontier of Denmark. Saxo's contemporary *Svend Aggesøn*, a well-read and learned man regarded as the first true Danish historical writer, who served as a housecarl to several kings, held the same opinion. He tells of queen Tyra's "splendid power", which protected the Danes against the fury of the Germans and earned her the name of "Denmark's Ornament".

Aggesøn also tells an interesting story of how the German emperor, seeking to obtain hegemony over Denmark, paid court to Tyra and endeavoured to persuade her to desert Gorm and become his wife. But she was crafty and gave a procrastinating answer to the effect that before she could leave her husband she would have to gather together sufficient money to purchase her release from her ignominious situation. In this way she gained time, which she used in order to secure the southern frontier of her country, so that when the emperor's representatives came to collect her they were met with a haughty refusal, for now the danger of conquest had been averted. There are other indications too that it was really Tyra who built up Denmark's power. Danes are taught at school to call Gorm *den gamle* ("the Old Man"), but the nickname given him in earlier ages was *den løghe*, which means "the Sluggish".

We have no reliable knowledge of the status of women in those days, but *Al Gazal*, an Arab poet who died in 860 A.D., has written about the journeys he undertook as the envoy of a caliph. He visited an unnamed Danish king, and he recounts in detail how he became fascinated by the queen and sought to win her favour, "and I obtained more from her than I had dared to hope". He came to the queen so often that he was afraid there would be trouble, but the queen said: "Such things are unknown with us, and there is no jealousy. Our women are with their husbands entirely by their own wish. The woman remains with him as long as it pleases her, and she leaves him when she is tired of their life together." Al Gazal goes on to say that before Christianity became widespread, no woman was unattainable to a free man, but she became dishonoured if she had a liaison with a slave or with a man of very low birth. This chimes well with the laws of the legendary king Frode, under which a free woman having sexual intercourse with a slave lost her freedom. At the end of the 12th century Adam of Bremen relates that women guilty of fornication were sold forthwith. Ancient Danish law consistently applied the rule that a child's status depended upon the mother's, and this was likewise adhered to if the father owned its mother. In other words, the mother had to be freed in order to make the child free. If a boundswoman had a child it belonged to whoever owned the mother.

It is probable that women of chieftain descent had the right to inherit land but that otherwise women could not inherit. Tradition has it that *Sweyn Forkbeard*, king of Denmark around the end of the first millenium A.D., and a great warrior who numbered the conquest of all England among his exploits, was kidnapped and taken to Jomsborg, a fortress founded by his father, probably on the estuary of the Oder. The Jomsvikings holding him demanded three times Sweyn's weight in precious metals in return for his release. The men were unable to raise the amount alone, and the women of Denmark therefore gave their ornaments and jewels to make up the weight of the ransom. As a mark of his gratitude, Sweyn Forkbeard is said to have granted the right of inheritance to women, allowing them to inherit half as much as the nearest male relative. At all events, the latter was the rule of inheritance for centuries, and not until 1845 was any kind of change made in it.

Christianity and Daily Life

Christianity spread only slowly in the Nordic lands. The earliest missionary, a Frankish monk named *Ansgar*, came to Denmark in 826, and little by little the old deities of Tor, Odin and Frey were ousted. On the great stone of Jelling king Harald relates that he converted Denmark to Christianity, and in the period from about 960 to 1060 wooden churches by the hundred were built in villages all over the country.

The new religion changed the situation of the individual with regard to many aspects of daily life. The church demanded continual participation in religious services, and it forbade the eating of meat on Fridays and prior to the great church festivals, including the 40 days before Easter. It also desired to regulate and intervene in the private lives of individuals, and here it met with resistance. The church's teaching that the supreme human virtue was total sexual abstinence evoked no response, not even from Danish priests, who wanted to marry and have children like other men. The church did not succeed in appropriating marriage, although church weddings were instituted so that people strongly seized by the new faith could enter upon matrimony with the church's blessing. Right through to the Reformation the mutual pledges of a man and woman, their betrothal or engagement, was regarded as equivalent to a marriage contract and was often accompanied by a wedding feast. The Marriage Ordinance of 1582 attempted to make a church wedding a condition of valid marriage, but despite this the peasantry continued for a couple of hundred years to marry according to the ancient custom of betrothal followed by intercourse. Not until 1799 did a church wedding become the only recognised form of marriage.

A wide measure of freedom in sexual matter long prevailed in Denmark, although the church gained much support for the view that a sexual connection between one man and one woman – monogamy – was the only permissible relationship. But in the Jutlandic Law of 1241, compiled by the wise old bishop *Gunner* of Viborg at the desire of king *Valdemar Sejr*, concubinage – the keeping of an illicit partner – was fully recognised. It says: "If a man have a concubine in his house and do openly sleep with her, and she have lock and key and do openly seek her food and drink from him for three winters, then shall she be a lawful spouse and true wife." And later: "The father shall bring his bastard to the *thing* and register it and proclaim that it is his child. Whatsoever he will give it, he shall deed to it. If he acknowledge paternity and do not deed to it, then it shall take a half portion with the children of his lawful spouse. If there be no children of a lawful spouse, then a registered bastard shall inherit fully from his father."

The church fought against the exposure of infants, which had been practised from time immemorial in periods when crop failure and therefore famine and distress had forced people to rid themselves of their newly-born, or when the number of children in the family had become too large for all the mouths to be fed. Families got rid of deformed children in the same way, for it was impossible to accept such a burden under the primitive conditions of life then prevailing. But the church condemned exposure and other forms of infanticide as sin, for it took the view that every new-born child had a soul that must be brought within the kingdom of God as swiftly as possible through baptism. The Gotlandic Law of the late 13th century says that "... every child born in our land shall be nurtured and not cast out. Every woman shall make room in her bed when she is in labour and shall call two female wit-

24

nesses, viz., the midwife and a neighbour, who shall testify that the child was stillborn if it is dead and that her hands did not help in this." The church strongly condemned concealment of childbirth, and a woman who gave birth and slew her child committed an unforgivable sin. Poor, single and secretly pregnant women were placed in a more wretched position than before, for ever since the time of the apostle *Paul* the church had regarded sexuality as wicked. An unmarried mother had committed a sin, and as Erik Arup says in his history of Denmark (1925), "it was Christianity that first brought sin into the Danish consciousness". She could be punished through exclusion from the church and later through public penance, i.e., acknowledgement of her guilt before the entire congregation and the imposition of acts of penance. For a poor woman this would mean exclusion from the community and thus isolation.

The Roman church gradually became very impatient and dissatisfied with the failure of Danish priests to comply with its requirement that they should remain unmarried, and in 1117 pope *Paschal II* sent a letter to the Danish king enjoining strict priestly celibacy, without any apparent result. Some years later Zealand peasants and chiefs actually founded a movement against married priests and demanded that they should put away their wives. Some of the priests who resisted were maimed or killed, and others fled. But the bishops endeavoured to help their priests and poured oil on the troubled waters, so that *Eskil*, archbishop of Lund, was able to continue living in wedlock and acknowledged both children and grandchildren. Many actions were launched over the years to get priests to live in sexual abstinence, but although Catholicism held sway in Denmark for about 600 years, it never did succeed in effectively enforcing celibacy. Even priests in religious houses, who were subject to mutual supervision, had children, while a priest outside the religious houses would have a housekeeper, known as a *deje*, and she was often in fact his wife. Throughout the Middle Ages, history tells us of both sons and daughters of priests.

Under Jutlandic Law, which prevailed until the introduction of the Danish Law of 1683, there are a number of rules offering enlightenment on the legal status of women during the Middle Ages. This law made the father the guardian of an unmarried woman, with either a brother or the nearest male relative as his deputy or successor. The father's family was nearer than the mother's. If the family prevented a woman from marrying because of her fortune, she could appeal to the king, and an adult female over 18 or a widow had the right to go to the *thing* and demand her guardian's permission to marry. But the guardian's authority was limited and it was possible to marry even without his consent. Both spinsters and widows had to have guardians, and a man who wanted to marry had to approach the guardian, but the woman herself had the last word. The property laws were such that a spinster was unable to sell inherited land unless she was so poor that it was necessary for her subsistence; but in such a case she had to take the advice of her relatives and could only sell her land a little at a time.

When a man brought his wife to his parents' house, and her property was not included in the joint estate, then in the event of his death she could not take away with her more than she had contributed in the first place. Moreover it seems as though everything except the inherited land of the spouses generally became common property in those days. If a wife was pregnant when her husband died, she was allowed to continue in undivided possession of the estate until after the birth of the child and was entitled to keep her children, but if she remarried the guardian took custody of the children unless they were infants. Thus the father's family had clear priority over the mother's, contrary perhaps to what had been the case earlier. Names indicating this are those of king

Svend Estridsøn († 1074 or 1076) and *Peder* and *Jørgen Bodil-søn*, two Zealand chiefs who lived in the 12th century.

In cases where one of the spouses of a childless marriage died, the estate was divided into two equal portions, the survivor receiving one and the other going to the heirs of the deceased. If there were children, the survivor inherited a portion equivalent to the children's but subject to complex rules according to whether it was the mother or the father who survived. However, there was no great difference between man and woman. Generally speaking, Jutlandic Law and the other Danish provincial legal codes (the Zealand and Skåne codes) exhibited a fairly reasonable attitude towards women, although they did take special steps to safeguard the family interest in holding landed estates together and in that connection neglected women's interests somewhat.

Moreover, Jutlandic Law contained a special rule not found in the other provincial legal codes. This concerned the right of the male spouse to chastise his wife, whom he was permitted to punish "with a staff or 'vaand' (a thin stick) but not with weapons". These were harsh times, and this rule leaves no doubt of the subordinate status of women despite the stipulation "not with weapons". While those women who owned property of some kind (which meant that they belonged to a powerful family) doubtless had rights, the situation of every woman in Jutland and Funen in relation to her husband was that the law specifically directed how he might beat her.

Some folk-songs mention the daily round of women and refer to food, slaughtering, beer, spinning and weaving, berry-gathering and so forth – all the activities falling under their jurisdiction: one song records the tale of a maiden, skilled in rustic pursuits, who rides to the king at the *thing* and demands to be married, as is permitted under the provincial laws if the family place obstacles in the way.

The song dealing with the death of queen *Dagmar* (at the beginning of the 13th century) is very dramatic. It relates how she is in labour and sends for little Kirsten, who is skilled in medicine. The latter has to deliver the queen of her child by what we call a Caesarian operation:

"We have found a son today,

"We have cut him from the side of Dagmar."

Women had always taken care of the sick and injured. Anyone reading about the past will now and then come across such references as the report of women tending the wounded at the battle of Stiklestad in Norway (1031). Much of the care of the sick was gradually taken over by the convents and monasteries, and indeed a considerable hospital system was built up during the Middle Ages, with St. Jørgensgårde (St. George's Courts) looking after lepers and houses of the Holy Spirit handling those suffering from other ailments.

The greatest name among Danish women of this period is that of queen *Margrethe* (1353–1412). She was the daughter of king *Valdemar "Atterdag"*, and when he died in 1375, her son who succeeded him was still under age. Margrethe ruled Denmark on her son's behalf until 1387, when he died. Her husband, king Håkon of Norway, had already passed away seven years before, and she had taken over the government of that country too. Denmark's worst enemies at that time were the German Hanse towns, to which a number of the castles of Skåne were in pawn. Margrethe secured the return of the castles: she also arrived at an acceptable accommodation with the counts of Holstein, who had likewise been a thorn in Denmark's flesh. When she had ruled Denmark for 14 years a faction of the Swedish nobility offered her the Swedish throne if she would help them to get rid of their German king. When this had been accomplished, the three Nordic lands became united by the Kalmar Union in 1397. Margrethe's goal was a strong, peaceful kingdom, and her laws sought, to an extent greater than was customary in that age, to ensure tranquillity and order to protect the weak. She may be adjudged a great political talent, displaying both vigour in action and, when necessary, moderation. But she by no means lacked toughness, especially towards her greedy vassals. Her successors totally failed to measure up to her standards, and the Union ultimately collapsed in 1523. Denmark-Norway and Sweden were enemies for almost the whole of the next two centuries.

One place where medieval townspeople, both men and women, could meet for mutual enjoyment was the *badstue*, a modernised but generally segregated version of which is known today in English-speaking countries under its Finnish name of *sauna*. It is not certain whether Danish villages or farms likewise had *badstuer*, but in Norway they existed on the farms at least, and in Finland a notable *badstue* tradition still survives and flourishes. In the small medieval villages that grew up around trading-points in the 12th and 13th centuries, special buildings were fitted out as sauna-baths. Hot steam was obtained by pouring water over stones heated to a high temperature, and the steam gave the patrons a sense of both well-being and cleanliness. The sauna offered numerous other facilities, such as shaving, hairdressing and beard-trimming by a barber. He could also perform cupping, which was intended to have a preventive effect against illness, and he knew the art of bleeding. But the sauna also functioned as a tavern, where food was served and a great deal of beer drunk. The sauna was a popular recreation which did not enjoy the highest of reputations. When at the beginning of the 16th century "the French sickness", also known as "the pox" (i.e., syphilis), spread in epidemic proportions all over Europe after the discovery of America, it became necessary to close the public saunas; although nothing was known at that time of bacteria as a source of infection it was nevertheless suspected that diseases could be disseminated through personal contact.

Throughout the Middle Ages and even beyond, the associations of merchants and artisans known as the guilds and livery companies played a role in promoting solidarity among the various occupations. The aim was primarily professional, and artisans kept an eye on one another's prices and quality, and also watched to make sure that non-members did not dabble in the trade. There were rules governing such matters as the number of journeymen a master might have; internal disputes were settled; guild brothers protected and helped each other when necessary; feasts were held. The church tried to combat the guilds, partly because of their extravagant wedding-feasts, and the government tried to break their monopolies; nevertheless they survived, though with different functions down the ages. Both guild brothers and guild sisters are mentioned in guild and livery company statutes, and a widow could carry on her deceased husband's trade as long as she refrained from remarriage and remained honest. An impression of the forthright tone used by the Copenhagen citizenry among themselves in the middle of the 15th century is afforded by the statutes of the Danish Company. The latter was an association of merchants and artisans, and at that time conviviality had supplanted its more serious purposes. "A brother who makes water within the guild premises shall give a barrel of ale; and wax to the value of two marks if he does it within the doors of the hall." And later: "A brother who speaks indecently to maidens or ladies or behaves indecently in the guild house, or performs indecently with his arse, shall be fined one barrel of ale." It is probable that fines of ale of which everyone partook were more popular than fines of wax, for the latter was used for making altar candles.

The Reformation, Its Oppression of Women and Its Witch-Hunts

The Catholic church had venerated the Virgin Mary as the one human being who had attained the highest perfection, and this was certainly not without an impact on the medieval attitude to women, even though men enjoyed a superior position in society. The Renaissance, with its humanism and individualism, its patrons of the arts among great merchant princes, its emancipated and learned women, but also its cruelty, did doubtless exert some influence upon the upper classes of the Nordic countries but not upon the populace at large.

Yet, the triumph of the Reformation was accompanied by profound changes in many aspects of social life, and not least in the view taken of Woman and Man. *Luther* vigorously asserted the superiority of the male, supported by the words of Scripture: "God created man before woman; therefore it is God's will that the man shall have authority over the woman and be her lord." Furthermore, by extolling marriage unreservedly, the former munk signalled a crucial break with the ascetic ideals of the Catholic church. Not to be married now became a positively inferior condition. Luther believed it was a woman's task to bear children, to gratify her husband and to exercise mercy. Women had been given large hips and a broad posterior in order to remain at home, sit still and look after the house. It was a man's duty and responsibility, for which he was accountable before God, to guide and govern her, for she herself lacked both strength and intellect to this end.

Widows and widowers were now to remarry as quickly as possible and beget children. At the same time, there was a

31

change in the relatively lenient medieval attitude towards breaches of the rules of sexual conduct. Adultery, for example, now came to be regarded as the work of the Devil. Thus, the Copenhagen Ordinance of Christian III stipulated that a husband guilty of adultery should be beheaded and a wife similarly guilty was to be tied in a sack and drowned. Similar rules applied if one of the parties was unmarried. Unmarried mothers were to be whipped at the public whipping-post, exhibited naked before the church door and then expelled from the town. Some towns actually subjected all the girls to lactation tests to discover which of them were pregnant or had given birth so that they could be punished. On top of this there was the church's excommunication of innocent "illegitimate" children, towards whom both the church and others nourished an intense ill-will. Society gradually adopted a calmer attitude after these criminal excesses, but condemnation of unmarried mothers continued well into the 20th century whereas immoral behaviour on the part of a man was not viewed with nearly the same gravity. It is probable that in country districts among the peasantry severe attitudes to sexual morality and harsh punishments for transgressions never entirely won the day.

Witch trials began soon after the Reformation, and the first two women to be burned in Denmark went to the stake on the island of Møn in 1540. The Catholic church had associated impurity and sin with the relationship between man and woman. Woman was man's great temptation, and since according to God's Holy Word the Devil was the cause of all sin, the belief prevailed that women were particularly liable to fall into his clutches. The intense zeal of newly-converted Reformers led to increased belief in the Devil and his power. Witch-hunts, however, raged in all Europe following pope Innocent VIII's bull of 1484.

In Denmark the bishop of Zealand took a leading part in

Cup-shaped marks outlined in chalk on stone, found in Jutland. The cup-shaped mark has been variously interpreted: e. g. as a grave-mound map, and as the imprint of troll fingers.

Bog-finds: (Left) More than 300 bronze rings sacrificed to the fertility goddess. (Right) One of the small fertility goddesses with a double collar around the neck. (Photos: National Museum).

Accurate reconstruction of the Maid of Egtved's attire found in a Bronze-Age grave in Jutland in 1921. Her short corded skirt provoked a furore among both archaeologists and the general public. Other finds show how widespread similar skirts were in both the earlier and the later Bronze Age. (Photo: Inga Aistrup).

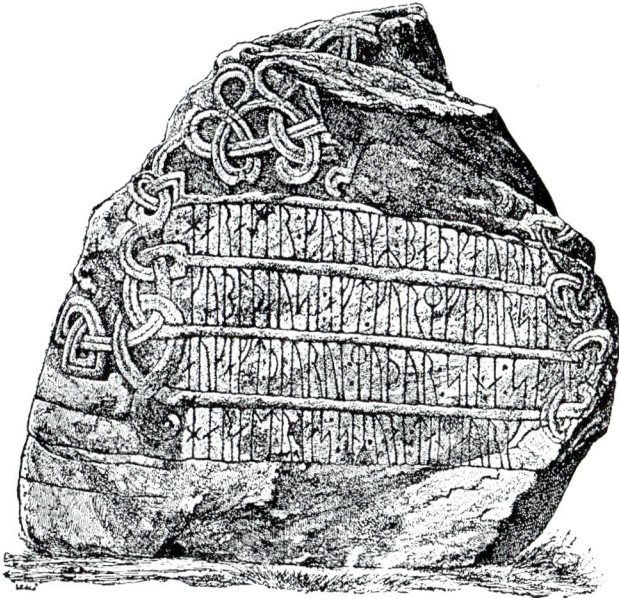

On the great sacrificial vessel from Gundestrup bog there are gods and goddesses – on one of the exterior plates (to the left in the picture) there is a love goddess, symbolised by the bird held in her hand. A handmaiden is plaiting her hair, while another woman is seated at her elbow. (Photo: National Museum).

Runic stones likewise tell us something about women. The larger of the two stones of Jelling (in the picture) was raised by King Harald Bluetooth (940–85) to his father, Gorm, and Tyra, his mother.

Persecution of witches raged all over Europe from the beginning of the 16th century and reached Denmark shortly after the Reformation. Women were considered to be in league with the Devil, as is evidenced by frescoes from the Catholic era.
Above: The Devil writing down women's gossip. Fanefjord church, 1475–1525. Below: A woman riding backwards on the Devil. Åstrup church, 1475–1500. (Photos: National Museum).

the hunting of witches and urged church congregations to keep a careful watch lest there should be a witch among them. Idle gossip, thoughtless remarks or tragic circumstances brought innocent women and some men under the accusation of having had intercourse with the Devil and practised sorcery. After trials in which interrogations were conducted under torture, many yielded and confessed simply to avoid pain. This provides the explanation of such mass burnings as occurrred when "recently in Als and its vicinity 52 sorceresses were burned".

Witch-burnings went on for over 150 years in Denmark, and not only women but some men too were accused of having, with the devil's help, put "the evil eye" on people to make them ill, of having bewitched cattle and in general of being in the Devil's power. Some of those accused appealed to the king and protested their innocence. In one such case in 1558 the burgomaster and council of Rudkøbing were ordered "to restore Gertrud Rasmussen as a Christian woman", and a number of other such instances are known.

In 1576 a change of legal practice was introduced whereby all cases of witchcraft were to be tried by a *thing*, not by courts sitting with a jury. The reason for this was that it could often be shown that innocent people had gone to the stake. The new rule brought some order into the situation.

A local squire in Djursland in the 1680s conducted an energetic witch-hunt which spread to the neighbouring districts, and a number of women were condemned to the stake. This attracted notice in Copenhagen, and the executioner was ordered to explain whether he had induced the women to confess by using torture, such as dripping burning brimstone on their breasts, putting them to the rack or inflicting pain in some other manner. The executioner had to admit that such had been the case. He had availed himself particularly of the "water test", which consisted of tying up the women and throwing them into the water: if they were innocent they sank and if guilty they floated. After this case it was decided that in future no witch was to be burnt before the supreme court had considered her case.

The intensity with which belief in witches, wizards and the Devil persisted is illustrated by the Danish Law of 1683 ruling that any sorcerer or sorceress having forsworn God and given himself or herself to the Devil was to be burned alive: this rule of law was in force until 1866.

But the real turning-point in the witch trials came with the Thisted case in the 1690s. A girl had suffered for a considerable time from a strange illness, and she came to be regarded as possessed of the Devil. Several priests attempted to exorcise her, but in 1695 her condition deteriorated, and other girls in the village displayed the same symptoms. A local priest at once decided that the girl was possessed of the Devil, and she confessed soon afterwards. Prayers were said and hymns sung over her and the other girls, and they were exhibited in the church, where they enacted extraordinary scenes before the congregation. But the Devil was undaunted, and still more girls became possessed. At last the guilty witches were identified and accused: their deaths at the stake seemed certain. But now the bishop of Ålborg intervened and set up a commission, which condemned the possessed girls as imposters, sentenced some of them to be beheaded, exonerated the alleged witch, and unfrocked the priest involved. The case came before the supreme court, which passed much more lenient sentences, none of them capital. There were even certain of the judges who believed that the root cause was really an illness. From that time on the courts no longer accepted tales of large-scale possession by demons or witches, and proceedings against witches quickly vanished from the courts, although the peasantry continued to believe in witches and took matters into their own hands.

Thus in the 18th century, for example, a goodly number of old women were beaten until the blood flowed, for according

34

to peasant superstition a witch's power could be broken in this way. As late as 1722 a mob of peasants burned a woman whom they suspected of having bewitched their children and livestock. The wretched woman was tied to a post in her house, which was then set on fire. After the trial that followed this crime the two chief culprits were sentenced to be beheaded and the rest sent to prison. The last witch-murder in Denmark took place in 1800, the victim being an 82 year-old widow who earned her living by begging. She came unsuspecting to a house where an itinerant "wise woman" was holding forth: there she was attacked and mauled until she was dead. The "wise woman" had previously said that she would be able to cure witchcraft if she could only get hold of the witch. For her deed she was condemned to beheading, while the men who had helped her merely received a few months in prison on the ground that they had acted out of fear of her. The last time an alleged witch was physically mistreated was in 1897, but as late as 1937 a woman was accused of being a witch.

The closure of monasteries accompanying the Reformation brought considerable problems for middle-aged and elderly spinsters without fortune or family, who now no longer had a place of refuge and who had no opportunity or desire to marry. Noble families were exceedingly displeased that their unmarried daughters could no longer enter a convent and be supported there. It was in their interest to keep their estates in as few hands as possible, and they generally regarded with misgivings their daughters' marriage, especially if it was below their rank. In order that land should not be disseminated too widely by means of the now so divinely ordained institution of marriage a law was enacted in 1547 providing that a noblewoman who married an unfree man, i. e., a commoner, must sell her land forthwith to someone of free birth. Lutheran retreat houses for noblewomen were also established to get these troublesome spinsters out of the way. Once they were safely immured in the home the inheritance problem was solved too, for a woman once received into a home could not inherit.

These partly secular homes for ladies caused a good deal of trouble as their inmates tended to be motivated by the desire not to serve God but to find subsistence. The ladies were accused of "frequenting loose company", and in 1565 the abbess of Maribo was commanded by royal charter to ensure that they led "a Christian and modest life, shunning all loose living and vice". Nevertheless, pastor Sadolin of Toreby, son of the bishop of Odense, had to be dismissed for having had sexual relations with one of the ladies of the home in Maribo.

A special practice associated with the appointment of clergymen evolved after the Reformation when it became customary for the applicant for an incumbency to have to marry his predecessor's widow in order that she and any children should be supported. Local authorities were very interested in cheap arrangements: however, appointments had to be confirmed by the king. This procedure could lead to some quite extraordinary situations. For instance, six priests succeeded one another in a minor Zealand parish during the 17th century. When priest no. 1 died, his widow married no. 2, who also died, the widow then marrying no. 3, who died likewise. It was then the turn of no. 4, but during this marriage it was the widow who died, whereupon no. 4 remarried. The latter's widow managed to marry nos. 5 and 6. Although this special form of female succession led to wide age-differences between the spouses, many of these marriages are reported to have been happy, though there were also priests who kicked against having to marry their predecessors' widows. One of them set these conditions: he would eat alone, sleep alone and not be contradicted by his wife. But she was quick of tongue and retorted that when she and her children had eaten, he could have the leavings, and that if he slept alone, then she would sleep with the schoolmaster. Finally, she would keep quiet one day, and on the next it would be his turn to be silent. They did marry; they were happy; but it was she who wore the trousers.

Not all priests were satisfied with their wives, of course. As late as the 18th century one of them complained about the way in which his wife treated him, with "slaps on the mouth, beatings and curses". He felt it embarrassing to come to church with a scratched face and swollen eyes. But many examples can be cited of priests' wives being similarly brow-beaten, and a good number of cases ended up with priests being dismissed for cruelty to their wives.

These continually renewed priestly marriages are perhaps especially striking because of their particular economic background, but the situation was somewhat similar among the other social classes.

One consequence of the new glorification of marriage was masses of children, while at the same time infant and child mortality was very high, the latter, however, being nothing new. All the sources suggest that prior to 1800 average life expectancy – i.e., the average number of years for which a new-born child could be expected to survive – was just over 30 years, unless catastrophes such as wars, great epidemics or famines over a protracted period reduced it even further.

Absolutism and Its Interference in Private Life

Denmark diminished in size after Sweden's conquest of Skåne, Blekinge and Bohuslen during the wars of 1657–60, and it was Dutch fears that Sweden would now become the dominant Baltic power controlling the Cattegat, the Sound and the Belts that prevented Denmark itself from being subjugated. A further contributory factor, however, was the great exertions of the people of Copenhagen in defending their city. Citizens and clergy were both indignant in the extreme over the vacillating and haughty conduct of the nobility during the war, and in this situation king *Frederik III* (1648–70) was able in 1660 to make himself absolute hereditary ruler of Denmark-Norway. The constitution then introduced was the most arbitrary in Western Europe in terms of law, but in comparison with other absolute states the government was actually relatively mild.

The new government brought interventions in many areas of private life, firstly by means of edicts and ordinances and secondly, more particularly, through the *Danish Law of Christian V* of 1683. This supplanted the ancient provincial legal codes, so that the nation was placed under a common system of law.

According to the latter all women were minors. However, widows were regarded as legal adults, but they had to have a guardian who could sign all major legal documents jointly with them and give them advice. Widows could themselves choose and dismiss their legal guardians. Unmarried women and married women were minors, but whereas a married woman remained in this situation it was possible for an unmarried woman owning, for example, a farm or carrying on a business, by concession to be regarded as a minor under trustee supervision. In exceptional cases she might be granted complete legal authority.

The rules of inheritance under Danish Law, like those of provincial law, gave a man double the inheritance of an equally closely related woman. However, parents could make a will dividing their estates equally between daughters and sons. The status of married women suffered a diminution when their right to retain inherited land as freeholders was withdrawn and inherited land became part of the spouses' common property, over which the husband had disposal. However, a married woman could establish a marriage settlement and in that way continue to own land that she might have inherited. A rule remained in force from earlier times whereby a childless wife was entitled, without her husband's permission, to bequeath half her portion of the common property for church purposes. The husband's permission was required if there were children of the marriage. But this rule had been retained more in the interests of the church than of women.

In addition, a change of usage with regard to names occurred without any legislation. Whereas the situation previously had been that a woman continued to bear her family name on marriage, it now became the custom for her to take her husband's name. But it was a long time before this practice established itself, and instances are known well into the 18th century of women who bore their own family names after marriage. This change of custom with regard to names may be regarded as a reflection of the restrictions imposed by absolutism both juridically and socially upon the independence and legal competence of married women. A woman was also excluded in principle from appealing to the newly-established supreme court unless the case concerned her own, her husband's or the children's life and honour.

Danish Law changed the husband's right of chastisement

by doing away with the rule of Jutlandic Law entitling the husband to beat his wife with "staff or vaand", but it introduced rules of domestic discipline to which both children and servants were subject. The children's duty to honour and obey their parents was sternly enjoined.

Children who were disobedient to their parents could lose their inheritance, and if a son cursed his parents or spoke to them "shamelessly" he could be put to hard labour for life in Bremerholm, the government shipyard and prison. For similar offences a daughter could be sent to the *Spindehus*, a prison for women. An ordinance of 1708 empowered parents to place vicious and disobedient sons in that section of the *Børnehus* ("children's home") known as the *Rasphus* to be disciplined. However, the poor law authorities had to investigate the reasons so as to ensure that the matter was not one of pure malice on the part of the parents; also, parents who could afford it had to pay for the child's admission. To what extent this form of punishment of children was actually practised is unknown, but the mere fact that the various institutions had a limited number of places available (400 in all at the *Børnehus*) and had numerous other tasks to perform as well suggests that the numbers cannot have been large. But both children and servants were thrashed by their fathers or masters, as many witnesses attested, and despite the fact that the law no longer gave husbands the right to beat their wives, witnesses in cases before matrimonial (ecclesiastical) courts testify that it did take place, and it was by no means uncommon for a wife to go to the court in matters of this type, especially in an age when divorce was unobtainable.

It was typical of absolutism that people's private lives were subject to interference if, for example, the government believed that individuals were squandering their fortunes by extravagance. Thus, there were numerous regulations aimed at preventing lavish celebrations of births. Danish Law enjoined clergymen to urge women in confinement to remain indoors for five or six weeks after the birth, and in the same year that the Law was enacted a special ordinance had laid down that word of a birth was to be sent only to parents, children and siblings, and that no extra help was to be brought in to assist in the entertainment of callers offering congratulations. Of course it was difficult to enforce rules of this kind, and the ancient custom of sending food to women in confinement persisted despite prohibitions in many ordinances, as did the rush of callers, who had to be entertained with coffee, tea, chocolate, wine and jam.

The first time the woman in confinement came to church after the birth, she had to be "churched" by the pastor, which meant that he met her at the church door with words of admonition: only then could she go into the church and take her place. An offering was made to the pastor at the same time, and a not inconsiderable proportion of his modest income came from this source. Danish Law said that churching was to take place wherever "it has hitherto been customary". There was resistance against the practice in the towns, and officers' wives considered themselves excused from it, while in some places even the wives of horse-troopers and dragoons evaded churching. An edict was promulgated in 1748 giving all wives whose husbands were of a certain rank permission to be excused from the ceremony, but they were, nevertheless, to pay some kind of offering to the pastor. This provoked a vast flood of petitions to be excused on various grounds – cold churches, the wife's state of health and so forth. Churching was accordingly done away with entirely in 1754 and now took place only on request, yet the pastor was still to give admonitions and express good wishes from the pulpit the first time a woman came to church after giving birth, and an offering was to be made. The tradition persisted for a long time in many country districts, as is shown by *Thit Jensen's* story (see pp. 177 ff.) in her book of reminiscenses *Hvorfra? Hvorhen?* (Whence? Whither?), of how as a little girl she

41

had watched her mother waiting at the church door. Thit had felt it to be unseemly and degrading. This was in the 1880s.

The legislation of the Reformation epoch had made sexual intercourse outside marriage (fornication) a crime (see page 25), and Danish Law also had strict rules on the matter. Fines could be imposed, and in the event of repetition even the death penalty "or other forms of supreme punishment as an example and deterrent to others". Adultery, meaning sexual intercourse with another person's spouse, was punished by a fine on the first occasion and banishment on the second, but a busband found guilty for a third time was beheaded and the guilty wife put in a sack and drowned. Yet, all were not equal before the law under absolutism. Danish Law conferred upon the king's children conceived of women other than the queen one of the highest social rankings immediately after the princes, and it laid down that they could not be prosecuted before any judge other than one appointed by the king. Kings of Denmark-Norway were hardly more immoral than the monarchs of other countries but perhaps there was more openness about their relationships. Particular indignation was aroused when kings married in church "with the left hand" – i.e., morganatically – and a number of them did so. Even though the law said nothing of any special privileges for the high nobility in these matters, some of them openly followed the royal example and acknowledged their "illegitimate" children, who were then sometimes even accepted into the ranks of the nobility.

There was a rule of Danish Law that a woman of unblemished reputation who became pregnant could demand that the father should marry her. But in 1734 the law was altered so that it only applied if the man had promised marriage either in writing with two witnesses to his signature or orally in the presence of two good men. Moreover the man must be over 25 years of age. If marriage took place the two parties must nevertheless pay fornication fines, which in the towns went into chancellery funds to help pay for the administration of justice and in the country accrued to the lord of the manor or master of the household: payment was often rigorously enforced. A prison sentence might be imposed in lieu of payment, and this was not the best basis on which to begin a marriage.

In any event, a special church punishment fell upon the woman, for she had to confess her sins publicly in church so that the priest could determine her contrition, pronounce forgiveness from the pulpit and lead her to the altar. Men generally escaped this punishment, from which both parties could be excused by permission of the king. But that cost money, so only the better-off could afford it. An ordinance of 1696 in fact exempted all non-commissioned officers and men of the army and navy both from public confession and from the fine for a first offence of fornication. An ordinance of 1767 abolished public confession of fornication, but offenders were now to expiate their crime with eight days on bread and water. This too could be avoided, however, by obtaining a dispensation costing ten *rigsdaler*; but this was a lot of money, especially for an unmarried mother in the country whose wages would be paid mainly if not exclusively in kind.

There was no obligation upon a father to contribute to the support of his "illegitimate" child, but in 1763 he was made economically responsible jointly with the mother for the child's upbringing. He was to pay, according to the judgment of the authorities and his own circumstances and fortune, at least half of the child's necessary maintenance until it attained the age of ten. Soldiers being in a special position, as already noted, they wanted to escape the maintenance contribution as well, but the authorities refused this on the ground that it was not a punishment but a natural duty rest-ing upon all parents whether married or not. When fornication fines were done away with in 1812, the government again stressed the obligation of parents to maintain their children.

It followed from the domestic discipline to which children were subject that the parents intervened a good deal in their relationships with the opposite sex. This applied most particularly to daughters, who were of course minors and as long as they were unmarried remained so under the guardianship of their father. The latter also had the right to refuse a betrothal, and a suitor had to "beg for his daughter's hand". Much unhappiness resulted from this. Novels, autobiographies and so forth reveal this: thus, for example, *C. E. F. Weyse* (1774–1848), perhaps the greatest composer produced by Denmark in the 19th century, was not accepted as a son-in-law by the rich merchant to whose daughter he had given music lessons. He tells in his autobiography of the black melancholy that gripped him and how for years he was unable to compose.

Another question is the extent to which children were forced into marriage they did not want. Here the matrimonial courts furnish a certain amount of information. The procedure was that if a man or woman was forced by parental or family pressure to give a promise of betrothal to some person whom it was wished to bring into the family, then he or she must protest *forthwith* to the family, neighbours and church congregation. In addition, he or she must approach the pastor and explain how compulsion was applied and also obtain witnesses to testify to the mode of compulsion. It goes without saying that all this was no easy matter, especially when girls were often married at 14, and instances are known of betrothal at 12. Betrothals were now to take place in the presence of the pastor and five other witnesses and to be entered in the church register. At the same time the parties pledged themselves to wed, and the betrothal could be broken off only by due legal process. Study of matrimonial court records discloses that some individials did manage to escape from unwanted connections. Twelve girls defeated their parents before the Århus matrimonial court between 1704 and 1734 by proving how they had been compelled by harsh words, threats, blows, beatings and so forth to give betrothal promises. Only a few cases are known of men having launched this sort of legal action, but no doubt compulsion was frequently used to bring about a marriage.

An enormous interest in rank was another characteristic feature of the age. Social ambition governed both men and women, but perhaps mostly women. For example, rules were laid down by the authorities concerning the manner of allotting pews in church, so that those who had been married longest were placed higher than others of the same rank. This sometimes led to altercations and scuffles in church. Two ladies of the military class quarreled over their seating to the point where the dispute actually had to be settled by a royal edict in 1735. One of the ladies was married to a lieutenant-colonel while the other was the widow of one. The latter had driven the former from the pew she had previously occupied, and had stormed and raged so that the wife had swooned and had to leave the church – this despite the fact that the latter's husband had been commissioned in 1715, while the widow's husband had not been appointed until 1718. The widow was commanded by the king to behave herself and in addition was ordered to donate 1 *rigsdaler* to the poor for having caused a public nuisance.

In another incident in the town of Sæby in 1696, three daughters of the burgomaster sat on each other's laps in church, bandying words and interrupting the priest, because all three wanted to sit in front.

There were also fixed rules that maidservants should sit according to their employers' rank, and a case concerning a noisy squabble between professors' maidservants and a group of townspeople had to be determined by the consistory in 1723. The complainant pastor received the reply that a professor had no right to lend his maidservant's seat to townspeople or others who did not belong to the university.

Among the many matters in which the government involved itself was that of dress. Detailed ordinances on this matter were promulgated for town-dwellers in 1783, and later in the year the peasantry received instructions as well. Among other regulations, townswomen were forbidden to use velvet, brocade, materials brocaded with gold or silver, and foreign lace. Silk was not prohibited, but maidservants were only allowed to have a cloak and a black skirt of silk. They were forbidden to have headdresses costing more than nine marks, and they were not to wear earrings. The government even took an interest in girls' confirmation dresses and in 1784 decided that everyone outside the peasant class should be dressed in white or black taffeta, woollen material or linen. Skirt and hair might be decorated only with red and white ribbons, and the neck was to be covered with a white neckerchief. Regulations of this sort had but little effect compared with the influence emanating from the court. If the ladies of the court dressed in velvet and feathers, neither law nor ordinance could prevent women of rank, whether by birth or marriage, from entering the competition, and others who could afford it did not hold aloof.

There was no necessity for issuing an ordinance prohibiting the attire of the peasantry from being too luxurious, but it was done nevertheless. Peasants could wear only home-made clothes of homespun or linsey-woolsey (linen mixed with wool). However, men had to have a jacket or waistcoat of "pedlar's fabric", i.e., fabric purchased from a pedlar's booth, and wives were forbidden to wear coats, skirts or neckerchieves of silk, but were permitted a bonnet of silk and a coat and skirt of pedlar's fabric.

The Pietist movement had an influence upon religious life at the beginning of the 18th century. At that time the church was ossified by dogma and orthodoxy, and no one needed to display such qualities as brotherliness in his *actions*, provided he adhered to the authorised doctrine of state and church. Influenced from German quarters' where there was a desire to transform Christianity into an inner spiritual experience and to manifest faith through neighbourly love, a number of people began philanthropic works such as establishing charity schools linked to the churches. Among these persons was Frederik IV's unhappy queen, who had to share the king with his morganatic wife. The king too was interested in the school system and had 240 schools established on Crown estates serving military purposes. As early as 1739 a royal ordinance enjoined the founding of schools all over Denmark and ordered the introduction of compulsory school attendance for all children, but implementation was prevented by considerations of economy combined with protests from congregations and landowners. Nevertheless a fair number of public schools (in the American sense) were established, often with private assistance.

The process of creating a school system in Copenhagen began in the early part of the century, and money was collected for this purpose in churches and from private individuals. In addition to giving free education these public schools might supply food and clothing to the children, who were to learn to read the catechism and the Bible as well as being taught writing and arithmetic. Girls were also taught sewing and spinning, but if they did not know their catechism or answer correctly questions from the Bible, they were punished by not being allowed to do handwork. Boys and girls were kept apart as far as possible and were not permitted to play together outside school time. Curiously enough, preparation for confirmation was always conducted jointly.

Alongside the public schools, charitable societies and others established a number of small private "girls' academies", notably towards the end of the century, and in 1801 there were 25 of these in Copenhagen for girls only and three taking both girls and boys. Ostensibly the girls' academies, in the spirit of the Age of Enlightenment, laid emphasis on an all-round education and instruction in a wide range of subjects. But only the surface was scratched, and "female accomplishments" such as flower-arranging and dancing were included along with the recognised subjects. In several of the academies the girls were supposed to learn three foreign languages, and the persons appointed as language teachers were not all equally well qualified. Many of these girls' schools were heavily criticised and received such nicknames as "parrot-learning schools".

Since time immemorial it had been customary among well-to-do families to employ private tudors or governesses, and to have a foreigner in this role was particularly grand. Frenchwomen were held in special regard, and indeed many of them were highly qualified and very skilful teachers: the word *mamsel* (= *mademoiselle*) became assimilated into the Danish language.

About half the child population of Copenhagen was attending school by about 1800, and Denmark was one of the first countries to introduce compulsory education in 1814 for all children between 7 and 14 years of age. Compulsory *school* education has never existed in Denmark, and even today parents have the right to have their children educated at home – and possibly to do it themselves.

Large families were general at all levels of society. This sepulchral tablet dates from about 1660 and depicts the priest's family of Hjerm. It relates how the priest's wife went through eighteen pregnancies and births in order to establish a family with seven children living. The number of miscarriages was not mentioned openly. It is also evident from the painting that special children's clothes are a relatively novel phenomenon.
(Photo: National Museum).

Opposite page, above: The cows stayed in the fields all through the summer, the wenches going out to milk them. In former times they carried the milk in pails on their heads so as to be able to carry on knitting while walking, thus wasting no time. Below: Dinner in a farmhouse at the turn of the century. The farmer sits at the head of the table, with his labourer and boy along the side while the wife and maidservant stand by ready to serve the menfolk.

The map of Denmark shows the distribution of this custom whereby the womenfolk, or at least the maidservants, stood to serve the food.
Drawings: Povl Abrahamsen.

Urban life too was hard and toilsome for women. Sanitary arrangements were squalid and tenement flats small and overcrowded. Copenhagen, about 1905.
(Photo: Copenhagen City Museum).

The Age of Holberg

Ludvig Holberg (1684–1754) was a prolific and versatile writer who tackled a great variety of topics from history, philosophy and social problems to the attitudes, way of life and customs of his own time. He came from Bergen in Norway, was orphaned at the age of ten and obtained degrees in theology and philosophy from Copenhagen University when he was twenty. He had had to earn his living as a private tutor, and he continued to do this alongside his writing while travelling for some years around Europe. At the time Holberg became professor of metaphysics – a subject he despised – he was an indigent and sickly scholar. His financial circumstances were so bad that the year before his appointment as professor he had accepted help from the poor-relief fund of Trinity Church. However, the moment his income was assured he was gripped by a "poetic rapture" and wrote satires and comic verse instead of learned works on history, geography and jurisprudence. He now saw the comic side of life and handled countless subjects with good humour and sound commen sense. He was the first playwright to write in the Danish language, and it is from this period that his highly esteemed comedies date.

Holberg deals with the status of women on a number of occasions, exposing absurdities and injustices.

In the comic poem *Zille Hans-Datters Forsvarsskrift for Kvindekønnet* (Zille Hans-Datter's Tract in Defence of the Female Sex) (1722), Zille writes of herself that at the age of eight she wanted to study and tried to persuade her father to allow her to do so. Then her brother Frantz could spin in her place, for he did not have her capabilities. Her father replied: "He is called Frantz, and you are Zille." Zille suggests that parents could wait until they know their children's capabilities before giving them names. She argues so well that her father is amused and gives way, but her mother weeps, for she has seen how their neighbour's sister has been driven quite out of her wits from reading the translation of Seneca by the learned noblewoman Birgitte Thott. When Zille had studied for six years, she could get through the "most obscure Latin book", and she asks why women cannot, like men, be appointed to official posts, become leaders of armies, ambassadors, lawyers or astronomers. The poem ends with the words: "If we were entrusted with more, we could do more." By then Zille has rejected both the argument of women's inferior intelligence and the one which holds that women are too refined by nature to be employed on "man's work".

Holberg received his inspiration for the character of Zille from Sille Gad, a fellow-townswoman. The latter learned Latin, Greek and Hebrew from her father, so she could have taken the university entrance examination at the age of 15 – but for a girl this was impossible. Sille was known to the professors and students of Copenhagen University for her erudition, but when she wanted to act as critic in a doctoral disputation she was refused. Her subsequent fate was a tragedy which says a good deal about the conditions under which women laboured in those days. In Bergen she got to know a Dutch seaman, by whom she became pregnant. In his absence she gave birth to a child which was said to have been stillborn. She hid the body, but it was found, and she was accused of infanticide. The lower court found her innocent, but the courts of higher instance and the supreme court too condemned her to life imprisonment. The king then pardoned her on condition that she confessed publicly, paid a fornication fine, remained in prison for another half-year and then left the country. In 1708 she joined her father in Copenhagen, where they both died of the plague in 1711.

In *Peder Paars* (1722) women discuss politics and read newspapers, while Marthe the children's nanny has theories about how trade can be made to flourish. Stork, head of the household, becomes very angry with his wife and the nanny for taking part in such goings-on, so he sets about them with a cane. He relates the circumstances to the pastor later on, but the latter cannot condone his severity and indeed sees nothing wrong in women reading newspapers – "most of it is lies anyway; they might as well read them". Holberg himself comments thus:

"Let those study who have minds to understand!
"Let those govern who a household can command!
"Let those who best can do so the tiller take in hand!"

The novel *Niels Klims underjordiske rejse* (The Underground Journey of Niels Klim) (1741) is another work one of whose themes is the issue of feminism. The book is a satire on the social conditions of the day and can be compared to Jonathan Swift's *Gulliver's Travels*. In one episode Niels Klim arrives in the ideal state of Potu (Utopia spelt backwards), where women receive the same upbringing as men and also have the same occupations and jobs. Those appointed to official posts are those best suited to them, and this applies in the army and navy as well. Niels Klim is astounded to encounter a presiding judge who is a maiden lady. She administers her office to the full satisfaction of the inhabitants of Potu, and her verdicts are always upheld by the supreme court. He expresses objections to the wonders he sees, and tries to explain to the natives that they go against "nature and the law of nations". But they tell him that he is confusing nature with habit and training, and his suggestion that women should be excluded from public office is rejected on the ground that it would be highly injurious to the state if half the population were ineligible for office. Another strange land which Holberg causes Klim to visit is Kokleku ("Cock-a-doodle-doo"), where the menfolk see to the kitchen, the weaving and the cleaning, and "receive blows", for it is considered that men are suited to this kind of work by virtue of their great stamina and muscular arms. Women take the most important civil, religious and military posts, though men can still be employed as common soldiers. It follows naturally in the upside-down world of Kokleku that it is the women who court the men, send them verses and gifts, and that "the latter feign coldness and modesty, for it is unbecoming for a young man to say yes to a young woman straight away". Of course Niels Klim is thoroughly baffled by this state of affairs and cannot understand how the men can put up with it, but they are accustomed to it and even believe that it is the natural order of things. Holberg set out to make paradoxes in these stories and he certainly amused his comtemporaries. He may also have caused some people to reflect that there could be different ways of organising society. Holberg himself probably believed that the equal-rights society of Potu was a feasible one. His repeated emphasis upon the significance of upbringing and education in the social placing of men and women.

Holberg was not the only one to air such ideas in those days. *Montesquieu* too, in his book "Lettres Persanes" (1721), declared that the causes of women's social subordination were to be found in upbringing and custom, so that he and Holberg may perhaps be regarded as the first sex-role theorists.

Although Holberg's very extensive literary production is often marked by irony, wit and subtlety, he also provides information about significant features of the society in which he lived and most notably about important aspects of women's status. He was much concerned about the latter, which can be seen from his comedies, in which it is often women who have the shrewdest or timeliest words to say. But Holberg's *Epistler* (Letters) also, consisting of brief essays on religious, historical, moral, literary and personal questions ("Why I Like Women's Company", "Why I Have Not Married") give evidence of this side of his wide-ranging intellect. In his old age he wrote stories of heroes and heroines. In the last of these (1745), for example, he compared queen Margrethe of Denmark to Elizabeth of England and Christian IV's daughter Leonora Christine – who was married to a traitor and spent 22 years in prison – to Jane Grey.

Holberg's pupil, the philosopher *Frederik Christian Eilschov*, who died in 1750 at the age of only 25, was also interested in the social status of women. During his short life he managed to write a couple of books and translate Fontenelle's *Conversations on More than One World between a Woman and a Learned Man*. The upbringing of girls is a topic to which he devotes particular attention. Girls should learn basic subjects but not mainly Greek and Latin. They do not need these, for it is hearts that they are to win, not jobs. Women's timidity and impatience he attributes merely to their sentimental upbringing, he says. Eilschov's views would, of course, have been of interest only to a narrow upper class, yet he did say something about the science of the age: "*We* are obliged to become adept at paltry trivialities, scientific dilettantism and sham knowledge, but Woman employs science correctly to its purpose, tossing aside all evasions and superfluities."

In the early 18th century there was scant interest in girls being taught anything more than a little reading. *Charlotte Dorothea Biehl* (1731–88) was given by her grandfather copies of Holberg's Peder Paars, his History of Denmark and his comedies. She wanted to learn Latin and Greek in order to understand the citations in the books and her grandfather promised to help her. But he said: "But you do not wear trousers and cannot become a professor!" When her grandfather died, her father tried to stop her studying, but she hid books in the fold of her dress and continued reading on the sly by the firelight. By the time she was nine she had read a good deal but she still could not write.

Charlotte Biehl's distinctive achievement is her translation of *Don Quixote* into Danish; but she also wrote books, historical essays about the kings of the age, plays etc. Her father, who was curator of the Charlottenborg Academy of Fine Arts and secretary of the art museum, was very strict with her. In her book of memoirs *Mit ubetydelige Levnedsløb* (My Insignificant Life) she writes: "Although I was almost 46 years old when my father died, I had never dared to go down to the palace garden, still less to meet anyone, without having first asked his permission." This book is in fact the only detailed autobiography of a woman that has come down to us from the 18th century.

Country Women

The Traditional Village Community

Danish rural society has been changing for many hundreds of years, although never as violently as in our own time. Before villages had properly formed themselves there were three classes of people: thralls, peasants and chiefs (see page 17). Thralls had in principle no rights and were subject to their lords' pleasure. They could not own anything or assemble at *things*. A Nordic poem from Viking times relates that the thrall has a wrinkled skin, stooping back, thick fingers and an ugly face. He is created to carry loads and haul fuel to the house. Peasants, on the other hand, have ruddy faces and clear eyes. A peasant is a free and prosperous man who knows how to drive a ploughshare and build a house. The chief is rich, has keen eyes, goes hunting with dog and horse, can throw a spear, can read runes, and is generous. This poem, it goes without saying, was intended for recitation in the chieftain's hall.

Not all thralls were equally downtrodden, but the position of field-slaves, both men and women, was wretched. Female thralls employed as house-servants might enjoy certain advantages even though they often suffered under their owners' right of chastisement and other caprices. From the 11th century onwards there was a sharp decline in the numbers of thralls, partly because the form of cultivation that had been based upon thrall-labour was no longer profitable and large estates could not be worked by badly-nourished and indifferent thralls. The church had urged the abolition of the thrall system and argued the cause of the oppressed, although without actually pronouncing a ban on the holding of thralls (though bishop *Absalon* (†1201), for example, gave two thralls their freedom in his will). Former thralls constituted the lowest stratum of society, and both men and women often worked as landless labourers, dependent upon their land-owning employer. Their only chance of achieving a more secure existence lay in obtaining user rights over a plot of ground and becoming cottagers (smallholders). They might then perhaps rent land from some landowner later on.

The great majority of country women were personally free. Peasants in Denmark were strangers to the serfdom under which peasants suffered on noblemen's estates else-where in Europe and in the twin duchies of Schleswig-Hol-stein (which belonged to the Danish king). The rights of country women were similar to the rights enjoyed by other Danish women, but the burden of labour they carried was certainly heavier, especially if they were married to copyhold peasants, who as well as paying rent generally had to perform *villein services*. When the copyholder himself was working for the landowner it was usually his wife who had to manage things at home.

An account of Norway in the Middle Ages indicates that the line between man's work and woman's work was drawn at the threshold of the home. The same cannot really be said of Denmark, however, where the vast majority of the peas-antry lived in village communities. It was quite practicable for some of the farm work in the flat or rolling Danish countryside to be done by women. But rural society was un-doubtedly male-dominated, as is shown by most of the sources from which our knowledge of the legal, economic and social conditions of Danish agriculture in the 17th and 18th cen-turies is derived. Women are scarcely mentioned save as com-panions of men on festive occasions or else when a corpse is to be escorted to the grave. Most of the articles of the statutes of rural villages are concerned with the farming operations of the open field era: cattle- and horse-rearing, the cultivation and enclosure of cornfields, fencing and ditching (drainage), the clearing of brushwood etc. Some degree of concern for the poor, the sick and the feeble was quite often to be found in the statutes, and this was certainly the sphere in which women were mostly involved: actively, as with those who took care of the sick and others in need of a helping hand; passively, because widows and other single women constituted the vast majority of the large numbers of distressed and indigent.

At the *village meeting*, the most conspicuous manifestation of some degree of peasant self-government, even the wives of yeomen farmers were not really welcome. On only a single occasion is there a mention of an intervention by women in men's business, and it was not well received. But it did occur that one or more yeomen's wives (not cottagers' wives: of that there was no question) acted as co-signatories when village by-laws were being adopted. In such cases, of course, they were always *widows* who had taken over the farms of their deceased husbands. There is one east Jutland village statute signed by one *Berethe Jacobsdatter* in 1672 along with 23 men; another one is signed by two women and four men. In some instance a grown-up son printed his mother's name on her behalf along with his own. (Most peasants could only write their initials, and someone more skilled in writing would then usually write out the name in full.)

Country Women under the Tenancy System

Most peasants were copyholders or tenants on Crown land or noble estates. The vast majority of manors were owned by nobles, but after the introduction of Absolutism in 1660 the number of common-born squires grew. The position of women left as widows by the death of a tenant farmer was improved in a crucial respect from the 1550s onwards, when they became entitled to retain the lease of the farm without paying the substantial fee that had formerly been exacted. If they remarried, then the new husband had to pay the special fee as before. In many districts it was a long time before the new regulations were applied. The best position was enjoyed by the widow with grown-up or almost grown-up sons, for she might reasonably hope that one of them would want to take over the lease of the farm either forthwith or in the near future. A son's deed of tenure, especially in cases where it had already been issued before the father's death, would sometimes contain a stipulation that he might marry only with his parents' permission or after the mother's death. A country woman's authority at the head of the household might thus be preserved after her husband's decease. And even though the deed of tenure was not always complied with, in the event of a son's marriage (many reasons for this can be imagined!) the phrasing of a deed of tenure now and then makes clear that the housewife necessarily lost her responsibilities and her rank to a daughter-in-law. A daughter might have been better!

It was exceptional for a deed of tenure to be made out to a woman. But widows of yeomen farmers could obtain the same rights with regard to the farm and its running as many older male lessees who while still alive secured the landowner's agreement to the farm's being promised to a younger peasant. In a number of cases a son or son-in-law signed a deed of tenure describing him as no more "than a faithful servant of his mother". Sometimes, however, a former yeoman farmer's wife would have to accept new responsibilities in her later years. Thus in 1733 the lessee of a farm secured a deed of tenure in which it was stipulated that his predecessor's widow, who was to be allowed bed and board at the farm as long as she lived in return for various forms of assistance, was both willing and capable, and that the new owners were to be satisfied with her.

That a sense of justice could assert itself is revealed by the consideration shown in certain situations by the squire – or perhaps more likely the bailiff (land agent) with his greater knowledge of the circumstances of individual peasants – as for example when an older tenant and his wife had to give up a farm. A younger country woman might in certain circumstances undertake responsibilities towards an older one. On one farm a young tenant promised his widowed mother the customary bed and board and a proper burial when the time came. But then followed the words: "... if contrary to expectation discord should arise between her and her son and his wife (if he shall have entered upon matrimony), so that she be forced to move away from them, then shall he and his wife ..." be bound to furnish the mother with benefits in kind as specified in detail. If the son should predecease his mother, then his widow in fact could find herself responsible for providing adequate accommodation and maintenance for her mother-in-law.

Deeds of tenure and records of the administration of estates disclose that the circumstances of farmers' widows could differ very widely. If the farm was well maintained, the soil well cultivated and arrears of tax inconsiderable, a young or middle-aged widow would have little difficulty in remarrying, especially if she did not have too many children to look after. A poor widow with many children would find it difficult to remarry. Bailiffs of estates seem often to have been at pains to find a young bachelor or widower willing to lease the farm and at the same time "marry the widow in possession". But an agent or bailiff might also come up against a widow who refused an offer of marriage. It was generally farmers' widows on Funen and in Jutland, where the economic situation of tenants was fairly favourable, who displayed the greatest degree of independence.

This is probably not unrelated to the pattern that evolved in the Zealand group of islands, where from the end of the Middle Ages to the beginning of the 18th century the menfolk were subject to *villeinage*, which meant that a man was bound to a farm for his lifetime and a peasant's son had to accept the tenancy of a farm if his lord required it. Even though villeinage did not extend to women, just the same their lives as wives or mothers of peasants bound to the soil were affected by this special hereditary relationship.

Villeinage was abolished in 1702, but already in 1733 it was replaced by the *adscription* or compulsory residence system under which the male peasant population was not permitted to move away from the home tract between the ages of 14 and 36. These limits were widened later on. Adscription, unlike villeinage, covered the entire realm apart from Bornholm. That the landowning class contrived to secure the introduction of adscription was undoubtedly due to the difficult times being experienced by agriculture, when in some places it could be touch and go to get tenant farms occupied. The peasantry were oppressed by taxes, dues and villeinage obligations, so that there were often attempts by individuals to leave the land. One of the landowners' arguments for adscription was that since they were obliged to supply troops for the militia, they had to ensure that the men did not leave their districts.

Although some landowners would have liked to impose adscription upon women as well, they never succeeded in doing so legally. From the beginning of the 18th century onwards both men and women wanting to move away from a parish had to have a passport issued by the priest and endorsed by the landowner with permission for removal. Although passport and travel could not be refused to women, this did in fact happen in a number of places, and in 1742 a special ordinance repeated the provisions of Danish Law to the effect that servants were entitled to leave their service after giving notice in due legal form. But now that adscription had been introduced for men the ordinance further provided that a man might obtain a certificate from his master granting him temporary permission to seek employment elsewhere but empowering the first master to recall him on due notice being given to the second. When some of the priests now began issuing similar documents to women this caused confusion as to the legal position of the latter, and it had to be established once more that they were not subject to adscription.

Voices were heard later on saying that women ought to remain on the farms where they were born until they reached their twenties, but this idea received scant sympathy from the government. That demands for such restrictions came up was due to the fact that women returning to the country after service in urban homes were likely to spread word of the different and better conditions to be found in the town. The result of this could be to tempt the menfolk away – and of course other women too – and getting labour could be a problem in the country, at any rate in certain districts and at certain times.

The position of widows in 18th century Denmark could vary between the wide extremes of reasonable prosperity and extreme poverty. An example of the former that can be cited is that of a widow who in 1759 was granted four "window-spaces" (measures of accommodation allotted) on a son-in-law's farm; he also gave her an annual allowance of 2 barrels rye, 1 barrel barley, 1 barrel malt, 1 porker, and 4 *rigsdaler* as well as 10 loads of peat and grazing for 1 cow and 4 sheep. This was an unusually generous level of support. When the farm – quite a large one – was divided between two grandsons in 1788 the widow was still alive, and the two tenants had to allow accommodation and support both to their parents and to the grandmother (one of them as sole tenant from 1793 onwards). When the widow died at the age of 90 she had been receiving maintenance for 40 years.

Many farmers' widows managed quite well, thanks to a second marriage or to assured accommodation and maintenance arrangements. But a regrettably large number of country women, especially cottagers' widows and other single persons, suffered poverty and distress. In Zealand in the period after 1750 there were as a rule more cottagers and landless folk than farmers in the villages. Thus in one village there were only 17 farmers living but 41 married couples of cottager status (as well as an innkeeper), of whom 22 could be regarded as farm labourers according to the records kept by the parish priest. Most of them were day-labourers though five had permanent employment; in three instances a landless man and wife served as farmhand and maidservant, but only two of the young couples worked in the same village. One aged cottager had been a soldier for 34 years(!), and of his almost equally aged wife the record states: "The wife must virtually feed them both by spinning, knitting etc." The pastor cites the tragic example of one married couple where the man had dissipated not only the assets of his farm but also most of the considerable fortune contributed to the joint property by his wife. After the couple had separated "voluntarily on both sides", she was left pregnant and with three children under age to look after. "He won't be coerced by love," wrote the pastor in concluding his sad tale.

Women's Occupations and Housewifely Duties

About 1770 a priest noted with justice: "When a cottager cannot feed and support his family and himself by his labour, the wives also hire themselves out as day-labourers, especially in the summer. As many as are able to do so weave, spin and knit both for themselves and for others." Of twelve widows in his parish, three received bed and board from relatives, three still hired themselves out by the day and one wove homespun, while five lived on charity. In another parish at this time it was reported: "All cottagers and landless folk in the parish are likewise day-labourers for the peasants, and the wives make a livelihood by spinning, making fishing-nets and knitting stockings, mittens, caps etc." In other places there were seamstresses who took charge of the attire of farmers' families. Many of them had their meals and stayed overnight on the farms.

Day-wages for women were much lower than for men. Not until the end of the 1750s, after a long period of low wages consequent upon agricultural depressions, do we find an appreciable rise in the day-wage, though the improvement was undoubtedly biggest for men. Both farmhands and cottagers often received corn as wages in kind, although this mode of remuneration was repeatedly prohibited by statute during the 18th century. The wages in kind paid to young women usually consisted of homespun, flax yarn or some other item that could serve for clothing.

Maidservants in the country always received only half the annual wage paid to men, which for most of the 18th century meant 6–7 *rigsdaler* in Zealand and in most regions of the country considerably less. There could be quite wide variations between one manor and another. Some landowners felt that maidservants' wages on peasant farms were unduly low. There was undoubtedly a link between this poor remuneration and the fact that many girls from the country betook themselves to the provincial town or to Copenhagen in the hope of finding better conditions. It was possible to hold down maidservants' wages on farms because right up to the present century it was customary for daughters to receive practically no cash wages at all. Neither, in many cases, did sons on farms receive any wage worthy of mention, but what they could rely on was assistance from their fathers when it came to taking over and paying for the lease of a farm. A farmer's daughter's chance in life, especially in the eyes of many parents, lay in her opportunity of marrying a well-to-do bachelor or widower. The relatively numerous cottagers' wives and single women who made an independent living as weavers or by sewing, knitting stockings and other woollen articles and the like, generally had "a modest competence", as it was often called. In fortunate cases they might supplement their incomes by lending the housewife a hand, especially on the somewhat larger peasant farms. Many "self-supporting women" of the olden days had to go out with a begging-bowl in bad years, or else send their children. For most of the time prior to the beginning of the 19th century there was no organised system of poor relief to apply to in most parishes.

Housewifely duties were many and varied, but there were usually maidservants and daughters who helped. In the era prior to the great agrarian reforms at the end of the 18th century potato-cultivation was still rare, but the *kitchen garden* was the country woman's preserve. There was often an older woman who looked after it and ensured that the inhabitants of the farm did not lack for the vitally important green cabbage and several other varieties of brassica were added later. *Orchards* were much less common, even on the islands. The cultivation of hops and the planting of fruit-trees were actually prohibited under the Danish Law of 1683, but only in parts of eastern Denmark was the prohibition of major significance. Certain herbs had been cultivated or collected since ancient times.

Breadmaking was woman's work, and so was the supplementary winnowing of corn for use as meal or flour. The husband or a labourer would generally cart the corn to and from the mill in good time before baking-day, but there were also hand-mills which the womenfolk could use if the wind failed. A full barrel of rye would yield a score of loaves each weighing about 6–7 kg. Sometimes it was the husband who would fire the oven with heather, brushwood, logs and bog peat, but the wife or a maidservant often helped. Although the oven took a long time to warm up, it made up for this by the residual heat given off through its thick clay walls, for this could be used for drying fruit, corn and malt, flax, bedclothes and wet wearing apparel, as well as the fuel for the next firing. On moorland farms where the firing was done with heather, the baking-oven was often situated at some distance from the farmstead.

The "mistress of the house" was, of course, responsible for meals, while the maids carried the food in. It was a widespread custom for the womenfolk to stand at the side of the table facing out towards the room while the husband sat at the head of the table; on the larger peasant farms the farm foreman occupied the highest place on the long bench, with the other hands below him, then the cottagers (day-labourers) and lastly the farm boys.

The *brewing of beer* was universal on farms. *Malt*, the raw material for brewing, was produced from barley, "the wife's special corn". The malt was dried in a kiln which was often connected with the kitchen or scullery fireplace. Since there was a danger of fire with a malt-kiln it was sometimes put in a special oast-house serving an entire village. The malt was often ground in a hand-mill. The vats had to be kept absolutely tight and clean to prevent any disagreeable taste. The maids had to be up early on brewing-day, for many pails of water had to be carried in and boiled up for the brewing. The mistress of the house herself took charge of the fermenting vat, in which the drenched malt had already been stirred. The beer-barrels were kept in a dark beer-cellar with thick stone walls. When people in poorer districts were too sparing with the malt and hops the beer was thin and would quickly turn sour.

Distilling by peasants was prohibited by ordinance as early as 1689, doubtless to the relief of many country women. Nevertheless illegal distilling did persist for about 150 years, despite renewed bans and tighter controls. Most men liked *brændevin*, the Danish distilled spirit, which could also be used as a medicine, for washing wounds and for relieving pain. *Mead*, which Danish peasants had drunk throughout ancient and medieval times, was no longer universal, but many housewives did make mead from "honey and flowers" and brewed it by a variety of methods when the honey had been got in from the beehives in the autumn. *Honey* was also important for its sweetening properties; sugar was expensive even when it came from Denmark's own West Indian colonies.

Milking was the responsibility of women. In the summertime, when the cows yielded the most milk and could be milked three times a day, maidservants often had to carry milk-pails home from the field by means of a yoke over the shoulders: in earlier ages they not infrequently used tubs carried on the head. If milking was done at different places on the common field the maid would have to squat on her haunches while milking, but three-legged milking-stools were nevertheless common. Once got home the milk was strained into barrels, which were usually placed on shelves under the ceiling-joists, where the milk stood and formed cream. A day later this was skimmed off by hand, and when enough had been collected the housewife or maidservant could start the *butter-churning*. It could take many hours before the cream turned into butter. The buttermilk which separated out when the butter was removed by hand or with a long-handled spoon was very useful to the housewife: the rest went to the pigs. The quality of the butter was not particularly high before the dairy era but was best on the manors, where there were dairymaids. *Cheese* was best made in the early summer, before the bustle of autumn set in. It could be made from fresh milk but also from skimmed milk, possibly mixed with buttermilk. *Whey* would be left over from the cheesemaking, and this could either be used for making gruel or go into the pig-bin.

Slaughtering was both man's and woman's work. *Sheep* were the commonest domestic animals in the old days, and it was women who slaughtered and skinned them. The sheep's head was a delicacy to be eaten straight after killing. Salted and smoked sausages could be made from mutton but most of it was salted down; a good share would be hung up for smoking or drying. Smoked or dried mutton-leg could be kept for a long time and sliced off as required.

Calf-slaughtering (mostly at the sucking stage) was woman's work. Pig-slaughtering was of greater importance and required a man's strength: when the pig was stuck, however, the maidservant caught the blood while the women filled it into black puddings, made various kinds of *sausage* and used the *lard*, which was seasoned with salt, onions and thyme. The most important part was the *pork*, which went into the salt-barrel; some of it would be smoked later.

Goose-slaughtering was done about Martinmas when the birds had been sufficiently fattened. It was often the wife who "stuck" the geese after the dirt had been cleaned off them the day before. Plucking was best carried out before the geese became cold. The wings were removed first: they made good feather dusters. The *down* of 24 geese would make a down quilt, while stripped feathers were used for making featherbeds. Many slaughtered geese were sold to the local town, frequently to regular customers. On the farms goose carcasses would be cut up and salted; sliced breast of goose was a popular snack to offer a guest. Not very many ducks and hens were kept, and chicken runs were unknown. *Eggs* were appreciated by wives, who by ancient tradition received egg-money for them, and if a sudden need arose for soup or something freshly-killed it was a matter of course that the housewife would kill and pluck a chicken.

At times of year when meat was short the housewife, notably in the northern and western parts of Jutland, could feel pleased that not only was there *dried fish* to be had but also the coastal farmers could drive to the fishing hamlets and buy fish such as cod, whiting, plaice etc., which the farm-folk would then busily clean and to some extent salt down. The herrings caught in the Limfjord district and around the islands of Zealand meant that *salt herring* and now and then wind-dried herring were available. Fresh fish such as sea-trout and eel was to be had as a rule only if there was a water-way or lake in the neighbourhood.

Country women were responsible for looking after the *clothing*. Wool was indispensable in this, and almost all the lengthy and complex operations involved, from shearing the sheep to spinning the yarn and weaving the cloth, fell to the lot of the womenfolk. Weaving might sometimes be done by men as well, however, and in some parts of Denmark both girls and boys were taught to knit.

Flax too burdened women with long and complicated tasks. It used to be grown in most parts of Denmark, but was gradually replaced during the course of the last century by cheap flax, almost ready for spinning, imported from the Baltic states. Cotton too was now imported, and this was both spun and woven in textile factories. The flax cultivation still practised in Denmark today is to be regarded as mainly in the nature of a hobby activity.

Candlemaking was decidedly woman's work. When sheep-fat was melted over a low heat, strained into a bowl and allowed to set, the white fat first produced could be used for festive candles; the yellowish fat from the next rendering made everyday candles, and a final re-melting yielded rough work-candles. The actual manufacture of the candles was quite a complex process. Candles were in fairly general use in Denmark until about 1900.

Washing clothes, an obvious task, was often laborious. It was not carried out all that frequently in olden times. Bed-clothes and linen were changed no more than once a month, and the womenfolk did not do their *main washing* in the brook or stream in the cold season of the year, for it was best that the clothes should be laid out to dry on an expanse of clean grass. *Fine washing* of the starched linen of which most women's clothing consisted in those days was the most difficult. Soap and rice-starch were used for this, and finishing had to be done with flat-irons and fluting-irons after the article had been dried.

Housecleaning was an operation of a very different character in an age when rooms had earthen floors and entrance-halls and sculleries were often paved with stone; however, many peasant farms acquired tiled floors in the 19th century, and wooden floors in the living-rooms and kitchen became common in the second half of the century. Earthen floors had sand scattered over them once or twice a day, and when the maidservant cleaned up she sprinkled the sand with water, swept it up with a broom and carried it out to the ashpit. The beds were made before the morning's sweeping-up. During *spring-cleaning* freshly-threshed straw would be put in the beds and probably also in the farmhands' room, which was usually by the cowshed, while the maid's room was often squeezed in beside the kitchen and sometimes did not have a window.

Country women had a heavy work-load. Not infrequently they took a share in field labour, mostly in the autumn, and in the age of villeinage they also helped with winnowing, peat-cutting, mucking out pig- and goose-pens, occasional hod-carrying and numerous other tasks.

From the French Revolution to the Fall of Absolutism

The Influence of the Revolution in Denmark

The ideas of liberty and equality of 1789 naturally reached Denmark and led to attacks on absolutism and its restrictions. Some of the early champions of freedom, such as *P. A. Heiberg*, were banished. But there was no response among women to the conceptions of female emancipation embraced by the Revolution. However, Mary Wollstonecraft's *Vindication of the Rights of Women* was translated from German into Danish in 1801. But this first written programme of the feminist cause, which was heavily influenced by Revolutionary ideas, produced no impact. As in the rest of Europe, the Napoleonic Wars provoked a general reaction, and in Denmark there were gigantic economic problems that led straight to the national bankruptcy of 1813.

Nevertheless, there was one field in which the Revolution did have an effect: opportunities for obtaining divorces were widened. Danish Law recognised only three grounds for divorce: adultery, prolonged desertion of the marital home, and a sentence of banishment or outlawry for life. Danish Law was very strict compared with other Protestant lands, but the king as head of the church had gradually acquired a good deal of power and could grant divorce by concession. Such concessions, however, were very exceptional prior to 1790. Attitudes to the question of dissolution of marriage are shown by a statement of the Faculty of Divinity at Copenhagen University in 1737: "Even if the spouses abhor one another irreconcilably, neither divorce nor separation can be permitted, but the church's disciplinary means are to be employed to induce them to cure or improve matters, and if these are of no avail, then secular punishment must be used." The reference to separation is probably due to the introduction by certain German Protestant states of legislation making separation possible if, for example, the wife was being ill-treated. But the Faculty expressed its disapproval of the by no means infrequent separations granted by the king, notably after 1720, both with and without the agreement of both parties. There was no legislation dealing with separation, and in contrast to other Protestant countries separation when granted was without time-limit. The effect of the events in France was that only a few years after 1790 divorces were occurring far more frequently by concession than by verdicts under Danish Law; furthermore it was becoming normal for separation to lead to divorce after three years, and sometimes after an even shorter period. This practice became fixed by a royal decree of 1796, which confirmed three years' separation and prescribed that efforts at conciliation should be made by the authorities before divorce could be granted. Apart from a decision of 1811 that the conciliation procedure should be carried out by the spouses' pastor, only insignificant points of detail were changed in these fields prior to the Marriage Act of 1922.

Hard Times – and a Cultural Golden Age

Hard times in the early 19th century brought distress to very large classes of the population. Thrift was imperative, and many women tried to earn a little extra income by handicraft work, just as they also sewed clothes more diligently than ever for all the family, even shoes being produced at home.

Yet this period saw such a flowering of literature and of intellectual life generally as to cause it to be termed a golden age. Romanticism triumphed over the rational attitudes of the Age of Enlightenment, and in historical chronicles and tragedies, in plays, poetry and novels, Woman was acclaimed for her courage, her loyalty, her gentleness and her mother-love, and at the same time elevated into a mystical being.

Salons now made their appearance in Denmark. These were not quite of the same character as in France perhaps, but at all events there were two notable women who assembled an array of prominent personalities of the day for social gatherings in their homes. The hostess at *Bakkehuset* in Frederiksberg was *Kamma Rahbek* (1775–1829), who created festivity and merriment along with music-making and brilliant conversation centering particularly on literature. The childless home of Kamma and *Knud Lyne Rahbek*, her husband and a man of letters, had an atmosphere of harmony and informality. Hospitality abounded, and friends came and went in a continuous stream. Kamma Rahbek was an avid reader of every kind of literature, with a command of Italian and Spanish as well as the three main European languages; in her later years she learned Latin and a little Greek as well. She was an ebullient personality with a great gift for finding striking phrases in which to clothe her observations and opinions. She loved her garden and went in for cultivating flowers to perfection, but bookbinding and box-making also engaged her interest. She was an indefatigable letter-writer, and several collections of her witty and graceful letters have been published. But she never wrote with publication in mind, and it is probably right to regard her as a homeloving woman who managed to attain great prominence among her circle through her openness, warmth and intelligence. Kamma Rahbek participated in the Copenhagen social round only on rare occasions, and apart from an annual shopping expedition to Hamburg she seldom left her home surroundings.

Friederike Brun's (1765–1835) salon was no less hospitable than Kamma Rahbek's but it was characterised by wealth and opulence, unlike Bakkehuset, where the entertainment offered often included merely tea – though it was excellent tea. In both salons the conversation was brilliant, but with the Brun family the numerous foreigners present lent the gatherings a distinctive atmosphere; and indeed, not very much Danish was spoken. The setting was either the mansion on Bredgade or the Sophienholm estate at Lyngby; the assembly would consist of members of the diplomatic corps, scholars and scientists, artists from various fields, young men and women of the Danish nobility, and recently arrived foreigners. Broadmindedness was the order of the day, so that neither cliques nor one-sided attitudes in politics or in matters of taste were allowed to dominate the proceedings. It was the hostess who saw to this, and if there were clashes between her friends she sought to gloss over them or make peace: it was a positive vocation for her. The entertainments also featured music and song as well as dance, plastic arts and mime presented by the young ladies of the house. Friederike Brun was highly unconventional and might decide, for example, to receive her guests lying on a sofa by artificial moonlight.

She was the daughter of the pastor of the German congregation in Copenhagen and had been married at the age of 18 to Constantin Brun, also of German birth and a wealthy merchant about 20 years her senior. She wrote poetry from her earliest youth, and when she was 16 her father proudly had her collected poems printed for his friends. She made her début as an authoress the following year with a description of her first visit to Germany. There were several children of the marriage, which seems to have been harmonious despite the fact that the couple had few common interests. Friederike Brun came by degrees to spend less of her time in Denmark than elsewhere in Europe, where she frequented various health resorts and was treated for an ear complaint that made her very hard of hearing. She was accompanied on her travels by a variety of friends, usually German poets, as well as her children and their tutor. Her husband's patience eventually wore out, and he wrote to her in Rome saying that she could either remain there and receive a yearly allowance or else cease her wanderings; if she remained, however, he wanted custody of their daughter *Ida*. She returned to Denmark in 1810 and settled down. It was from then until her death at the age of 70 in 1835 that she assembled celebrities from Denmark and abroad at her parties. Her entire literary production is written in German. It comprises sensitive and entertaining accounts of her travels, descriptions of the artistic circles of Rome and several collections of her poems. The latter are considered to be derivative. Her autobiographical notes, which were published in Danish early in the present century, shed light on such matters as the culture, controversies and personalities of her day. She also gives an account of her daughter Ida – who married the Austrian envoy, count Bombelles – and her artistic development as a celebrated singer. Friederike Brun was a friend of *Madame de Staël*, who characterised her as "a rallying-point and a warm hearth for the beautiful and the good".

"The Much-Discussed Topic of Women's Liberation"

There are one or two indications that the early 1840s saw an emerging interest in women's liberation, or "ladies' emancipation" as it was then known. An article about women's aptitudes and place in society appeared in the periodical *Korsaren* in 1841. It supported women's participation in politics and advocated agitation for emancipation. But four months later *Korsaren* deplored having reaped nothing but ingratitude for its support of women. It drew attention also to the unique situation in England, where queen Victoria and her husband drove to Parliament together, "and there she speaks and he listens ... how easily other ladies could do the same if they had this freedom!" The editor concluded: "The emancipation we formerly proclaimed will not come about quickly: everything will stay as it is for the present."

The first part of *Paludan-Müller's* verse novel "Adam Homo" appeared in the same year, written during a two-year tour of a number of European countries. In this work the emancipated baroness Mille appears clad in a velvet jacket like a man. She smokes, shoots and goes skating. The baroness speaks of women's emancipation as "the great principle of the age" and says that thousands of women will sacrifice their lives for it. Although Homo the student evinces contempt for the principle, Mille likes him and proposes marriage. He deserts his gentle mistress Alma, the opposite of the baroness. This was the first time that an emancipated type of woman – as understood by Paludan-Müller at least – had been described in Danish literature.

The following year, a short play was produced by *Jens Christian Hostrup*, clergyman and author. One of the characters in it is Sib, a young girl who does not wish to be addressed as *jomfru* or *frøken* (two different Danish forms of "Miss"). Sib, who wants to go to the theatre, says that she is a human being and wishes to be addressed as such. She wants to be liberated from the constraints and chores of family life. She speaks of the emancipation of women, which will make all human beings equal and abolish distinctions between men and women.

Students took up the cause as well and produced a vaudeville called "Ladies' Emancipation, or the Grisette at the General Meeting". The title is ample indication that the students were making fun of feminist issues.

Thomasine Gyllembourg (1773–1856) was a writer of the day who was regarded very highly by many and was certainly very much read. She was married at the age of 17 to P. A. Heiberg, another writer twice her age, and was the mother of Johan Ludvig Heiberg (see page 81). The marriage was not harmonious, and when her husband's severe criticisms of the

75

government caused him to be banished from the realm, Thomasine succeeded in getting a divorce after a hard struggle with him. She subsequently married baron Gyllembourg, an exiled Swede. She did not begin writing – anonymously of course – until she was 54, but her output, especially of short stories, was large. She draws upon her middle-class Copenhagen background to describe human entanglements and individual circumstances, giving prominence to the domestic virtue of women. In the last of the short stories, *To tidsaldre* (Two Eras) (1845) one of the characters mentions the "much-discussed topic of women's liberation".

Thus we can say that women's emancipation was at least spoken about in Denmark even before the revolution of 1848.

The Approaching End of Absolutism

After the Napoleonic Wars, the Duchy of Holstein remained part of Denmark but at the same time joined the Confederation established by the ruling princes of Germany. It was decided that all the member-states of the Confederation were to have assemblies of estates, and king Frederik VI of Denmark promised the Congress of Vienna that he would comply. But not until the post-1830 liberal movements gathered strength was the temporising Danish government induced to redeem its promise. It realised that consequences would ensue in the rest of Denmark, and so before any demand for such a measure had been raised, the government announced that assemblies of estates were to be introduced throughout the country. Nevertheless, it was not until 1834 that an arrangement of four assemblies, whose function would be advisory, was introduced. It was laid down beforehand how many members should be chosen respectively by citizens, landed proprietors and peasants (including tenants cultivating large holdings), and neither the franchise nor eligibility for election was equal or universal. In Copenhagen, for example, only one professor met the election qualifications while 75 liquor distillers did so!

The assemblies of estates assumed particular importance in two spheres. Firstly, the people at large became accustomed to open discussion of public questions, and secondly parish and county councils were established after negotiations with the estates. At the same time regular voting to the town councils of the provincial towns was introduced, these having previously been self-elective and without any real power *vis-à-vis* the burgomaster appointed by the king. Here too it was the better-off classes that received the franchise, but the measure did have the effect of giving a say in public affairs to broader circles of the population.

In 1845 the law of inheritance was amended to improve the status of women by placing them on an equal footing with men unless they were sons and daughters of the testator. Male and female issue were still to inherit in the proportions of $\frac{2}{3}$ and $\frac{1}{3}$ respectively. This inconsistency was the result of a compromise after the Jutland assembly of estates had twice rejected a proposal for complete equality, and not many years were to pass before men and women became equal with regard to inheritance.

Broad National Trends

Denmark was still predominantly an agricultural country, and as late as 1834 the urban population formed no more than 21 % of the whole, Copenhagen accounting for 120,000 of these and Odense, the biggest provincial town, for 8,000. There was virtually no industry: no more than 23 steam-engines were to be found in factories at the end of the 1830s, for example, so that scarcely any real industrial workers existed at all.

The large number of women who supported themselves were employed in agriculture mainly as servants, and besides performing household and childminding tasks, they were expected as peasant women to give a hand both indoors and out. To the wives of cottagers and farm labourers this meant that they became day-labourers whenever peasants or gentry had a use for them. Many unmarried women worked in urban households as well; for example, more than one third of Copenhagen households had female servants in 1801. Both in business and in handicraft trades it was axiomatic that wives helped, and they had apprentices and often journeymen living in. Some small retailing was directly in the hands of women: itinerant tradeswomen hawked needles and pins, mirrors, combs etc., and there were women who peddled fruit, eggs and poultry. Since time immemorial there had been women who made a living by going round recounting stories and fairy-tales or singing in the streets and alleys, but in 1805 "all crying and singing in the streets of songs, books and tales" was prohibited.

Mathilde Fibiger and the Early Feminist Debate

In 1848 the liberal movement spread from France to other countries of Europe and in doing so affected many women. In Germany the ruling princes had to give way to the demands of their liberal citizens, and the people of Schleswig-Holstein wanted a free constitution for Holstein and North Schleswig to enable the latter to be included in the German Confederation. War broke out, ending in a Danish military victory over the Schleswig-Holsteiners but also rendering German intervention in Danish affairs a strong possibility.

In the midst of the war Denmark received a new constitution which abolished Absolutism and introduced a limited monarchical form of government with an elected two-chamber parliament having special rules of eligibility for the first chamber or Upper House (*Landsting*) and restricting political rights so as to deny both franchise and eligibility to servants without their own households and all women. The June Constitution of 1849 was extremely democratic compared with contemporary constitutions in other countries.

The question whether women should have political rights was not considered in any fundamental sense. Professor Tage Algreen-Ussing, the jurist, declared without contradiction: "It is universally acknowledged that minors, children, women and criminals should not have the franchise."

One of the women gripped by the liberal ideas of 1848 and burning with nationalistic spirit during the three years' war became the pioneer of the Danish feminist movement. This was *Mathilde Fibiger*, a young officer's daughter who in 1850 under the *nom-de-plume* of Clara Raphael wrote *Tolv Breve*

79

(Twelve Letters), a book which raised a storm of controversy over the feminist question.

Mathilde Fibiger had a tense relationship with her father's second wife, and finances at home were very strained, so she took a post as governess to the family of a forest superintendent on the island of Lolland when she was 18. Here she felt very lonely and was irritated by the family's narrow views and preference for discussing daily trivialities and the doings of neighbours. If she tried to bring up issues that interested her, she found no listeners. And so she wrote the book, which gives an account of herself and her experiences with the Lolland family but comprises more particularly a young woman's laments over her situation and her demand for intellectual freedom: "For the first time in my life I feel sorry that I am not a man. How poor and empty is our life compared with theirs! Is it just that half the people should be excluded from all intellectual pursuits? Or did our Lord really create us of poorer stuff than men (as I have heard one fascinating gentleman of the neighbourhood declare in all seriousness), so that we are to be content to carry out automatically the trivial labour allotted to us in this life? Does our mind then possess no power and our heart no enthusiasm? Indeed they do, but the real life within us has not come to awareness, our spirit is captive and prejudice stands guard outside her prison . . ."

This passage exemplifies her skill in self-expression and reveals the basic idea and tone of the book. Her youth and unworldliness are reflected in Clara's (and Mathilde's?) love for a young baron and her refusal of him when he proposes marriage. She wishes to dedicate her life to ideas, and no one can serve two masters. He understands and respects her, then goes off to the wars, beseeching Clara to allow him the place of a brother in her heart. If he comes back his desire is to help and support her in fighting for her ideas, and they shall stand as man and wife in the eyes of the outside world. "For God and each other we shall live together like a fond brother and sister."

Mathilde Fibiger sent her manuscript to the director of the Royal Theatre, *Johan Ludvig Heiberg* (1791–1860), the leading aesthete and poet of the age. He was impressed and volunteered to write a foreword and to arrange publication. The book appeared, a heated debate broke out, and for half a year newspapers and magazines published innumerable contributions by the known and the unknown, by women and by men, for and against the little book. Mathilde was far from being sufficiently robust to weather the storm she had raised. The person who said nothing at all was J. L. Heiberg. He totally failed his protégée, for his wife *Johanne Luise* (1812–90), the much admired prima donna of the Royal Theatre, smelt a rat in her aging husband's excitement over Mathilde, with whom he had a number of meetings. To keep the peace at home he held his tongue.

The newspaper controversy was followed up by a series of pamphlets, including efforts by Mathilde Fibiger herself – though not under her own name – to explain and defend her point of view. In an article entitled *Fire Breve om Clara Raphael til en ung Pige fra hendes Søster* (Four Letters about Clara Raphael to a Young Girl from her Sister), *Pauline Worm* reproaches her for not having taken up the question of the upbringing of girls. At least half the schools for young girls are mere superficial "rote-learning academies", and the teachers whom families often jointly employ for their slightly older daughters seldom last more than a year or so. Pauline Worm also asserts the value of marriage and of love between women and men. In brief, she was considerably more constructive and down to earth than Mathilde Fibiger. She was born in 1825, had been a teacher from the age of 16 and while quite young had published a grandiloquently nationalistic collection of poems. She had speculated over the status of women ever since childhood, and at the age of nine had tried to get her uncle, a deputy to the Jutland assembly, to propose female suffrage and eligibility. For she had discovered that one of the biggest landowners of the district where her father was a pastor did not have the same political rights as other landowners because she was a woman. Pauline Worm in fact was the first woman to deliver a public lecture (1865).

Radically different viewpoints were introduced into the discussion by the young socio-economic author *Frederik Dreier*, who regarded family life as a main cause of the male-dominated and frequently isolated position of the female sex. His pamphlet bears the satirical title *Blik på det verdenshisto-riske Værk 'Clara Raphael' og den derved fremkaldte Dame-litteratur* (An Examination of the Historic Work 'Clara Raphael' and the Feminist Literature Provoked Thereby), and this alone shows how he castigates the naive and un-worldly Mathilde. But one of the questions he raises is the possibility of contracting and dissolving marriages more freely; he discusses the supplanting of small-scale enterprises by large ones and suggests that much of the work carried out by women in their homes could be done more advantageously on a large scale. Why, he enquires, "should there not be com-munal kitchens, where food could be prepared with a vast saving of manpower?" Dreier would also make the upbring-ing of children a communal undertaking which, he says, could enable for example "three mothers (to) tend and care for ten children just as well, apart from the suckling, as they now each bring up one, which would be a great saving of time and energy; in addition, and this is extremely important, we should acquire an infinitely richer body of knowledge con-cerning the upbringing of children, of which there is still scarcely a trace ...". He goes on to say: "The associated mothers will have more time and opportunity to participate in other communal tasks and pleasures. (This is) something which almost everyone, to speak frankly and unrhetorically, would acknowledge to be a great advantage." But visions of this sort were far removed from the issues in which people of the day were interested and did not become of current concern until well into the present century. For the rest, Dreier was at one with Pauline Worm and others in criticising the education received by the better-class "salon ladies" and believed that only a few aspects of the entire discussion were relevant to working women. Dreier was Denmark's first socialist theoretician. He was only 26 when he died in 1853.

Mathilde Fibiger ended her days as a tragic figure. Among those who aided her was *N. F. S. Grundtvig*, the founder of the folk high school movement (see pp. 105f.), who had called her "a Danish girl who heard the call of the Shield Maid to break a lance for truth of mind and heart". She found refuge in his home and lived there for several periods.

When in 1852 a national open-air meeting was to be held in the vicinity of the farm where Grundtvig lived, Mathilde asked the committee in charge if she might make a speech. She was promised that she could, but her name was not to appear in the newspapers and she was to speak last. There was a considerable fuss over the affair even in her own family, but Grundtvig and his wife supported her. The upshot was that she made no speech.

Mathilde Fibiger now led something of a wandering life earning her living as a private tutor in Jutland and Zealand, sometimes living in a small room in Copenhagen, sometimes in the country. She wrote a little, but without much success, and scraped a bare existence from her teaching, from translation work and from sewing. In 1856 *Caroline Amalie* (1796–1881) the queen dowager granted her a small life pension, and when the telegraph system was established and wanted to employ women as in other countries, Mathilde, prompted by a friend, decided to try to achieve a more secure existence in that way. She was Denmark's first female telegraphist and was employed under a telegraph manager in Århus who did not look kindly upon female staff. A new manager was soon appointed, however, and her situation improved greatly. Mathilde Fibiger had never been strong and she died of tuberculosis at the age of 41. She played no part in the organised women's movement. She did declare her sympathy with the *Dansk Kvindesamfund* (Danish Women's Society) and became a member, but she was unable to participate actively in its work.

The New Age: Women Organise Themselves

Change in Women's Status

In one of his stories Hans Christian Andersen calls 1857 "the extraordinary year", and he relates how the train-oil lanterns were extinguished and gas took over. This was the year when the boroughs were deprived of their prerogatives, so that for example tolls no longer had to be paid at the town gates, the guild system with its privileges was abolished, freedom of trade was introduced, the Sound Tolls were done away with and changes were made in the legal and economic status of women.

A problem had gradually arisen for a growing number of unmarried women inasmuch as they did not enjoy personal legal authority and could make financial dispositions only through a guardian, normally the father or a male relative. Whereas the daughters of the middle classes had formerly been able to find enough to occupy them within the family, they were now often becoming an economic burden as industry gradually began to take over a part of the work previously done at home. Private tutoring or governess work had been regarded as the only acceptable occupation for a young girl from a "better-class" family, but at the same time it was difficult to find other vocational opportunities for the unmarried. This must be regarded as one facet of the background to change in women's status. The other was the growing understanding that the concepts of freedom and equality, as reflected for example in the new constitution, must be extended to include women as well. When in 1857 the Majority Act giving unmarried women the right to control their own affairs came before Parliament for consideration, *Orla Leh-*

mann, the National Liberal leader, said that he regarded this law as a link in a longer chain whose main objective must be to give women a more liberated status in all economic matters. Full legal rights were a debt of honour owed by men to women and would have a beneficial effect on the latter's self-esteem. He regarded the lack of legal rights as both a consequence and a contributory cause of a view of women's nature and being which was at variance with reality and was unbefitting in a civilised and Christian society.

On the same day that the king signed this act he also signed two other statutes of importance to women. The first was an amendment to the law of inheritance making it equally applicable to men and women in every respect; the second was the Trade Act, which gave to widows, deserted wives, and divorced, separated and unmarried women over 25 years of age the right to carry on a business on the same terms as men. In addition, widows were permitted to carry on the business of their deceased husbands, though they lost this right if they remarried. Finally, said the Act: "The making of millinery and of garments for persons of the female sex and for male children under ten years of age, the sewing of linen goods, bonnets, neckbands and the like shall be regarded as trades open to women."

These laws were enacted without any feminist pressure, for there was broad agreement and understanding as to their necessity. Nevertheless, the Clara Raphael controversy did probably have some influence: at any rate it was mentioned in Parliament during the debate on the Trade Act. Parliamentary moves were also afoot to improve the educational standards of female teachers, and women were beginning to be trained in order to enter government service.

Establishment of the First Feminist Organisation

However, more than ten years were to pass before a women's rights organisation was formed after the pattern of those established in a number of European countries from the mid-sixties onwards and as early as 1845 in the United States. John Stuart Mill's *Subjection of Women* was published in a Danish translation by *Georg Brandes*, the man of the modern literary breakthrough, shortly after the English edition (1869). Its castigation of English marriage laws and especially the demand for equal political rights for women provoked renewed discussion of and interest in the social status of women.

The leading figure in the establishment of the first feminist organisation was *Fredrik Bajer*, who was later awarded the Nobel prize, and his wife *Matilde*. Bajer had had links for some years with the Swedish periodical *Tidskrift för Hemmet* (Home Journal), which ardently pursued feminist questions, and he worked diligently to get subscribers for it in Denmark. Through a Dane in Geneva the Bajers heard that an international women's league had been formed there with branches in six countries. Negotiations began for the founding of a Danish branch, and this came about in 1871 in the shape of *Dansk Kvindesamfund* (Danish Women's Society). However, the new Society soon dropped the Geneva connection, for the word "international" was a liability in the days of the Commune, besides which there was internal friction in Geneva.

The constitution of the Society stated that its objective was "to assert the rights of women in intellectual, moral and economic respects and so also make females more responsible and active members of their family and nation, especially by facilitating their securing her right to financial independence". Under the leadership of Matilde Bajer the organisation endeavoured to live up to the latter aspiration by establishing vocational schools for women, which were greatly needed. First of all a school of commerce was opened for women desirous of being trained for office and shop work. Next came a "Sunday school for Women of the Working and Servant Classes", where there was instruction in Danish, arithmetic and writing. There were also lectures for the pupils every other Sunday on issues of the day. In addition a school of draughtsmanship and applied art was opened in 1875. These schools received subventions from a variety of funds and continued in existence for many years, eventually as independent institutions. At the same time the Society followed up the work through an employment information office, a registry office for domestic work and a general employment agency. The Society's members, of whom there were 121 in 1880, had their work cut out for them!

Fredrik Bajer, who had become a member of the Lower House of Parliament, worked to improve the position of married women, supported by the Society. He introduced a bill that would give married women the right to dispose of the money they had earned themselves; it was well received by the public at large, doubtless because most of them knew of instances where husbands demanded their wives' hard-earned shillings and drank them up. However, it was touch and go whether the proposal would get through the Upper House, and it was passed only because of the support of several conservative lawyers. After several attempts by the Society and Fredrik Bajer, the next step towards full legal rights for women came in 1899, when they became entitled to dispose of their own fortunes and the husband's control over the joint estate was abridged somewhat. Yet they still had no say with regard to the children, and a husband could, for example, remove them from home without so much as telling his wife where they were. Not until 1922 did married women obtain equal authority over their own children, and it was as late as 1956 before the parents acquired equal status as guardians of their own children.

Another important matter attracting enormous attention was that of women's political rights, and in 1883 the Society declared its intention of working for "full rights of citizenship", though nothing was in fact done. Other women soon took up the task, for the Society was afraid of finding itself enrolled in the ranks of the political opposition to Denmark's Conservative government. The Society "reefed in its sails during these years and kept firmly secured all the hatchways that might lead to political contention".

Working-Class Women Also on the Move

Aversion to Trade Unions among Women

In the 19th century there were not many industrial workers in Denmark and the different methods of compiling statistics make comparisons difficult. The great increase in the number of women in industrial and handicraft occupations seems to have taken place during the last 20 years of the 19th century, and in 1901 8.3 % of women between 15 and 70 years of age were employed in these fields. In 1880, according to the population census, there were 29,000 women so occupied, and by 1901 the figure had risen to 66,000.

When a branch of the "International" was established, divided into sections, an organisation for working-class women came into existence for the first time, but this "Women's Section" has left no traces. A new organisation, *Den frie kvindelige forening* (The Independent Women's Society) came into being when the three socialist leaders of the "International" were arrested and convicted. They had supported a strike of bricklayers and insisted on holding a mass meeting on the Copenhagen Common, although the police had prohibited it and intervened vigorously (*Slaget på Fælleden* – The Battle of the Common). This happened 1872.

The immediate purpose of this women's organisation was to collect money for the three imprisoned leaders; it also wanted to improve the status of women in society and help and support its members. The collection was successful, and meetings were held on feminist issues. But not all the seed fell on fertile soil, and the weekly *Socialisten* expressed disbelief that there were "citizens who fanatically discuss women's rights ... It is a downright lie, for it has been stated many times that in this Society they have nothing to do with politics at all but leave such matters to the men." The Society seems to have been mainly concerned with publicity and to have discussed more or less the same issues as were on the programme of the Danish Women's Society: the organising of women on an industrial basis, which might have helped the members, does not seem to have featured prominently among its activities. However, the Society did last for a number of years.

Yet another women's organisation, the *Socialkvindelig Forening* (Women's Social Union), was founded in 1874 for the express purpose of forming trade unions for women "in order thus to implement fully the idea of emancipation". A year later its objective seems to have changed, the gist of it now being "mutual aid and support in sickness and other emergencies and the establishment of a loan fund". There was disagreement on the issue of special women's trade unions or joint trade unions for both sexes, and this is still the case today, over a hundred years later.

There was a whole range of problems that all industrial workers had to face in the 19th century, the chief of these being the amount of the wage and of any relief during unemployment and sickness, but also including the length of the working day, working conditions, jobfinding and so on. A female worker's wages were about 35 % of a journeyman's and about 54 % of an unskilled male worker's in the period 1860–75. A study of average wages in Copenhagen in 1882 shows that women's daily wage was 1.37 *kroner*, that of the unskilled 2.37 and of journeymen 3.04 *kroner*, which means that women received about 58 % as much as the unskilled and 45 % as much as journeymen.

There were scarcely any really skilled women workers: most were unskilled or semi-skilled, but they were often given work for which men would have received higher wages, and it is an established fact that male wages in a trade employing both men and women were lower than in related occupations employing male labour exclusively. Where work was done only by women, wages were particularly low, notably where the women were working at home under contract to business firms or, for example, did sewing for private individuals.

It seems not to have been widely acknowledged by women how important it was for both male and female workers to organise themselves in order to improve their conditions. There are statistics of organised labour collected by *De sam-virkende Fagforbund* (The Federation of Danish Trade Unions) from the period immediately prior to the turn of the century showing that there were 7,243 female members all told. After various calculations and estimates and a comparison with an industrial census of 1897 this shows the proportion of female workers organised as 20 %. The equivalent figure for men at that time was 76 %.

Towards Equality on the Labour Market

When the first trade unions appeared on the scene there were few who saw any place in them for women. The statutes of *Enigheden* (Unity), the cigar-makers' trade union of 1871, for example, included a passage aimed directly against women. It read: "Any cigar-maker who teaches a woman to roll bunches or cigars, except his wife, may not be a member." This is all the more remarkable inasmuch as women had been working in the tobacco industry for many years. Members of the weaving trade, however, viewed matters differently, for they had experienced instances where manufacturers had utilised female home-weavers as strike-breakers. They tried in vain on numerous occasions to get women organised, succeeding at last in 1886, when the initiative came from the women themselves in connection with what was the first women's strike in Denmark. It occurred at a steam weaving-mill where wages and working conditions were particularly bad. Rates of pay for certain jobs were actually reduced, and negotiations between the manufacturer and the female weavers broke down. Nearly 200 women walked out and went as a body to the *Vævernes Fagforening* (Weavers' Trade Union) in search of support. They received it not only from the weavers but from the executive committees of all the trade unions, and collections were made for them. The strike lasted four weeks and ended with an extremely modest improvement in the women's wages, for labour was plentiful at that time. But now the women were disunited among themselves, and there were disagreements with the trade unions over strike pay and dues. The upshot was a split among the women, some of them joining the Weavers' Trade Union and others forming a separate union for women. This state of affairs lasted for 11 years and caused many internal problems, but in the end the women's union decided to throw in its lot with the men.

Another strike took place which changed the attitude of the cigar-makers towards women. Three hundred cigar-makers struck, and the women who worked as bunch-makers for them were laid off. The men were probably anxious lest the manufacturers should employ women to take over the strikers' work, for *Enigheden* invited all the women of the trade to a meeting, at which the chairman said: "By a regrettable error of judgment men and women workers have hitherto harboured animosity towards one another, regarding each other as rivals . . . But our socialist doctrine has made us recognise that all workers are as one in face of capitalist injustice. This doctrine has also opened our eyes to the equality of women and men, and the female worker doing the same work as a man must consequently be paid the same wage." A women's section of *Enigheden* was established shortly afterwards, but during a protracted tobacco workers' strike in 1883 the manufacturers had some success in employing women in place of the strikers. These will certainly have been unorganised tobacco workers, so that it was urgent that many more women should become organised. A sickness and relief fund for female tobacco workers was formed during the strike, possibly in order to overcome the aversion to trade unions, and this was subsequently turned into a trade union proper when its total membership had passed the 200 mark. The latter figure was reached in a couple of years, and when a nationwide tobacco workers' federation was formed, the women's trade union was at once able to join with about 400 members. But a situation in which *Enigheden* still had a women's section from earlier times co-existing alongside the new trade union (with its male president!) could only be transitional, and both organisations were soon brought under the umbrella of *Enigheden*. Many words were wasted over this during the years. It may be added that at the turn of the century the tobacco workers' federation was the first to achieve equal pay for men and women doing the same work.

The great majority of working women were to be found in the clothing trades, but their interest in trade unions was not great. However tailoresses, who had the best education, were an exception. The passivity of the many seamstresses may be accounted for by the fact that most of their work was done at home, not in a sewing workshop or factory. Furthermore, there was a special "sweat-system", as it was called, whereby the journeyman-tailor undertook work for a factory or master-tailor and then sub-contracted it to others, often women, who carried it out at a lower rate of pay than that which the trade union was trying to maintain. Both the employers and the middlemen, or "sweaters", were interested in the continuance of the system, for they made good profits from it.

In 1883 the tailoresses formed an organisation, sharing their male president for a while with the male tailors' trade union. An advertisement by the new organisation illustrates conditions at the time: "Unemployed members can collect

meal coupons from the lady president, Madam Ankersen."
The tailoresses joined the *Dansk Skræderforbund* (Danish Tailors' Trade Union) in 1889, but did not meet with any particular goodwill, even from the union leadership. Journeymen were reluctant to recognise the women as colleagues, and the women often felt themselves to be neglected by the union. Eventually there was a breach, though this only lasted a year, after which *De kvindelige Herreskræderes Fagforening* (The Tailoresses' Trade Union) functioned as an independent women's organisation affiliated to the Tailors' Trade Union right up to 1930. Many times over the years there were discussions and negotiations with a view to a merger with the Tailors' Trade Union of 1883, but the women were reluctant. It was only when the ready-made clothing seamstresses became better trained so that the work of journeymen and seamstresses overlapped, and when the trade became industrialised, that it was agreed to bring together all the men and women working on men's ready-made clothing in the Tailoresses' Trade Union, which was then renamed *Fagforeningen for Herrekonfektion af 1883* (The Men's Readywear Trade Union of 1883).

Efforts were made to organise the large body of seamstresses employed in various trades, and meetings were held to encourage them to show some initiative. As most of them were home-workers it was not easy to make contact with them. The small unions which did manage to struggle into existence had brief lives. But by the end of the 1890s there were trade unions for seamstresses in the readywear, linen and corset trades with memberships totalling not much more than a hundred all told, even though several thousand women were employed in these trades. In 1899 the three unions merged to form *Syernes Forbund* (The Sewers' Trade Union), which was joined later by new unions, and in 1915 the seamstresses joined the Tailors' Trade Union.

The organisation that was to assume particular importance

for female workers began in 1885 as *Foreningen for Vaske- og Rengøringskoner* (The Union of Laundresses and Charwomen). It soon adopted the name *Kvindeligt Arbejderforbund* (The General Union of Women Workers), although it was a Copenhagen union and not a trade union consisting of different branches. The objective was to organise female workers not already belonging to unions. After an initial period of lively agitation and meetings it languished, and by 1892 all that was left was the executive committee of five members! But then *Olivia Nielsen* took over as president, and in the years that followed she succeeded in organising female workers at the Tuborg Breweries as well as the match and coffee-substitute factories. By negotiating with these three firms the trade union achieved improvements of 4–6 *kroner* per week in wages, while a ropework employing only women flatly refused to negotiate, resulting in a strike. It lasted eight weeks and involved 85 women, but the outcome was an increase of only 1.20 *kroner* in the weekly wage. The strike attracted considerable press coverage, partly because women had struck only once before and partly because the firm brought in strikebreakers, notably from Sweden, an entire shipload coming from Stockholm. There were clashes several times when the workers left in the evening under police protection. During the stoppage the employers tried to strike a blow against Olivia Nielsen personally by bringing an action against her for some articles in the newspaper *Socialdemokraten*. The action, however, involved Olivia Nielsen's husband as well, for in the eyes of the law he was his wife's guardian. Undoubtedly the aim was to obtain a verdict against the husband in order to show the workers the risks they ran if their wives engaged in trade union activities. However, the case was dropped when the strike ended. Olivia Nielsen continued as president until her death in 1910, by which time the General Union of Women Workers numbered about 2,000 members with branches all over Denmark. The

Mathilde Fibiger (1830–72), the pioneer of the Danish feminist movement.
(Photo: Royal Library).

From the first Nordic feminist meeting in Copenhagen, 1888.

Executive committee of the Tailoresses' Trade Union during the strike of 1899.
(Photos: ABA, The Labour Movement Library and Archive, Copenhagen).

Olivia Nielsen (1854–1910), mother of seven children, was the first important female trade union leader. Her presidency of the General Union of Women Workers lasted from 1892 until her death. (Photo: ABA).

Women brewery workers at a 1 May demonstration in 1907. (Photo: Cph. City Museum).

The founders of the Domestic Workers' Union, 1904. (Photo: ABA).

The daily life of working women: A mangling-woman and her children, who acted as her assistants. The latter took it in turns to stay at home from school in order to turn the mangle. Copenhagen 1908. (Photo: ABA).

One of the many dressmakers' workrooms in Copenhagen at the turn of the century. (Photo: Cph. City Museum).

Union still exists today as an alliance of several women's trade unions and has about 90,000 members.

The pioneers of the struggle for humane conditions for women workers had to do battle on several fronts. First there were the employers, then the female workers' own passivity and lack of interest in collective action, and finally there was often outright opposition on the part of male workers. But the early women's trade union movement was notable for its vitality and self-confidence, qualities that were particularly in evidence among the tailoresses and the General Union of Women Workers.

The Chastity Controversy

When a new Danish edition of John Stuart Mill's *Subjection of Women* appeared in 1885, a foreword had been added by *Georg Brandes* in which he dissociated himself from the political emancipation of women because he believed that they would support reactionary opinions: of far greater importance was the emancipation of women in sexual matters.

After a survey of the development of the family based upon *Friedrich Engels'* book "The Origin of the Family, Private Property and the State", Brandes drew the conclusion that the relationship between men and women was unlikely to have reached its final form. Society will be less concerned in the future with regulating the relationship between men and women but more with care of the children. Brandes asserted that asceticism is "a misfortune, a thing against nature, a sacrifice repeatedly offered up to a worthless prejudice", and of the conjugal state he says that "it may well have done much good as an animal trainer".

This introduction was reproduced in its entirety in the newspaper *Politiken* and triggered off a tremendous uproar among feminists. The Danish Women's Society having just started publishing the periodical *Kvinden og Samfundet* (Woman and Society), under the editorship of *Elisabeth Grundtvig*, it invited *C. N. Starcke*, who later became a politician and professor of philosophy, to write an article contesting Brandes' views. Starcke did not believe that the future trend would be toward free sexual relationships as Brandes thought but that society was likely to impose much more control over men by making them responsible for the maintenance of children born out of wedlock.

Elisabeth Grundtvig entered the debate with a lecture delivered at the request of the Danish Women's Society's executive and entitled "The Present Demand for Moral Equality", in which she explained how social attitudes had hitherto required chastity of the unmarried woman and fidelity of the married, while the same society made no such demands upon men. If there was to be sexual equality between men and women, then the question had to be answered whether women were to become like men or men like women. The lecture was printed in "Woman and Society", and two further contributions followed in the next issue of the magazine. Brandes now got the chance to attack, and first he ridiculed the feminist cause as expounded in the last two articles, then turned his fire upon Elisabeth Grundtvig, whom he accused among other things of misquotation. She reacted strongly and instituted proceedings – not against Brandes, for he had acted anonymously – but against *Politiken*, which was ordered to pay a fine of 100 *kroner* for defamation.

The issue of equality between men and women in wedlock had already been raised by Henrik Ibsen in 1879 in "A Doll's House". Bjørnstjerne Bjørnson's play "A Glove" of 1883 advocated premarital chastity for both men and women, while before this Bjørnson had proposed a more liberal sexual morality for both sexes. He took Elisabeth Grundtvig's part and pronounced Brandes' articles against her as the rudest he had seen for a long time: this broke the friendship between Bjørnson and Brandes. The chastity controversy continued, not only in Denmark but in Norway and Sweden too, with countless contributions from all sides. In Sweden an association of women was even formed whose members pledged themselves "not to marry any man whose past was not pure".

There were differing views within the Danish Women's Society as to whether the Society should concern itself at all with "the demand for moral equality", and an extraordinary general meeting was called to discuss the issue. At the meeting *Nielsine Nielsen*, the first Danish woman doctor, declared that it would be inconsistent of the Society not to claim equal rights socially, economically and politically and yet to do so in the field of moral conduct, which she did not consider to be the feminist movement. Her speech provoked much opposition, for there were many who were well pleased with the Society's espousal of moral issues and felt that criticisms of the work done so far were unjustified. One result of the chastity controversy and the support given to Elisabeth Grundtvig was that the Society lost some members in Copenhagen but on the other hand gained some elsewhere in Denmark. The Society's modest membership rose from 732 to over 1,000 during the course of the year 1887.

Women's Education and Employment

Better Schools and Teachers

The great figure in the task of developing better girls' schools and proper training of women teachers was *Nathalie Zahle* (1827–1913). She herself took up her first governess post at the age of 15 and soon discovered the inadequacy of her background: she accordingly prepared herself for the only examination that existed for women teachers at that time. This was the *institutbestyrerindeeksamen* (academy principalship examination), which she passed when she was 24. Shortly afterwards she obtained permission to establish a girls' higher school. In 1851, by a combination of borrowing and immense personal sacrifices she started a course for private teachers, with a school for children attached to it. Nathalie Zahle herself called her course "a preventive measure against bad teachers". Her activities were wide-ranging and include the founding in 1862 of a training college for women teachers in *almueskoler* (primary schools). It was only a couple of years earlier that teaching in public schools (see page 47) had been opened to women teachers, and then only in girls' classes, but a few years later the regulations were amended to permit them to teach boys. The salaries of women teachers were lower than those of their male colleagues, being generally fixed at about two thirds.

Pauline Worm (1825–83), who during the Clara Raphael controversy had been loudest in declaring the importance of a proper girls' education, was now herself the head of a girls' academy. It was she who had drafted the proposals which had formed the basis on which examinations for women primary school teachers had been introduced in 1859. The test omitted mathematics, physics and gymnastics, replacing them with needlework. Not many took the test during the first ten years – only 12–14 every year – and all of these were employed in urban schools rather than replacing assistant teachers in the country as Pauline Worm had wished. From 1894 onwards teacher training became identical for men and women, except that women were required to take needlework in addition.

But there was no state teacher training college for women. Women had to resort to private colleges such as Nathalie Zahle's, for state colleges were only for men. This was one of the questions that greatly exercised the Danish Women's Society. "Why do you really want these state teacher training colleges?" a government minister once asked a member of the Society. "After all, our private colleges are excellent." Her retort was to the point: "Yes, but they are six times more expensive." Not until 1918 did the government take over the Ribe Seminary and open it as a teacher training college for women.

When the university entrance examination was opened to women in 1875 (see page 108), Nathalie Zahle reluctantly agreed to establish a preparatory course for it. She was in fact not in the least interested in the idea of young girls spending their time learning Latin and Greek but did realise that it would be useful to have a course for girls without private means to enable them to prepare themselves for university. Private education would prevent many girls from becoming students as it was too expensive. As soon as the new school-leaving examination was introduced for boys, Nathalie Zahle arranged for girls to be allowed to enter and herself organised a course for it.

Nathalie Zahle was an exceedingly gifted organiser and succeeded in attracting a number of excellent educationists to her establishment, but it would be wrong to conceive of her as a really creative educationist in her own right. To some extent her ideas about schooling coincided with Grundtvig's, and the children and young people in her schools were made to learn something. At the same time there was a degree of freedom, though accompanied by duty and order.

The feminist movement, of which Nathalie Zahle was not personally an adherent, nevertheless was touched by her influence, not least through her many pupils who graduated from her schools. Many of the latter became heads of schools themselves, and both Nathalie Zahle's school and teacher training college and a number of her pupils' schools still exist today. But they are now mixed schools with upper secondary departments and higher preparatory examination courses. A special girls' school examination, formerly a *raison d'être* of many of the schools, has long since been abolished.

Nurses

Nurses received no sort of formal training, and the task of nursing and tending hospital patients was performed by female ward orderlies and attendants whose reputation was by no means the best. They were considered prone to intemperance, idleness and thievishness. It caused something of a sensation, therefore, when *Ilia Fibiger*, the sister of Mathilde and 13 years her senior, voluntarily enrolled herself as an assistant nurse at the Frederiks Hospital during the cholera epidemic of 1853. Respectable citizens considered it downright scandalous that an unmarried woman of good family should undertake the nursing of strangers. But Ilia held out for six years and only then was promoted to "attendant in charge". By her example she opened the way for a new type of nurse, and in 1863 a hospital medical superintendent began to appoint "ladies for training in nursing". The *Diakonissestiftelse* (Nursing Sisters' Institution) was founded on the initiative of queen Louise in the same year and took up the matter of nurses' training. Something of the narrowness of view prevailing in that age is revealed by the uproar which broke out among the sisters when the Institution's first medical superintendent insisted that they should nurse men as well as women: headed by their matron they declared it incompatible with their modesty. An appeal was made to the queen, who said that the sisters were within their rights in refusing to nurse men. The medical superintendent resigned, and the queen quickly appointed a successor, who was able, shrewd and adroit. It did not take him long to persuade the sisters that their attitude was ill-advised and untenable, and so in the end they agreed to tend both men and women.

The Copenhagen municipal hospital now likewise introduced training for nurses, but it was not until 1899, when the nurses' professional organisation called the *Dansk Sygeplejeråd* (Danish Nurses' Council) was established, that up-to-date and systematic theoretical and practical training was offered.

Female Employment

Some indication of the nature and extent of women's work outside the home may be gleaned from a statistical summary of 1890:

Liberal professions	8,186
Mails, telegraphs, railways (government services)	163
Agriculture	30,878
Industry	40,729
Trade and transport	8,957
Fishing	73
Different kind of women workers	6,373
Diverse contract works	16,045
Servants	121,184
TOTAL	232,588

In relation to total population this means that just under one third of all females over 15 years of age had some form of paid occupation. The only sector showing a vast difference compared with earlier days was agriculture, where the figures had been failing particularly for women but also for men throughout the period for which statistics exist. The figures for almost all other sectors were rising, notably where industry in its widest sense was creating entirely new occupational categories.

Folk High Schools and Women

In Denmark there is a special school for young people founded on the ideas of *N. F. S. Grundtvig*, a priest who was also a poet. In his writings Grundtvig (1783–1872) had advocated a Danish "folk high school" in which young people would be able to find a form of education different from that of the grammar schools and the universities. This "school for living" would teach Danish history, poetry and social problems. However it was not Grundtvig himself who made his "historical and poetical" school for young people a reality, but he did inspire others, and in 1844 the first folk high school was opened in North Schleswig.

This was a "peasants' school", one of whose objects was to provide young peasants with the background they needed in order to represent their estate in public assemblies. No one, oddly enough, stopped to consider that girls too might be able to learn something from the high school, and not until 1863 when eventually there were 15 high schools with a total of about 500 pupils, did the great educationist *Christen Kold* open a summer school for girls in his high school on Funen. Eighteen girls turned up the first summer, and soon the numbers had risen five- or sixfold. Other high schools all over Denmark followed this example, and attendance at a high school came to signify an intellectual revival for young

105

country girls just as for boys. It often made a mark on them for life and gave them interests beyond the daily round.

There are now about 80 folk high schools in Denmark with somewhat varying ideologies – three of them, for example, are workers' high schools – and the aggregate number of pupils reaches about 10,000 every year. They are normally divided into summer and winter terms, but now men and women are educated simultaneously in the schools, and naturally issues of contemporary importance are dealt with.

Admission to University

The Door Opened by an Individual, Not by the Feminist Movement

A college in the United States, opened in 1833, accepted females (and negroes) as students from its inception, and the first American woman doctor qualified in 1849, though only after a series of vain attempts to obtain recognition by a medical school in order to gain admission. In Switzerland the University of Zürich was opened to women in 1867; in Sweden this happened in 1873; London University admitted women on equal terms in 1878.

In Denmark this particular trail of female advance was blazed by *Nielsine Nielsen*, a young shipmaster's daughter from a small Funen seaport. In 1873 she happened by chance to read in a Copenhagen newspaper a brief paragraph in the fine print to the effect that women in the United States could now study medicine and that there was already one woman practising as a doctor in one of the states. This made a strong impression on her – so strong that she swore an oath to herself to do everything in her power to become a doctor. She was then 23 years of age and had been working for several years as a private teacher, but this work did not satisfy her. After various investigations and enquiries she made contact through an acquaintance with a mayor, *C. E. Fenger*, who had previously been medical superintendent of Frederiks Hospital. He was very sympathetic to the idea of women doctors and indeed had complained about the fact that no woman had yet commenced medical studies in Denmark. Fenger became Nielsine Nielsen's protector and helper in the years that followed. He advised her to apply to the Ministry of Ecclesiastical Affairs and Public Instruction for permission to take the university entrance examination with a view to studying medicine afterwards, and he delivered the application to the Ministry personally in January 1874. Nielsine Nielsen never received any reply, but in July 1875 she read in the newspaper that by royal decree women could now be admitted to study at Copenhagen University on the same terms as men, though women studying theology could not take the final examination but must enter for a special religious examination.

By this time Nielsine Nielsen had already been preparing for the university entrance examination for a year and a half and was studying under an ideal teacher. This man taught impecunious young men without charge to help them to take the entrance examination, and he accepted his new pupil with pleasure. Other women followed, and a little class of four was formed, though two dropped out later. Nielsine Nielsen had to work as a private teacher herself in order to make a living. An ardent member of the Danish Women's Society named *Marie Rovsing* heard of Nielsine Nielsen's plans and her financial situation, and she formed a secret circle of feminist women to provide support for Nielsine and so enable her to devote herself to her studies full-time. Nielsine never knew the identities of her benefactresses. For that matter she knew nothing about the Danish Women's Society and her desire to be a doctor owed nothing to any notions of emancipation. A warm friendship developed between Marie Rovsing and Nielsine Nielsen despite the difference in their ages, and Nielsine joined the Society and subsequently became one of its leaders.

Processing of the Application

As soon as the Ministry of Ecclesiastical Affairs and Public Instruction had received Nielsine Nielsen's application it had sent it to the University Senate for comment. The latter wanted to have the purely legal side clarified first and accordingly made enquiries of the Faculty of Law and Political Science, which stated that women had no entitlement under the law to be enrolled in the University. But since on the other hand the law neither directly nor indirectly forbade the admission of women, the question must lie within the competence of the highest University authorities to decide. Any ruling concerning such admission must be consistent with the objective of the University: "To promote and extend the pursuit of scholarship as demanded by the spirit of the age." This opinion was passed on to the Medical Faculty, where most of the professors were favourably inclined and the dean gave his recommendation with the remark that the Faculty could not be expected to provide special lectures or practical training for women, who would be on an absolutely equal footing with male students. One professor alone dissociated himself from the dean's view in a long letter, one of his arguments being that "since the Faculty ought to have the weal and woe of its students at heart, we should therefore do everything possible to spare them from these persons, who in disregard of every sense of decency and propriety will seek to satisfy their sexual appetites by attending medical lectures along with the students"; further on he says, "Admittedly it can be argued against me that the state may be said in some sense to have taken indecency under its protection when it permits and regulates prostitution, but the latter is regarded nowadays as a necessary evil, while women doctors may be called a somewhat unnecessary evil, from which every Danish man would surely wish his country to be spared."

When the matter finally came before the University Council there were 25 votes out of 34 in favour of the admission of women, though with two important special provisos. One was that no examinations or academic degrees were to give women admission to public office while the other debarred female students from receiving scholarships or similar benefits.

The theologians were so uneasy about the entire business that they had a special religious test introduced for women in place of the final examination as well as a rule against female students of divinity speaking from the pulpit like the men. However, no one ever actually took the special test, and when a woman began studying divinity many years later she applied to take the ordinary final examination and graduated as a Bachelor of Divinity in 1916.

Once the University had opened its portals to women its example was followed by the other institutions of higher education such as the Polytechnic Institute (now the Technical University of Denmark), the Royal Veterinary and Agricultural College, the College of Dentistry and the College of Pharmacy. Few women applied for the first two of these but many women became dentists and pharmacists.

The First Women Academics

The first two women students were admitted to the University in 1877, both of them going in for medicine. Their male colleagues accepted them well, and there were no difficulties. But they were unable to become members of the Students' Union, which held a dramatic general meeting on the question. When the more liberal Students' Association was founded in 1882 it was taken for granted that women students were eligible for membership. But the Students' Union held out against women right up to 1898.

Nielsine Nielsen became a physician in 1885 and after doing hospital work for some years established herself in practice in Copenhagen. Her friend passed her examinations the following year, and 21 women had graduated in medicine by the turn of the century. Twenty-three had graduated in arts or science and one in political science but none so far in law.

The average annual student enrollment in the period 1885–89 consisted of eight women and 368 men, but when the state upper secondary schools were opened to girls in 1903 and the *nysproglig studentereksamen* (university entrance examination with modern languages) was subsequently introduced, the number of women students increased every year. The average enrollment for 1905–09 consisted of 58 women and 414 men and for 1915–19 of 223 women and 726 men.

The Medical Faculty for a long time retained its special attraction for women. The graduates of the period 1905–09 included 22 in medicine, 15 in arts or science, 4 in political science and/or economics, and 4 in law. But the first woman to obtain a doctoral degree did so in the Faculty of Philosophy in 1893, and it was not until 1906 that a woman obtained a doctorate in medicine.

When the first woman took the university entrance examination, the clear aim of almost all of them was to obtain an academic education; these were mature women in their mid-twenties, who gradually attained their goal often at the cost of privation and immense difficulties. Later on the upper secondary school and thus the university entrance examination became a continuation and conclusion of school life for many middle- and upper-class girls. The percentage of girls who became students rose year by year, while that of women students taking final university examinations fell. Thus, in the ten years 1915–24 between one third and one quarter of all first-year students were women while 204 women and 2,662 men graduated during the same period. It should be observed that the figures are not strictly comparable, but they do afford an impression of the orders of magnitude involved. Fifty years after women had gained admittance to university, over 4,000 had taken the university entrance examination but barely 400 had completed a course of university study.

Employment Opportunities

The subsequent careers of women with an academic education varied widely. Graduates in medicine had the best chances: they could obtain teaching posts in hospitals and become registrars or establish themselves in general practice. Graduates in arts or science had opportunities of teaching appointments in private schools, and when the state upper secondary schools were opened to girls in 1903 it was laid down at the same time that vacant teaching posts were to be filled by women in approximate proportion to the numbers of female pupils. The salaries of male and female teachers were far from equal, however.

The few graduates in political economy had difficulty in finding employment. The Department of Statistics employed women in minor clerical posts inferior to those available to men with an academic education, and women did not get promotion. But female graduates in politics or economics did have a chance of being appointed to the Inspectorate of Factories on an equal footing with women engineers.

It was a long time before any woman went in for studying law, for a supreme court ruling of 1888 had established that women could not act as counsel. The background to this was that a woman holding the *exam jur.*, a non-academic legal qualification now abolished, who was employed by a barrister as his managing clerk, appeared in court for him but was turned away – which a man similarly qualified would not have been. She instituted proceedings but lost, and this verdict was confirmed by the supreme court as already noted. The first woman to graduate in law did so in 1905, and it was through her efforts that women achieved the right to act as counsel. Subsequent Acts of 1908 and 1916 opened various subordinate legal posts in the public service to women.

The question of equality of the sexes in applying for public service appointments came under consideration by Parlia-

Georg Brandes (1842–1927), literary critic, supported the feminist movement but subsequently disappointed it by dissociating himself from the political emancipation of women.
Matilde Bajer (1840–1934), founder and first president of the Danish Women's Society 1871–72.

Elisabeth Grundtvig (1856–1945), one of the leading figures of the Danish Women's Society. She gained particular renown for her part in the chastity controversy.
Pauline Worm (1825–83), authoress and teacher, was known all over Denmark for her lecturing activities, especially on feminist questions. (Photos: Royal Library).

Line Luplau (centre) surrounded by other persons also involved in her struggle for women's suffrage. Fredrik Bajer is on her right, with Matilde Bajer at his side. Sitting on Line Luplau's left is Nielsine Nielsen, the physician. Painting by Marie Luplau *Fra Kvindevalgretskampens Tid* ("From the Age of the Women's Suffrage Campaign"), hanging in the Danish Parliament.

The Danish Women's Society's young standard-bearer at the head of the suffragette procession on the occasion of the constitutional amendment giving women equal political rights, 1915. (Photos: Royal Library).

Jutta Bojsen-Møller, president of the Danish Women's Society for 16 years, is seen here with Matilde Bajer and others at the head of the deputation of which Henni Forchhammer acted as spokeswoman when it presented an address to the King on Constitution Day, 5 June 1915. (Politiken Photo).

The 1887 graduating class from Nathalie Zahle's school, with Gyrithe Lemche on the left of the picture. The average number of female students per annum during the five years 1885–89 was eight, compared with 368 men.

The first three women to participate as experts in meetings of the League of Nations: Christine Bonnevie, Norway, Anna Wicksell, Sweden, and Henni Forchhammer. The last-mentioned was a leading figure of the Danish Women's National Council, being president from 1913 to 1931. Bodil Begtrup (born 1903), an economist and former ambassador, was an important figure in both the Danish and the international women's movements. (Photo: Royal Library).

ment in 1904 in conjunction with a legal modification of the position of the Department of Statistics. Two Members of Parliament put forward a proposal that the Department should open all its posts to women. The Lower House carried it unanimously, but the Upper House wanted it to be discussed by an *ad hoc* committee and the whole question of women's eligibility for public office to be brought under consideration. As part of the latter process the committee ordered a study of which appointments could suitably be filled by women and the conditions of service that would be appropriate. The Danish Women's Society was asked for its views and replied that while certain specific appointments were unsuitable for women, e. g. in the military service, in principle a woman ought to be on an equal footing with men in appointments to office or employment in other public service posts. The effect of marriage on appointment to or continuance in office ought theoretically to be the same for men and women, but the Society was convinced that the great majority of female officials would choose the home rather than the job after marriage. The views of the University were canvassed as well, and all the faculties except Divinity had no doubts about placing women on a par with men and took it for granted that they should receive the same remuneration and not be hindered from being appointed to or continuing in a post because of marriage.

Pressure of time prevented the question from being taken any further during the 1904–05 Parliamentary session, but it was raised once more during the next session. The Lower House again adopted the proposal, which was thereupon buried in a committee of the Upper House. During the deliberations of the Upper House one conservative landowner said: "If this measure is passed, then we shall hear the swift steps of tiny feet and the rustle and swish of skirts . . . in government building. This is something we have never had before." A true but empty statement.

Not until after the First World War were laws enacted formally giving to women almost total equality with men in
these matters, and these were some of the momentous
changes whose adoption was assisted by the women newly
elected to Parliament.

The Biggest Women's Organisation – The Danish Women's National Council

The Background

Women who were campaigning in the United States for the temperance movement and against negro slavery assembled at Seneca Falls in 1848 for the first women's congress, from which sounded forth the call for full civil rights for women. Here the celebrated "Declaration of Sentiments" was signed as a document of feminine emancipation. Forty years later the National Woman Suffrage Association issued invitations to an international meeting in Washington to honour the pioneers, the "heroines of Seneca Falls". Another aim was to try to form an international council of women to enable women of all social classes, religions, occupations, races and nations to get to know and respect each other. It was also hoped to get women to cooperate to improve the status of women, for the benefit of themselves and of society, of their countries and of the whole world. The "Golden Rule" of doing onto others as you would have them do onto you was adopted as the organisation's motto. Seven European countries and 29 American women's organisations united to form the International Council of Women (ICW). The Danish delegate was taken ill and was unable to attend the meeting.

The ICW held its next international meeting to coincide with the Chicago World's Fair of 1893. *Kirstine Frederiksen*, president of the Danish Women's Society, attended it and returned home full of ideas for gathering the various women's organisations and institutions into national federations which then could formulate detailed statutes for their cooperation. The task of creating a Danish Women's Council to be affiliated to the international organisation proved somewhat complicated, and it was 1899 before this was brought about with seven affiliated organisations representing a fairly comprehensive range of women's interests. As well as the Danish Women's Society these included *Den danske Jordemoderforening* (The Danish Midwives' Union), the *Københavns Kommunelærerindeforening* (Copenhagen City Women Teachers' Union), *sammenslutningen "Den Danske Pigeskole"* (the "Danish Girls' School"organisation), *Tegne- og Kunstindustriskolen for Kvinder* (School of Draughtsmanship and Applied Art for Women), *Københavns kvindelige Gymnastikforening* (Women's Gymnastics Association of Copenhagen) and *Kvindehjemmet* (The Women's Home), which latter is still in existence and is a social institution for helping women in difficult circumstances, especially those with children. The Danish Women's Council has retained its broadly-based structure down the years and has been of great value in making representations to the government or the authorities. The Council changed its name later to *Danske Kvinders Nationalråd* (DKN), or the Danish Women's National Council.

It has always been a prime objective of the National Council to work in concert with the International Council of Women in a variety of fields that naturally change with the times. At the purely practical level what happens is that Danish committees are established corresponding to the ICW standing committees on such topics as peace and the arbitration of disputes, woman suffrage, women's occupations, women's legal status, moral equality, public health and child care. International cooperation on such issues is practised both at congresses and at other meetings and also, most notably, through exchanges of written information and the answering af questionnaires. The affiliated Danish organisations having a special interest in the work of one or more of the committees are brought into it, and this may result in representations being made to particular authorities or to the government on behalf of both the National Council and various of its affiliated organisations.

Work for Peace and for the Victims of Two World Wars

Votes for women and work for peace were the issues that concerned the Danish Women's National Council at the time of the Second Hague Peace Conference in 1907, and its representatives at the Conference gave voice to the desire of Danish women for peace in the world. In the midst of the First World War *Henni Forchhammer* (1863–1955), president of the National Council, managed to secure Danish participation in the international women's conference in The Hague which led to the foundation of the International Women's League for Peace and Freedom. During the Second World War the Danish section of the League attained a membership of over 22,000 and did a great deal of publicity work, notably on international problems and the importance of cooperation between peoples.

In Denmark during the First World War the National Council helped to alleviate female unemployment by establishing a study-room and a high school course lasting some months for unemployed women. Food supply difficulties occasioned the arranging of courses for housewives in the preparation of such victuals as were to be had, and sewing courses to teach women how to repair garments eased the burden of hard times. These tasks were subsequently assumed by the government.

During the war Henni Forchhammer was the only member of the ICW executive who came from a neutral country, so that it became her task to preserve the links between the national councils of the belligerent countries and afterwards to negotiate the resumption of international collaboration. After the armistice the Danish Women's National Council participated in the relief work whereby German and Austrian children were placed in Danish homes, a special feature being its support through its president for the work done by *Karen Jeppe* (1876–1935), a Danish citizen, for Armenian women and children, and by *Fridtjof Nansen* (1861–1930), the Norwegian explorer, to rescue Russian women refugees in Constantinople who had resorted to prostitution as the only means of keeping alive.

The Danish Women's National Council was strongly interested in the League of Nations concept long before it became translated into actuality, with the result that from 1920 onwards it was working for the inclusion of women in the delegation to meetings of the League in Geneva. In this way Henni Forchhammer became a member of the Danish delegation from 1920 to 1937 and was the first woman to speak in the Assembly. Her special concern was the fight against the trade in women and children – at that time a most appalling and highly organised traffic. Another Danish woman, an eye specialist and a member of the Social Commission of the League, made a notable contribution to the work of aiding blind children, and when the social status of women was being considered in 1935–37, the Danish government sent the internationally-renowned women's rights campaigner *Anna Westergaard* to the League of Nations at the suggestion of the Danish Women's National Council and other feminist organisations. Henni Forchhammer retired from the presidency in 1931 and was succeeded by *Kirsten Gloerfelt-Tarp*, an economist and a skilful organiser, who held the post until 1946.

During the Spanish Civil War the National Council strongly supported a Danish Quaker in her work of helping Spanish children, and in 1939, working in concert with the League of Jewish Women and the International Women's League for Peace and Freedom, the Council got about 300 Jewish children out of Central Europe and placed them in homes in rural Denmark so that they could learn farming and later settle in Israel. Unfortunately some of the children were taken by the Gestapo in 1943 and sent to the concentration camp Theresienstadt.

During the Second World War and the Occupation the National Council undertook a multiplicity of tasks. When the "Winter War" of 1940–41 was raging between the U.S.S.R. and Finland, help was given to Finnish children, many of whom came to Denmark. There was also much work to be done in Denmark itself, and as the unifying organisation for the numerous feminist interests the Council was able to promote the launching in 1940 of the *Danske Kvinders Samfundstjeneste* (Danish Women's Social Service) under the presidency of *Kirsten Gloerfelt-Tarp* (1889–1977). In this situation organisations other than those affiliated to the National Council joined in with offers of labour, among them being women's trade unions. There were collections of used clothing and "white rags" (which after being processed could be used for medical purposes), and all over Denmark special committees sprang up one after the other for collecting wild fruit from which jam was produced at about 250 cooking centres. In addition, clothes repair centres and a home help service were organised as job-creation measures: the home help service is now run by the government on a permanent basis. Other moves included the establishment of daycare centres for infants.

Supply difficulties persisted after the capitulation, and through its new president, *Bodil Begtrup*, the National Council took the initiative in launching the *Danske Husmødres Forbrugerråd* (Danish Housewives' Consumers' Council, now known as the Consumers' Council), which was able to represent the interests of consumers on the numerous committees and boards which had influence over postwar emergency legislation and its administration. The Consumers'

Council proved itself as events unfolded to be a highly useful and vigorous body (see pp. 172ff.).

The work in which the National Council had participated at the League of Nations was continued under the United Nations in different forms, and Bodil Begtrup attended the General Assembly in London in 1946 and subsequent meetings at the U.N. headquarters in New York. Bodil Begtrup played a vital role in establishing the United Nations Commission on Women and was its first president in 1947. The work in the United Nations has continued ever since, and every year the Danish government invites the Women's National Council to nominate an adviser on equal rights questions as a member of the Danish delegation to the U.N. General Assembly.

Many Other Fields of Activity

Unemployment and the general illiberal mood of the 1930s led to intense attacks on the equal rights laws of 1919 and 1921 (see pp. 141ff.), and the Danish Women's National Council therefore established the *Danske Kvinders Erhvervsråd* (Danish Women's Occupational Council), which may be regarded as a forerunner of the *Ligestillingsråd* (Danish Equal Status Council) established by law in 1978. The Occupational Council intervened in many instances to prevent dismissals of women from both public and private posts in circumstances such as marriage or pregnancy, protested against unfair treatment of women in appointments or promotions, drew attention to discriminatory advertisements and to discrepancies between government notices of job vacancies and the Non-Discrimination Act of 1921 when certain jobs were advertised by sex and not by qualifications.

One matter which engaged much of the attention of the Occupational Council was that of the "closed clerical class", which contained a large number of women. In the public service there were – and still are in certain places – two classes of office staff, the executive and clerical classes. The former of these, in which incumbents had the benefit of proper training, consisted almost exclusively of men, while women were placed in the clerical class, from which it was more or less impossible to transfer to the executive class and receive the training from which opportunities of advancement would flow. The chances of promotion for clerks were infinitesimal. Yet it was not easy to bring the Non-Discrimination Act to bear upon the situation because in principle both classes were open to both sexes: it was simply that in practice there were almost no male clerks or female executives. The Occupational Council succeeded in affording assistance to only a few women in cutting their way through the thickets for regulations into the executive class, and it was not until the labour shortage of the 1960s that the anti-feminist rigidities of the system were broken up.

Another initiative of the same sort was the establishment in 1936 of the *Danske Kvinders Politiske Samråd* (Danish Women's Political Council), whose aim it was to generate greater interest among women in participating in political activity so as to involve more women in local and state government. Among other measures a pamphlet entitled "The Community Calling" was published and a debating society launched. The latter held monthly meetings at which some current political issue would be ventilated by means of brief contributions by women from each of the political parties whereupon a general discussion followed.

A further important task undertaken in the 1930s comprised a nationwide campaign for better child nutrition in collaboration with *Den almindelige danske Lægeforenings Hygiejnekomité* (The Public Hygiene Committee of the Danish Physicians' Union). Women's clubs all over Denmark organised hundreds of free publicity meetings at which a local doctor would speak and a home economics adviser give a demonstration of sound diet followed by a film about baby nutrition.

Women's Social Problems

During the 1940s the National Council itself established two committees, or rather commissions, because the government did not see any reason to intervene in important women's problems. In collaboration with the Danish Women's Society and *De danske Husmoderforeninger* (The Federation of Danish Housewives' Society) a committee was set up in 1944 to examine the situation of widows, and four years later it published its report, containing firstly the results of a question-naire enquiry into the circumstances of about 500 Copen-hagen widows and secondly a series of proposals for economic and social assistance to widows. Some of the proposals in-spired subsequent legislation – although not until after a government commission had once again delved into the mat-ter. The Ministry of Social Affairs provided secretarial assist-ance to support the work of the National Council.

The problem of single mothers was also considered by a commission established by the National Council and the Women's Society in 1948. The Ministry of Social Affairs fur-nished secretarial assistance while the Copenhagen City Of-fice of Statistics processed the results of a questionnaire, as had been done in the case of the widows' enquiry. A report was published in 1953, and a number of its proposals were used as a basis of legislation.

Like the Danish Women's Society, the National Council has concerned itself with other social issues such as pressing for restrictions on children's employment, the opening of more day nurseries, kindergartens and youth centres, the ap-pointment of school doctors and the establishment of a uni-versal school dental service. The Danish branch of the Save the Children Fund was founded at the prompting of the Women's National Council.

The National Council has achieved a position *vis-à-vis* the government where it is used by the latter as a consultative body on any legislative matters, international questions and so forth affecting the interests of women.

The National Council is normally represented on commissions, councils and boards concerned with questions affecting women and the family in a broad sense. Thus, the National Council had two members on the Commission of Enquiry into the Status of Women in Society (1965–74), and on the Equal Status Council that comprises the chief result of the Commission's work the Council is represented by three out of a total of seven members.

The National Council launched a number of activities in connection with the United Nations International Women's Year in 1975 and was represented at the International Women's Conference held in Mexico City. Problems of developing countries have occupied a prominent place in the work of the National Council for a number of years, and the Council has been directly involved in several projects and is represented in the Danish International Development Agency (DANIDA).

The National Council has involved itself in numerous other problems such as the nationality of married women, marriage laws, abortion and the taxation of married women; in this way it has been able to encourage movement towards equality for Danish women both in form and in fact.

The Danish Women's National Council as an Organisation

In 1980 the National Council is an umbrella body embracing more than 40 organisations totalling over half a million members. At the annual general meeting of representatives of the member-organisations a president, vice-president and other executives are elected to conduct day-to-day business.

One of the tasks of the executive committee is to keep abreast of public events of particular interest to women, especially in the field of legislation. When the executive committee believes there is cause for protest, comment, statement or independent proposals, the executive committee will normally put the issue in question to the affiliated organisations in writing so that within a given time-limit they can either associate themselves with what is proposed, suggest changes or decline to be involved.

The many interests represented by the National Council extend from the purely feminist ones such as have been embraced by the Danish Women's Society for over a hundred years through rural and urban housewives' organisations affiliated to the Association of Country World Women (ACWW), to women's sections of political parties and purely professional organisations such as the *Dansk Sygeplejeråd* (Danish Nurses' Council), *Kvindelige Lægers Klub* (Women Physicians' Club), *Jordemoderforeningen* (Midwives' Union), *Kvindelige Akademikere* (Women Academics), *De københavnske kvindelige lærere* (Copenhagen Women Teachers), *Husholdningslærerne* (Home Economics Teachers), *Kvindelige Kunstneres Samfund* (Society of Women Artists) and a single women's trade union, the *Husligt Arbejderforbund* (Domestic Workers' Union). There are also religious organisations such as the *Katolsk Kvindeforbund* (Federation of Catholic Women). The Danish branch of the Women's International Zionist Organisation, the Women's Circle of the Salvation Army, and the KFUK (= YWCA); as well as these there are temperance societies, charitable organisations, Soroptimist Clubs affiliated to the Soroptimist International Association, the *Grønlandske Kvindeforeningers Sammenslutning* (Federation of Greenland Women's Associations) and others.

The National Council holds two or three meetings every year on matters of current concern and seeks by this means to strengthen cooperation between the organisations. In addition, for almost 20 years courses lasting several days have been organised on such topics as women and politics, obligations to women in developing countries and the increasing frequency of working women at a time of rising unemployment. Faroese women have twice selected topics and participated in courses, while Danish women have twice visited the Faroes under the auspices of the National Council and so obtained an insight into women's status there.

The organisation's link with the ICW continues to occupy a primary place in the work of the executive committee. The ICW is recognised as a consultative non-governmental organisation by the United Nations, the ILO, UNESCO and other bodies. The European regional organisation of ICW (ECICW) also engages the attention of the executive committee through its two fixed annual meetings and occasional conferences. Furthermore, the National Councils of the Nordic countries collaborate closely through annual meetings and other joint arrangements and in submissions to the interparliamentary Nordic Council. Thus, for instance, the National Council works in concert with the Nordic Council on school textbooks and other educational materials. There are also links with the European Community, and prior to the referendum of 1972 the Women's National Council mounted a large-scale publicity drive without itself adopting a position on the issue of Denmark's membership.

The leadership of the Women's National Council endeavour by immense personal exertions and on an extremely tight budget to promote the interests of women both nationally and internationally, in the economic, family, professional, social and cultural spheres so that women may take an active part in the development of society and help to shape its character.

The Struggle for Political Rights

Discord among Feminists

The general political situation of the mid-1880s was marked by profound clashes of interest. The government was confronted by a Lower House with an opposition majority but commanded the support of an Upper House which was able to block any law. The Danish Women's Society worked very cautiously and had no wish to commit itself on issues that could bring it into the party political arena, even where these concerned women's rights, and this provoked displeasure among some of its supporters. Furthermore, there were others who felt that the Society was too closely associated with the better-off middle classes.

In 1886 this led to the formation of the *Kvindelig Frem-skridtsforening* (Women's Union for Progress) under the leadership of *Matilde Bajer*, the first president of the Danish Women's Society. Unlike the latter, the Union accepted only women because it was afraid that men would have an inhibiting influence on the willingness of women to participate in the activities of the Union generally. The special objective of the Union was to discuss political questions from all angles, and on the most burning issue of the age, namely defence, it favoured a reduction of expenditure for military purposes. Other causes which it took up were the feeding of children in primary schools, the "maidservant question" (their reliability, competence, cleanliness etc.), married women's rights and similar matters. Yet another highly popular and pressing cause was in the spotlight – the provision of public toilets for women in Copenhagen, a matter which previously had been neglected by the city fathers, possibly because of a misplaced sense of modesty.

Johanne Meyer, a journalist with the *Socialdemokraten* newspaper, succeeded Matilde Bajer in the leadership. The newly-formed Union dared not as yet declare officially that its aim was full political equality for women, but when a large-scale international exhibition was to be held in Copenhagen in 1888, the Union for Progress took the initiative in issuing invitations at the same time to a Nordic feminist meeting whose programme was to include women's political rights. During the days when the congress was being held the Union published the first issue of "WHAT-WE-WANT. The Journal of Feminism, Peace and Labour". Its editor was Johanne Meyer, formerly also a member of the Women's Society. The paper also became the mouthpiece of *De samlede Kvindeforeninger* (The Confederation of Women's Unions), a newly-formed coalition of seven trade unions including the *Kvindeligt Arbejderforbund* (General Union of Women Workers), *De kvindelige Herreskrædere* (The Tailoresses), the tobacco workers and the weavers. Another organisation joined the following year: this was the *Kvindevalgretsforening* (Women's Suffrage Association), founded by *Line Luplau*, a member of the Women's Society.

The First Bill for Local Suffrage

A Bill had been put forward in the Lower House by *Fredrik Bajer* in 1886 for women's suffrage on the same terms as men in elections to the Copenhagen City Council. The proposal also extended to married women, who for this purpose were to be regarded as "having disposal over their own estates, even though they may live with their husbands in community of property". The Bill was buried in a committee, but when Bajer decided to revive it the Union for Progress hastened to submit a supporting petition to Parliament, and a little later the Women's Society sent in a petition as well. It was signed by 1,887 women, including 619 female taxpayers. (At that time there were about 4,000 women paying tax in Copenhagen).

When the Bill was brought in again the Lower House approved it after a lengthy debate but the Upper House rejected it. However, the Speaker of the latter stated that it might be appropriate to consider it in the context of a general reform, but not in the shape of the present Bill. This caused Bajer to remark in a report on the affair: "It fell, but it fell forwards!"

In the next Parliamentary session in the autumn of 1887 Bajer presented a new Bill applying to the whole country and conferring the franchise (though not eligibility for election) upon widows and single women. Married women were thus not covered, for the previous Bill had provoked much resistance in Parliament through their inclusion. The Women's Society lent its support to the Bill by handing in a national petition bearing about 20,000 signatures; but a particular impression was made when a special petition came from the small market town of Varde and its surrounding district signed by 1,702 women. No one had believed that the cause of emancipation had adherents in western Jutland. The moving spirit here was a clergyman's wife, *Line Luplau*, and to have achieved this result in a fairly short time was something of a feat.

The Lower House approved the proposal, but the Upper House gave it a difficult passage. *Carl Ploug* (1813–94), a prominent politician of the day, declared that he might be able to agree that women owning substantial property in a local district might be granted a say in the management of the latter, but that to give local suffrage to all unmarried female taxpayers would end up with its being extended likewise to "widows taking in laundry for a living, 24 or 25 year-old seamstresses – in short, to people on the brink of poor relief". Moreover, Ploug continued, women were neither ready for the franchise nor did most of them care about it. "It is true that Parliament received a petition from seventeen or eighteen hundred women in Copenhagen last year and another from Varde this year. Let us now go on to assign an equal importance to the esteemed ladies of Varde and Copenhagen. I would not offend the one at the expense of the other but will content myself with observing that it is here in Copenhagen, of course, that the widest extremes prevail; it is here, I contend, that the most radical, most fanatical and most fiercely ambitious women are to be found; but that they exist on the west coast of Jutland – that I had never heard, nor do I believe it." Ploug held to the view that society's interest could not be served by drawing women away from their proper sphere of charitable works in order to wrangle with politicians in a political club. He moved a resolution reading: "The Upper House being convinced that the enfranchisement of women would be in the interests neither of themselves nor of society at large, it proceeds to next business." This Parliamentary device for dropping the matter was successful. Naturally Ploug's utterances drew a reaction from women. Johanne Meyer, writing in WHAT-WE-WANT, declared: "He should have said, 'Women ought therefore to be brought in, since the organising of our society is an affair of the heart. For we ought not so to order our society that hundreds of working people's children have to rely upon the parish for their daily bread and their daughters upon immorality for their livelihoods; neither should we have laws that favour one class at the expense of another; but above all we ought not to exploit one sex for the benefit of the other." A number of protest meetings were held, too, including a mass meeting in the Deer Park to the north of Copenhagen, and in general a great deal of activity went forward with a view to arousing the interest of women in equal political rights. The Union for Progress established a "Socio-Political School for Women", with courses in civics, history since 1848, the law of domestic relations, constitutional law, ethics and psychology, for the purpose of endowing women with the knowledge needful for making fruitful use of political rights.

At the time of the election to the Lower House in 1890, Line Luplau suggested that candidates should be questioned regarding their attitudes to equal political rights for women or other feminist issues. She succeeded in getting the various women's organisations to support the idea and in finding women willing to ask the questions. Every organisation formulated its own questions, and the Women's Society asked whether the candidate would work for improvement of the status of women and for the rights of women to take part in local elections while the Women's Suffrage Association enquired about attitudes to full political rights for women.

Liberal and Social Democratic candidates favoured amelioration of the legal status of married women and local political rights for women while being less positive about full political equality, it being considered that women were only moderately interested in the latter. Almost all Conservative candidates gave negative responses on both local and national suffrage for women. And at one place the chairman of a meeting illegally refused a woman the right to speak.

Despondency Spreads

Repeated efforts were made during the 1890s to get the local government electoral laws changed. The Bills put forward differed slightly from one another, so that there were variations in the categories of women who would have received the franchise and become eligible for election. Some covered the whole of Denmark; others applied only to the Copenhagen City Council. But the fate that befell them in Parliament was quite repetitive: passed by the Lower House and thrown out by the Upper. Politically the path of progress was blocked, as it was for all other reform legislation at that time.

The new women's organisations gradually lost heart, for the situation appeared to them hopeless. The real inspiration and leadership had been supplied by Line Luplau, who now lived in Copenhagen. Her death in 1891 caused the Suffrage Association to wither away, and in 1895 both the Union for Progress and the periodical WHAT-WE-WANT died. The Confederation of Women's Unions was likewise dissolved during the general despondency and loss of faith in quick results.

The situation looked rather different to the Danish Women's Society, which had many strings to its bow and whose president, *Jutta Bojsen-Møller* (1837–1927), was full of ideas and initiative. Thus in 1895 she sought by personal appeal to influence all those Members of Parliament who were opposed to local suffrage for women. She succeeded in getting two members of the Lower House to put forward the Society's very moderate electoral Bill, which would have given local suffrage – but not eligibility – to female taxpayers. Again the Bill foundered in the Upper House, where the ten Conservative members whom Jutta Bojsen-Møller thought she had won over by her "crusade" dwindled to only five and they abstained!

Renewed Activity:
New Women's Suffrage Organisations

A Bill for changes in the franchise for the Copenhagen City Council was proposed in 1898 by the Minister for Home Affairs. It contained nothing about women's suffrage, but in the Lower House the Bill was amended and adopted in a new form that placed men and women on an equal footing, with the result that the Upper House acted in its customary fashion by throwing it out.

This was seen by feminists as a provocation, and a considerable bustle of activity was triggered off. An alliance of women's organisations, the *Danske Kvindeforeningers Valgretsudvalg* (Danish Women's Unions' Suffrage Committee) was quickly formed with the sole object of securing the local

and national enfranchisement of women. Among those af-
filiating themselves were not only the Copenhagen Circle of
the Danish Women's Society and the *Kvindelig Læseforening*
(Women's Reading Club) but also an array of occupational
organisations such as the Midwives' Union, *Københavns
Kommunelærerindeforening* (Copenhagen City Women
Teachers' Union), *Cirklen* (The Women Artists' and Authors'
Circle), *De kvindelige Herreskrædere* (The Tailoresses),
Sølvpolererskeforeningen (The Women Silver-Polishers'
Union), *Kvindernes Handels- og Kontoristforening* (Women's
Business and Office Workers' Union); and there were others
which joined later.

Even before the Upper House had had time to reject the
amended proposal of the Minister for Home Affairs, the new
joint organisation had made an approach – without success –
to the relevant Parliamentary committee asking that the Bill
should be brought into line with what the majority in the
Lower House had adopted. Shortly after this both the Liberal
Reform party and the Social Democrats introduced legislative proposals for changes in the local franchise that included votes for women on the same terms as for men. The
Suffrage Committee gave its support, and branches of the
Danish Women's Society all over the country submitted a
petition.

Activity was wide-ranging. The Suffrage Committee approached the individual members of the Upper House when
it was considering a Bill for extending to independent unmarried female taxpayers the right to vote but not to stand as
candidates in elections to the Copenhagen City Council, and
a majority was mustered in favour. But since the proposal
was linked to another which was rejected by the Upper
House, the outcome was negative. Nevertheless, it was an encouragement, for it did now look as though local enfranchisement was in sight.

When a new Minister for Home Affairs appeared on the

scene the Suffrage Committee went straight to him to ask him to bring in on his own a Bill for local suffrage and eligibility for women. He was unwilling to do this but promised to support any such measure introduced by others. A number of members of the Lower House were then approached, but they took the view that women should be enfranchised as part of a comprehensive reform of local electoral law.

Even after the change of the Danish political system consequent upon the victory of the principle of Cabinet responsibility in 1901, when only eight Conservatives won seats in the Lower House and the king had to appoint a Liberal ministry, many years passed before equal local political rights for women became a reality. Numerous Bills were presented, but none could get past the Upper House, where the Conservative majority could not stomach the idea of the vote's being exercised by married women or servants. It was 1908 before local electoral reform was implemented.

In the meantime, however, a number of statutes were brought in conferring certain political rights upon women. Church vestries were established by law in 1903, and women were eligible both to vote for and to be elected to them provided they applied for inclusion on the electoral register. In 1904 a law dealing with primary schools was passed and a system of school commissioners established. Widows with children attending a country school were given both voting rights and eligibility in this connection. A law establishing child welfare committees to deal with neglected and difficult children was enacted in 1905, and the members were to be appointed by the local authorities. Women were eligible for these committees. The fourth and last such law to be passed before the reform of local government concerned relief funds to aid persons in distress. Unmarried female taxpayers over 25 and wives of male taxpayers were permitted both to vote and to stand as candidates in the elections to the committees administering these funds.

Equal Local Citizenship for Women at Last

The government Bill which was adopted in 1908 gave both the vote and eligibility to women over 25 who paid tax themselves or whose husbands paid tax either out of the joint funds or out of the wife's own property. But after being first introduced in 1906 the Bill had to be amended, for the Conservative majority in the Upper House would not relinquish the privileged franchise, restricted to those who paid the highest taxes. The government had to make certain concessions, and the privileged franchise was maintained for the county councils.

Both in the Danish Women's Society and in *Landsforbundet for Kvinders Valgret* (The National Alliance for Women's Suffrage), established in 1906, the question was now eagerly debated whether special women's candidate lists should be compiled or whether women should be encouraged to join the political parties and make their mark there. The latter was favoured by the vast majority, but there were some who said that if they could not get on to a county council without being a member of a party they would rather stay off it.

The excitement surrounding the first election after the reform was intense. How would women use their vote, and how many of them would be elected? When the results of the March 1909 elections were reckoned up it was found that 50 % of women voters had voted compared with 76 % of men, and this was felt to be satisfactory. But only 127 women had been elected compared with 9,682 men, so that there was considerable disappointment among the champions of women's suffrage. Moreover, in some places the Women's Society had put up special women's candidate lists and had everywhere had only one woman elected.

The subsequent trend up to the Second World War showed a steady rise in women's exercise of the vote, which gradually attained a point about 10 % lower than men's, but the numbers of women elected to the councils did not increase. A nadir was reached in the elections of 1925, when only 90 women were elected. In 1937 the figure was 117: stagnation in other words.

It generally turned out that once women had got on to the local councils they tended to be re-elected and that they made themselves respected through the excellent work they did. The big problem was getting them adopted by the constituency associations, which had many interests to take into account. Furthermore, women often displayed a certain diffidence about making speeches in assemblies composed almost exclusively of men, but anyone putting up for election had to do it.

Full Political Equality

The only women's organisation totally committed to equal political rights for women at the turn of the century was the Danish Women's Unions' Suffrage Committee. The Danish Women's Society was suffering from internal schisms and contented itself officially with championing local enfranchisement. But its president, Jutta Bojsen-Møller, and the Copenhagen Circle of the Society worked in close concert with the Suffrage Committee, the Society's local circles being self-governing and "Mother Jutta" an extremely independent person. It was not until 1906 – the same year that the Society hosted a IWSA congress in Copenhagen – that its objects clause was amended to include full political rights. But during this long period of hesitation a number of new suffrage organisations were established.

A *Politisk kvindeforening* (Women's Political Association) was formed in 1904 with the aim of publishing and discussing political affairs, but it soon turned into a suffrage organisation pure and simple, and changed its name to the *Københavns Kvindevalgretsforening* (Copenhagen Women's Suf-

135

frage Organisation). Despite its name it took a particular interest in the establishing of similar organisations elsewhere in Denmark, and in a short space of time there were a number of independent women's suffrage organisations all over the country. They joined together in 1907 to form a national federation comprising eventually 160 organisations with over 11,000 members. The Women's Society had about 7,000 members and 112 circles in 1910. The national federation published a periodical called *Kvindevalgret* (Women's Suffrage), while *Kvindestemmeretsbladet* (The Women's Franchise Magazine) was already in existence at that time, being published by yet another organisation called *Kvindevalgretsklubben* (The Women's Suffrage Club). Women's suffrage groups were also being formed in country districts. The women's suffrage movement received political support from another quarter when *Foreningen af Mænd for Kvinders Valgret* (Men United for Women's Suffrage) was established. It was 1913 before that happened, by which time the issue had in fact been settled, but the initiative for it sprang from *Den internationale Mandsliga for Kvindevalgret* (Men's International League for Women's Suffrage), which was formed in 1912.

These many organisations were exceedingly active. They held meetings and endeavoured to activate women, submitted petitions to the government and Parliament, sent deputations to new governments, questioned candidates at election meetings about their views on women's suffrage, arranged "weeks of agitation" all over Denmark and, in short, exploited every opportunity of drawing attention to the demand for the enfranchisement of women. During the election of 1909, for example, the Women's Society got a poster put into the polling stations saying "Universal suffrage does not exist in Denmark as long as women do not have the vote."

It made a profound impression in Denmark when the Grand Duchy of Finland, then under Russian rule, gave

136

women full political rights in 1906. Women in Norway had been granted a limited local vote in 1902, and in 1907 a law was passed extending this to Parliamentary elections.

Sympathy for the cause gradually increased among the political parties. The Social Democratic party was the first to adopt full political rights for women as part of its programme. *Frederik Borgbjerg*, later to become Minister of Education, introduced a constitutional amendment Bill in 1907 abolishing the privileged franchise for the Upper House. At the same time the vote was to be granted to women, servants and persons over age 21. We do not have universal suffrage, said Borgbjerg, when half our people – i.e., women – are excluded. The amendment had no chance at all as long as there was a Conservative majority in the Upper House, but it did set a target.

Opposition to women's suffrage dwindled little by little to a hard core of Conservatives, although there were a few members of other parties whose objections persisted and who thought it best to wait until the results of local women's suffrage were in. But then, astonishingly, the resistance of the most inveterate opponents of women's suffrage began to thaw under questioning. The reason was simple: the opinion had become prevalent that women were more conservative than men. *Georg Brandes* stated this view explicitly in an article in "Women's Suffrage", and a similar attitude lay behind a Conservative proposal in 1908 for the introduction of *compulsory* voting in local elections. It was argued bluntly that now that women had the vote they ought to be obliged to use it.

Several proposals for a new Constitution came up for consideration. For example the Social-Liberals, in accordance with their party programme of 1905, put forward a Bill to confer both suffrage and eligibility on women. However, it failed even to get as far as the Upper House, though for reasons unconnected with women's suffrage.

Women's organisations continued to be active, and during the elections to the Lower House in 1910 they contrived to question all the candidates on their attitudes to the cause. Only one now remained opposed, a landowner from Vonsild named Bramsen. He was reluctant to force the vote upon women, saying: "It will make things a lot more difficult to have to drag your wife along with you to make your vote count."

The Liberal party twice tried in vain to surmount the Upper House barricades by means of a Bill to increase the number of members of the Lower House and give women equal rights with regard to the Lower House while retaining the privileged franchise for the Upper House, so that the latter would have to be changed later. A number of women's trade unions supported this.

Several other constitutional amendments were proposed, supported by women, accepted by the Lower House and rejected by the Upper. After the Lower House elections of 1913 the outlook improved somewhat. The Social-Liberals now formed a minority government with Social Democratic support, and in the Upper House the government parties and the Conservatives were in balance with 33 members each. When a constitutional Bill came before the Upper House after many amendments, the 33 Conservatives walked out, leaving the House without a quorum. The Prime Minister accordingly appealed to the country, and the supporters of the constitutional Bill were returned in greater force, so that full political rights for women were now assured – but then the war broke out and there were other things to think about.

Enfranchisement and the Procession of Women

Gyrithe Lemche, editor of the Danish Women's Society's journal "Woman and Society", had repeatedly expressed her dissatisfaction over the linking of women's suffrage with general political demands. In her view the issue was far too important to become part of the campaign against electoral privileges. She wanted women to be constitution-makers, i.e. to have political rights first, so that they could exert influence over the forthcoming new Constitution. For "the recognition of women as political citizens is not a secondary consideration as people generally would have it . . . It signifies nothing less than a change of system." But this idea of bringing in the new Constitution at two tempi found no favour at all among politicians.

The new Constitution was ready for the king's signature on 5 June 1915, and many women wanted to mark the day in some fashion. In a committee with representatives of the Danish Women's National Council (see pp. 115ff.), the special suffrage organisations and the Danish Women's Society, Gyrithe Lemche, now president of the Society's executive committee, proposed that a procession of women should be arranged to arrive at Amalienborg Palace at the historic moment when the king was to sign the Constitution. The proposal was adopted, but the invitations sent out to participants contained neither the word "thanks" nor "pleasure". Instead, they declared that the procession of women was to be "testimony that we appreciate and value the right of citizenship from which men of all parties are at one in wishing us to be excluded no longer".

The procession that wound its way decorously from the assembly-point to the Palace square was impressive and well-organised, with the Danish flag at its head followed by the banner of the Danish Women's Society surrounded by 30 young women clad in white. About 20,000 women are estimated to have taken part. The spokesman was *Henni Forchhammer*, president of the Danish Women's National Council, who headed a deputation to present to the king an address in which the word "pleasure" did appear. The king offered his thanks, and in his reply remarked "that there is one place

139

where we cannot do without women, and that is the home".
Prime Minister C. Th. Zahle likewise expressed thanks for the
address and bade the women welcome as Danish citizens. He
declared his belief that women would love peace and support
social legislation.

The procession then made its way to Parliament, whose
members welcomed the women by standing to receive the deputation. The Speaker of the Lower House declared that it
had been a great pleasure to correct the inequality previously
existing and that Parliament looked forward with confidence
to the entry of women into the affairs of the community.

The only two women's political organisations then existing
did not want to participate in the procession. *Højres Kvinder*
(Conservative Women) was not against having the vote but
probably regretted the loss of privileges for the well-to-do.
The *Socialdemokratisk Kvindeforening* (Social Democratic
Women's Union) was on the preparatory committee but
withdrew because it preferred to participate instead in the
Social Democratic constitutional procession and festival. But
there were some who said afterwards that they had easily
managed to get to both celebrations!

Non-Discrimination Laws

The 1921 Act – A Statute in General Terms

Some posts in the public service were opened to women graduates as described on page 112. A woman was appointed to a post as district medical officer in 1914, and in 1915 a woman economist became an employment exchange manager; there were a few women police officers as well. *Thora Pedersen* of the Wages and Salaries Commission had taken the initiative in distributing a questionnaire to the ministries and other departments of the government with a view to discovering the usefulness of women compared with men of equivalent education. The replies varied from a mere "no" to lengthy disquisitions expressing such views as that women were unsuitable for responsible positions because of their lack of administrative capacity, and that women should resign from government appointments in the event of marriage, and certainly if they had children. But there was a postmaster who believed that women were just as useful as men and they were more obliging and likeable than men.

A law providing for equal accessibility of jobs and appointments to men and women was introduced by Prime Minister Zahle in 1919. It aimed at equality in all except military appointments, but the Upper House had misgivings with regard to the office of pastor. The theological faculty of the university had none, and neither had six of Denmark's seven bishops, while the Minister for Ecclesiastical Affairs likewise felt that it ought to be made possible for women to be ordained. At a meeting of the Danish Women's Society he expressed regret that the Lutheran Church had been unable to bring women into its work and he called it "a legally organised male church". But vestries all over Denmark were clearly opposed

141

to women pastors, and the Upper House was reluctant to defy them. The Act was passed in 1921 and gave women equal access to all public service posts and offices except military and religious.

The law was formulated in very general terms and so occasioned conflict and discussion. Its intention was that no regard should be paid to the sex of applicants in filling appointments to the public service. But attempts were made, notably by local authorities and especially during the periods of unemployment in the 1920s and 1930s, to avoid appointing women and to hinder the advancement of those in post. This was particularly noticeable with women teachers, especially those who were married to men teachers. The history of the Danish Women's Society tells of many legal actions, resolutions, meetings, and representations made to local authorities, ministers and so forth in order to help individuals in difficulty and get the Act complied with. But the Act was not popular, and as late as 1939 male civil servants in the Ministry for Home Affairs demonstrated against the appointment of a woman lawyer by receiving their new and first female colleague arrayed in funeral attire.

The Act stated that it was illegal to dismiss women or refuse them employment on the ground of their being married or having children. The question was debated eagerly, and some lawyers expressed doubt as to whether the Non-Discrimination Act applied to married women. But a high court judgment of 1942 established that it was contrary to the Non-Discrimination Act to refuse to employ married women. The case arose when a Copenhagen suburban local authority, because of the pregnancy of one of its office staff, resolved not to employ married women in future. The trade union of the employee concerned *Handels- og Kontorfunktionærernes Forbund* (Union of Commercial and Clerical Employees) brought an action against the local authority and won it.

142

Exceptions to the Non-Discrimination Act – Pastors and Soldiers

The Danish Women's Society and the Danish Women's National Council made representations on many occasions for women to be eligible for *clerical office*, and as early as 1925 the then Minister for Ecclesiastical Affairs had brought in a Bill to enable certain benefices to be filled by women, but this was rejected. In 1946, however, Parliament was faced with a specific case where a congregation submitted an application for a particular woman theologian to be appointed as their pastor. Parliament then brought in an amendment to the Act, but in such terms that no congregation could be compelled to have a woman pastor against its will. But in the specific instance in question the bishop under whose authority the congregation fell would not ordain women. In Parliament there was no inclination to compel the bishop to act against his own convictions, so that a special law had to be passed to set aside the diocesan boundaries. When this had been done the bishop of Odense was able to ordain three women in 1947. Nevertheless, matters did not quiet down at once. The bishop of Odense received many scurrilous and some even imprecatory letters, and 514 pastors threatened to resign their livings in protest. In the event none of them did so, and tranquillity reigned for a time. But then in 1955 a pastor in one of the Jutland provincial towns appointed a woman theologian to act as curate, and as the bishop under whose authority the pastor came did not approve of women in clerical garb there was a tremendous uproar, so that the big problem of this little town became front-page news all over the country. The issue was solved when a bishop living a little further away took over responsibility for the congregation and ordained the curate. Since then peace has prevailed on this front, and there are about two hundred women functioning as pastors throughout Denmark. Two women have occupied the position of Minister for Ecclesiastical Affairs – mother and daughter, in fact, both of them theologians.

The second exception to the Non-Discrimination Act is the *military profession*, in which the feminist organisations have shown no particular interest. But there were many women who wanted to undertake tasks that would involve giving personal help and support to the civil population in the event of war, and even before the Second World War the Danish Women's Society, for example, established links with the *Dansk Luftværnsforening* (Danish Civil Defence Association), which undertook such functions. After the outbreak of war a special women's committee was formed under this Association, and in March 1940 the *Danske Kvinders Beredskab* (Danish Women's Emergency Service) came into being as an organisation of women who placed themselves voluntarily at the disposal of the official authorities in the event of war or catastrophe and had training in the provision of emergency services. About 40,000 women joined in a short space of time, and a large-scale programme of training had to be launched. Fortunately Denmark was spared the effects of direct hostilities, but the Women's Emergency Service came into action on numerous occasions, helping for example the relatively few families who were bombed out, managing the catering arrangements for civil defence exercises, meetings and courses. When the Danish Jews were deported in 1943 the Service was given the task by the government of taking care of the houses and apartments thus left without supervision, and in the closing days of the war when thousands of prisoners from the German concentration camps were moved via Denmark on their way to Sweden, the Service at very short notice fed the entire mass of starving people.

The Women's Emergency Service today has about 9,000 members and functions within the framework of the Civil Defence League. Its training is designed to enable them to intervene in catastrophe situations, to clear up and to furnish humanitarian help.

When the *Hjemmeværn* (Home Guard) was established after the war, some of the women who had taken part in the Resistance wanted to be allowed to join. This did not happen, however, and special women's corps were formed instead – first the *Danmarks Lottekorps* (Danish Women's Voluntary Army Corps) and the *Kvindeligt Marinekorps* (Women's Naval Corps), then later the *Kvindeligt Flyverkorps* (Women's Air Corps). Under the Defence Act of 1960 the three corps were affiliated to the Home Guard, and their commanders and instructors have titles, ranks and pay in line with those of their male counterparts in the Home Guard, which has increased in size in the last few years. The latter applies also to the women's corps, so that the Women's Army Corps now has about 7,500 members, the Air Corps about 1,600 and the Women's Naval Corps about 1,550.

The question of equality for women with regard to national service has often been canvassed, and the special position of women in this sphere has played a very prominent role in the thinking of opponents of equality. The *Venstres Ungdom* (Liberal Youth) raised the question seriously in 1970 and at a national party conference in the same year the party chairman, Poul Hartling, subsequently Prime Minister, gave his full support to the idea of national military service for women. But this is a matter that has not come before Parliament. Since 1971, however, women have been able to receive training and be appointed on a contractual basis as privates in the army and air force and as ratings in the navy. They are not trained in actual fighting and weapons handling, but they do receive instruction in the use of firearms for self-defence. It comes as a surprise to some of those who apply for this professional military training that they have to begin by doing virtually the same things as their male counterparts: route marches, patrols, camps, hand-grenade training, parade-ground drill and so forth. Some of them give up, but for others it has been an experience to discover little by little as their training proceeds that they are able to keep up with it and to become aware at the same time of qualities in themselves that they had not previously known. These experiences are of fundamental interest, for they tell us something of the potential for development inherent in the female sex when faced with demands outside the traditional sex-role patterns. That the same thing applies to the sex which is still regarded as dominant can be no surprise, for men have worked, and still do so, in practically all fields from child care to cleaning and food preparation.

Women have proved very satisfactory as members of the forces, and some have chosen to go on after their basic training with the result that there are now a few women officers in all three services.

The Equal Pay Act in Public Service

In 1917 a Salaries Commission was set up to establish principles for salaries, pensions and other conditions of public employees. The Danish Women's Society requested that female public employees should be represented on the Commission, and Thora Pedersen, a teacher, was appointed as representative of the Danish Teachers' Union. In her professional capacity she was the spokeswoman of about 4,000 women teachers in primary schools, who constituted the biggest group of female public employees. There were about 1,400 other women in government service as well, most of them in the telegraphs administration. Thora Pedersen was the only woman among the 21 members of the Commission, and she found herself strongly opposed by her male teacher colleagues when she demanded equal pay, with possibly a breadwinner supplement to be paid only to persons with children. Her male colleagues were particularly anxious to maintain the principle laid down in the Primary Schools Act of 1908 under which women were remunerated at the rate of 2/3 of the men's salaries. On the other hand the official side was in agreement with Thora Pedersen in her very skilful arguments that salaries should be equal for men and women holding the same posts. An enquiry was launched into women's remuneration on the private labour market, where firms declared that where men and women did the same job the wage was also the same, but it was exceedingly seldom that the work was identical. As far as superior positions were concerned, women only got them when a firm employed women exclusively.

One of the arguments against equal pay was that women were more economical with their money than men and had fewer needs. Anyone could see that, so it was said. Moreover, men were breadwinners – but the fact that such obligations might fall upon a woman was not recognised by the Commission.

Thora Pedersen gave way on the question of breadwinner obligations and agreed that married men should receive a cost-of-living supplement. The Public Employees Act of 1919 introduced equal pay for women and unmarried men, and it introduced a special concept of the breadwinner into legislation which caused a great deal of trouble and took many years to root out.

Even before the salaries law had been enacted, local authorities all over Denmark were threatening not to employ women as teachers in future if they were going to be as expensive as men, and they sabotaged the Act in various ways. For example, a fair number of female teaching posts were recategorised as male. The Danish Women's Society was very active in supporting women teachers and protested both locally and, on repeated occasions, to the Minister of Education; it also passed resolutions and held meetings, while

Thora Pedersen wrote articles on the issue in teachers' professional journals. In Copenhagen, where there were more female than male teachers, the number of female teachers fell by 61 between 1921 and 1926 – but women were still in a majority.

The breadwinner rules of the Public Employees Act were based on the idea that men and women ought to have the same basic wage, with a cost-of-living supplement paid to breadwinners, who were defined under the Act as all married men, widowers, widows, separated or divorced men and women with households of their own or with breadwinner obligations towards children under 18 years of age. Unmarried persons with breadwinner obligations towards children were also breadwinners under the Act, but only if they had their own household (dwelling).

This conception of breadwinning could produce quite ludicrous consequences. One example was that of the woman civil servant in Copenhagen whose husband became mentally ill and had to be taken to hospital. She paid his fees there and had children to maintain, but she was not a breadwinner in the legal sense. Then her husband died, making her eligible as a breadwinner since she was now a widow!

It is illuminating that this concept of the breadwinner provoked intense dissatisfaction among both public employees and the women's organisations, especially when the turn of economic events caused the cost-of-living supplement to form an increasingly large proportion of the total salary.

In 1946 the Public Employees Act was amended, and the Ministry of Finance was empowered to decide that a married female employee could receive the full cost-of-living supplement if her income was wholly or partly essential to the economy of the home. The Ministry of Finance interpreted the rule very strictly, however, and refused to recognise an employee as a breadwinner if the husband was fit and capable of work but was studying, for example – the argument being that he could simply stop doing it. From 1954 onwards, however, the Ministry began to grant the full supplement in cases of this sort.

But then in the same year an event took place that gave Parliament a fright. A group of unmarried public employees with dwellings of their own proclaimed publicly their intention of getting married and separating again immediately afterwards. In this way they would become "breadwinners". Parliament thereupon hastily introduced an amendment to the law abolishing the rule that persons previously married automatically became breadwinners provided they had their own dwellings. At the same time Parliament expressed sympathy with unmarried persons maintaining children, but did not avail itself of the opportunity of placing them on an equal footing with previously-married persons with children, who had the right to full supplement even without having a dwelling. Equal pay was eventually introduced by the Public Employees Act of 1958.

Housewives' Organisations

Prehistory

It is no accident that the first housewives' organisation was associated with Askov High School and Ladelund Agricultural College or that it took the form of a union of rural housewives.

Danish agriculture had experienced a crisis in the 1880s because of the fall of corn prices on the international market, and this led to a reorganisation of production. Denmark changed little by little from an exporter to an importer of corn and switched over to livestock production and the development of dairying. This was successful because Danish farmers were enlightened and receptive to the teachings of science. They joined together in producers' cooperatives and farmers' associations, which appointed advisers to guide the members and inform them about experimental work in agricultural economics.

To the farmer's wife, therefore, there was nothing remarkable in the idea that if the diet of pigs and cattle needed to be properly balanced, so did that of human beings. But to disseminate the requisite enlightenment among the population at large necessitated the training of personnel, which involved establishing schools of home economics. This was understood by *Birgitte Berg Nielsen* (1861–1951), a teacher who had practical housekeeping and dairy industry experience as well as having spent three years studying at the Royal Veterinary and Agricultural College. She was one of the pioneers of home economics teaching in schools and of a systematic approach to it, and she herself founded a home economics school with a training college for teachers attached. She spoke at Askov Folk High School in 1899 about the importance of home economics schools, and some of the women of the district were so interested in the question that they made efforts to get such a school established. Nothing came of these endeavours, however, except for a few female itinerant teachers giving demonstrations of new dishes and explaining nutritional theory.

But in 1906 the group of interested women came into contact with two young teachers who were looking for a suitable place to set up a rural school of home economics. The school was accordingly started near Askov in 1907. Local housewives came to it on courses as well, and in 1908 the *Malt Herreds Husholdningsforening* (Malt District Home Economics Association) was established, with the head of the rural home economics school, *Rebekka la Cour Madsen*, as president. She continued in that capacity for 27 years.

The first home economics school had already started up at Sorø in 1895, the prime mover in its launching having been *Jutta Bojsen-Møller* (1837–1927) of Sorø Folk High School. As well as being assistant matron of the School she had recently been elected national president of the Danish Women's Society, and she had personally suffered from a sense of ineptitude and ignorance in household affairs. She used to tell, for example, of the time when as the 20 year-old wife of a pastor she had entertained the bishop to dinner and served chervil soup in which there were supposed to be poached eggs, but the eggs caked at the bottom of the pot and the bishop had to have fried eggs with his soup. The gravy for the roast duck went wrong as well and consisted of liquid fat and paste. Jutta Bojsen-Møller was very attracted by the idea of home economics schools, and she influenced *Eline Eriksen*, her matron at the high school, to establish the Sorø School of Home Economics in collaboration with the 22 year-old *Magdalene Lauridsen*.

The latter was a pioneer in the field. Inspired by a study-visit to England, as early as 1900 she launched itinerant courses and evening schools for country housewives, and the Farmers' Unions found these innovations so interesting that they undertook to sponsor them and urged Magdalene Lauridsen to train teachers to carry the work forward. This led to the founding in 1902 of the Ankerhus Home Economics Training College for Teachers at Sorø, whose wide-ranging activities Magdalene Lauridsen spent the next half-century developing: the school and teacher training college are still in existence.

More similar schools were now being opened one by one all over Denmark, offering opportunities of employment for trained teachers over and above those already existing as itinerant teachers and on evening courses for the Farmers' Unions. As early as 1906 the Association of Danish Home Economics Teachers was formed at the instance of Magdalene Lauridsen, and it was from this quarter that the next advance proceeded. At a meeting of the Association in 1916, *Jens Warming* (subsequently a professor of economics) spoke of the importance of housewives' organising themselves into groups or societies. He had already written articles detailing the wide range of tasks which housewives might be able to execute more easily by collaborating with one another, and he was the first to use the term *husmoderforening*, or housewives' society. It was the economic side of the housewife's role that particularly interested Warming, and he laid stress on the savings that would ensue for the nation if, for example, housewives could be given instruction by means of courses, guidance by counsellors and advice through the medium of a members' bulletin, all underpinned by the various branches of science bearing upon the running of a household. Inspired by all this, the Association of Home Economics Teachers now addressed an appeal to the wives of all chairmen of parish councils in Denmark urging that housewives should band together, either by parishes or local districts, in a joint effort to raise the level of their skills.

152

The challenge was taken up in only a few localities, but by 1921 there were nevertheless a total of eight home economics associations dotted around Denmark, including the one in the Malt district. Negotiations between them resulted in the forming of a joint organisation.

The Federation of Danish Home Economics Associations

This joint organisation soon developed means of assisting the work of local associations, including lists of speakers and practical advice on association activities. Suggestions for courses included food-preserving, baking, food preparation, gardening, sewing, shoe repairing, cleaning clothes and bottling: detailed schemes were obtainable on request. Continuation school instruction in domestic work could be arranged for young girls on one afternoon a week in collaboration with local authorities. The government defrayed three quarters of the costs of such instruction. The joint organisation also prepared price-lists of articles that could be bought more cheaply in bulk, such as fruit-bottles, preserving-jars, caustic soda for soapmaking, wool for yarn and cloth, and tested garden seeds. It was suggested that the associations should try to have home economics sections incorporated in exhibitions held by farmers', smallholders' or other associations so that articles produced at home, from field, garden, kitchen or sewing-room, could be displayed. Lastly, the associations were advised to undertake the testing of household machinery and appliances. If the requisite tests could not be made on the spot, the joint organisation would carry them out.

The objective of the Federation of Danish Home Economics Associations is constantly "to work to foster the proficiency of women in filling their place in society and the home, to promote a sense of responsibility in this respect, and

153

to safeguard the interests of housewives and the home ..."
The joint organisation has worked with these ends in view
and has always been ready to tackle new problems of current
concern.

One somewhat unusual feature is that in almost 60 years of
existence the organisation has had only three national presidents, all of them country housewives. *Ellen Villemoes Andersen* (born 1895) served for 32 years, and by the time she
retired in 1966 the organisation had 26,840 members distributed over 282 local associations. In 1979 there were about
16,000 members and 234 local associations.

The first home economics adviser was appointed on a part-
time basis in 1922, and a year later a teacher of sewing was
appointed. But the federation dues were far too low to pay
the salaries, and in 1924 an appeal was made to the Ministry
of Agriculture, which took four years to grant a subsidy
amounting to 40 % of the salary. The subsidy today amounts
to 70 % for all advisers, plus a supplement for pension contributions and travelling expenses. By 1979 the organisation
had appointed 14 advisers, who not only arrange courses,
demonstrations, study circles and meetings but also give lectures and provide members with a telephone advisory service
on countless matters including the purchase of household
appliances. Some of them are specialists in economics, nutrition, interior housing design and technical matters. They
visit homes on request and for example will draw up plans for
kitchen design. The work done by advisers is similar to that
carried out in the other two organisations for rural housewives. When local chairmen are planning programmes of activity for their branches they often seek advice and guidance
from advisers, who keep abreast of current trends by taking
part in courses and by furnishing information about films,
slides and other useful material, as well as from *Statens Hus-
holdningsråd* (The Danish Government Home Economics
Council).

Studies of housekeeping accounts and of diet constitute a field which has been of great importance to all three rural housewives' organisations. A number of members undertake to keep accounts under detailed guidance, and this provides an insight into housekeeping expenditure, including the amount spent on items bought from outside sources and the role played in the consumption-pattern by goods produced at home. The purpose of dietary studies is to evaluate both Joule-consumption and the nutritional composition of diet, and in order to arrive at comparable results they have to be conducted on rigorously scientific lines. Specially-trained advisers have done a great deal of work in this field, and even though the material is rather flimsy – about 500 studies having been carried out among organisation members between 1927 and 1971 – it does offer a basis for discussing the nutritional situation and has given the individual household the opportunity of correcting defects in its consumption-pattern.

The joint organisation, along with the other housewives' organisations and others, has involved itself in one particular cultural sphere by arranging exhibitions of old needlework. A visit to the other Nordic countries inspired Ellen Villemoes to try to preserve and reawaken the cultural heritage represented by old-time needlework and textile articles, and when the interest of the National Museum was engaged a joint effort was made. A special society called *Danmarks folkelige Broderier* (Danish Folk Embroidery) was founded in 1954. The members of the organisations for rural women went through old chests and other hiding-places in search of needlework dating back before 1870, and a start was made with small-scale exhibitions to see what might be of interest to the National Museum. These brought to light a cultural treasure of previously unsuspected dimensions, and bigger exhibitions were arranged. About 25,000 embroideries have been shown in local exhibitions, and from these the National Museum has selected some 13,000 examples of traditional folk art to be recorded and photographed for its archives. Much inspiration has been supplied for modern embroidery, including the teaching of needlework.

One of the numerous annual events in the Association's calendar is a two-day national conference with 400–500 participants, at which the current scene is surveyed, new activities are introduced, petitions possibly submitted to the government or other official quarters, new leaders elected, and so on. It is customary to invite someone prominent in public debate to speak and possibly to lead off discussion of some topic. Since 1940 the joint organisation has had its own periodical entitled *Husholdningsbladet* (The Home Economics Journal), to which members must now subscribe. It forms a link between leadership and individual members, contains a great deal of information and useful advice, and gives reports of meetings.

The Home Economics Committees of the Federation of Danish Farmers' Unions

As already noted, the Farmers' Unions began arranging home economics courses under itinerant teachers shortly after the turn of the century, but it was 1922 before women became properly involved in this work through the formation of a Jutland home economics committee. *Rebekka la Cour Madsen* became its chairman and its first task was to get women to join the Farmers' Unions and either to form home economics committees or to establish special home economics associations with a view to cooperating with the Farmers' Unions and receiving assistance from them in various ways. Women do not pay subscriptions directly to the Farmers' Unions. The committee work is put on an equal footing with that of other specialist committees in accordance with a principle of equality "showing that there are two partners in a farm household", as a jubilee report puts it.

156

The first home economics adviser began work in 1923, and in the beginning great emphasis was laid upon investigatory and testing activities with a view firstly to assembling background information for housewives on such matters as the relationship between price and quality of goods and secondly to building up a case for the establishment of an institution for testing household commodities. For example, sago and oatmeal and various types of rice were tested, and bread and other articles were baked using American and Danish flour in various types of oven. The preserving of meat was a practice then current, and a good deal of time was devoted to discovering the correct procedure. The then-existing hand-operated kitchen appliances for washing up and peeling potatoes were also examined, and so was the washing of clothes, and in this connection countless analyses of water-samples were carried out to determine degrees of hardness. Little by little external activities connected with the expanding work of local associations and committees made more and more inroads upon the time of counsellors, so that the testing functions dwindled in importance, especially after The Danish Government Home Economics Council became involved in the latter. Nevertheless a certain amount of testing and similar work has always been done on the local level, as for example in 1976–78 when the results of an interview-enquiry into eating habits during pregnancy were processed by an expert on nutrition, so enabling guidance to be offered to any pregnant woman requesting it.

Other regions of Denmark had similar work going on at the same time as Jutland, and the desire for cooperation led in 1925 to the establishment of a national home economics committee. But the strongminded women at its helm were not always in harmony, so that the committee was dissolved in 1947 – only to be reconstituted in 1955.

The breadth and variety of the work that goes on locally may be illustrated by an account of activities on the island of

Funen in 1978. Funen has 12 committees or associations to-talling 5,180 members. These held 177 meetings and other events on matters of household and consumer information ranging from nutrition, shopping guidance, economics and knowledge of commodities to interior housing design, work schedules, rationalisation and so forth. Several of these meetings were held in a shop to enable those taking part to see different kinds of goods and evaluate them in the same way as in a buying situation. At other meetings use was of course made of slides, films and overhead projectors, and where the subject lent itself to it the meeting would take the form of a group discussion, brainstorming session or round-table conference. Two hundred events of a social, cultural or public information character were arranged. There were lectures on literature, sometimes with readings, travellers' tales from many lands, and discussions of such topics as "Modern Man in a Crisis Situation" or "Family and Society". There were also numerous visits to museums and to artists to see their products, to factories and other establishments, to social institutions and so on. Moreover the 12 committees ran 133 study circles and specialist courses in such subjects as dressmaking, textile printing, weaving, languages, gymnastics, public meeting technique and public speaking. One series of lectures was entitled "Is Democracy in Danger?", another "Danish Society and the Rule of Law", and a third "Who Were our Forefathers and How Did They Live?".

The Home Economics Committee of the Federation of Danish Farmers' Unions employs 35 advisers and comprises 60,000–70,000 members, most of them rural housewives or women connected with the land in some way. The farmers' union has a periodical called "Country Journal" with a circulation of about 110,000 always containing a special section with informative articles and other material addressed particularly to women and bearing upon the activities of the home economics committees.

The Home Economics Committees of the Danish Family Farmers Association

Ever since the foundation of the Smallholders' Association (now The Family Farmers Association) in 1902 women have been involved in its work, which includes the dissemination of technical, social and cultural information. Women participated in courses on animal husbandry, plant cultivation and gardening, for wives have always taken a share in the running of farms, especially the smaller ones, and married couples have had to work together in order to exist. In those days a smallholder's wife often bore the marks of the daily grind, both outwardly and inwardly, while still quite young.

After the First World War the local smallholders' associations began to form special home economics committees which soon worked together at local or regional level. It was by no means rare at that time for both the local and the new regional committees to have male chairmen. A few advisers were appointed in the 1920s.

The question of forming a national organisation became a matter of immediate importance in the 1930s when both the Federation of Danish Home Economics Associations and the Home Economics Committee of the Farmers' Union made a proposal for cooperation between the three Associations with a view to solving various practical questions. Among the points at issue were coordination of procedures for carrying out dietary studies, joint applications for government subsidies for exhibitions at cattleshows, concerted nomination of representatives to committees, councils etc. Moreover, for example, the Ministry for Home Affairs asked the Smallholders'Association to nominate a member to the commission preparing the establishment of The Danish Government Home Economics Council and subsequently to nominate a representative to sit on the Council itself.

The joint organisation was accordingly formed in 1937,

and the national home economics committee was constituted to consist of the chairmen of the provincial home economics committees. *Marie Hansen*, of Gevnø, was elected as national chairman and quickly made known that she would prefer to preside over a committee composed of women. Those present at the meeting believed that members ought to be free to choose persons other than provincial chairmen as members of the new home economics committee. Men disappeared from these committees a few years later.

The home economics committee and the local committees have had the same economic relationship to the Smallholders' Associations as the corresponding committees of the Farmers' Unions. The then president of the Smallholders is reported to have said at the outset: "You women shall have what money you need, but you shall jolly well economise as well." Nevertheless there must have been certain disagreements, for in 1943 the home economics committee asked the Smallholders' Associations to consider the question of women's membership rights so as to bring uniformity into the rules of the local organisations. The committee proposed a joint membership card for man and wife without any separate subscription for married women, while single women and widows would have to pay. It was then decided that the membership card should be valid for man and wife and that the subscription should be the same regardless of whether there was a spouse. At the same time it was made clear that man and wife had equal influence over all Association affairs.

The work done diverges only negligibly from that of the Federation of Danish Home Economics Associations and the Farmers' Unions Home Economics Committees. though perhaps a particular degree of initiative has been shown over the years in the approach to social questions. For example it was the smallholders' wives who pointed out during the war that homes in which young persons were employed ought to remember to give them ration coupons on days off. It may be

As many as seven children was common in working class families, as shown in this picture from 1879. The authoress Thit Jensen (1876–1957) became a champion of sexual enlightenment and other causes. Her lectures on such topics as voluntary motherhood made her famous throughout Denmark. (Photos: ABA, Royal Library).

The Mothers' Aid has been a central organisation giving ante- and post-natal help and advice since the 1930s. In 1976 the organisation was integrated into a new welfare structure centred upon municipal social welfare departments. (Nordfoto).

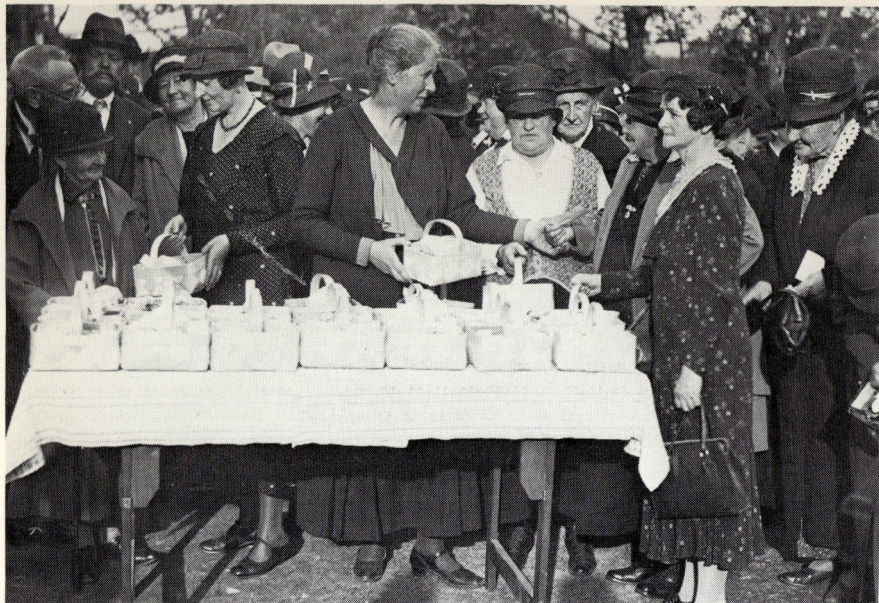

In the 1920s the Social Democratic movement established a women's committee, which among its other activities carried out a certain amount of humanitarian work. Here we see an outing for old people, with baskets of food being distributed, during the depression years of the 1930s. (Photo: ABA).

Thousands of women all over Denmark were brought into action by the Danish Women's Social Service during the Nazi Occupation. Nothing was allowed to be wasted, and enormous quantities of jam were made for distribution. (Politiken Photo, 1942).

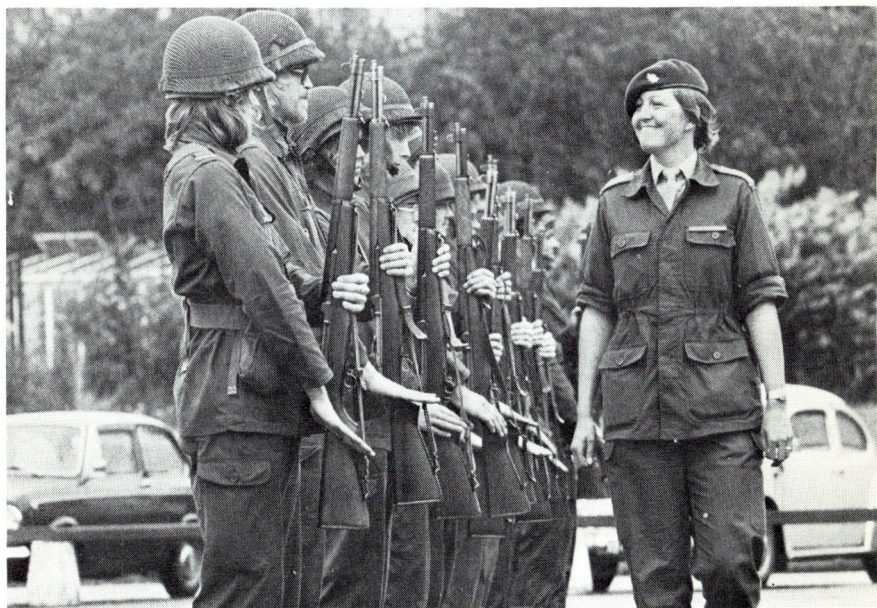

Members of the Danish Women's Voluntary Army Corps distributing food. (Photo: ABA).

Military training was opened to women in 1971: here the first woman sergeant is seen in action. (Photo courtesy of the Danish Defence Command).

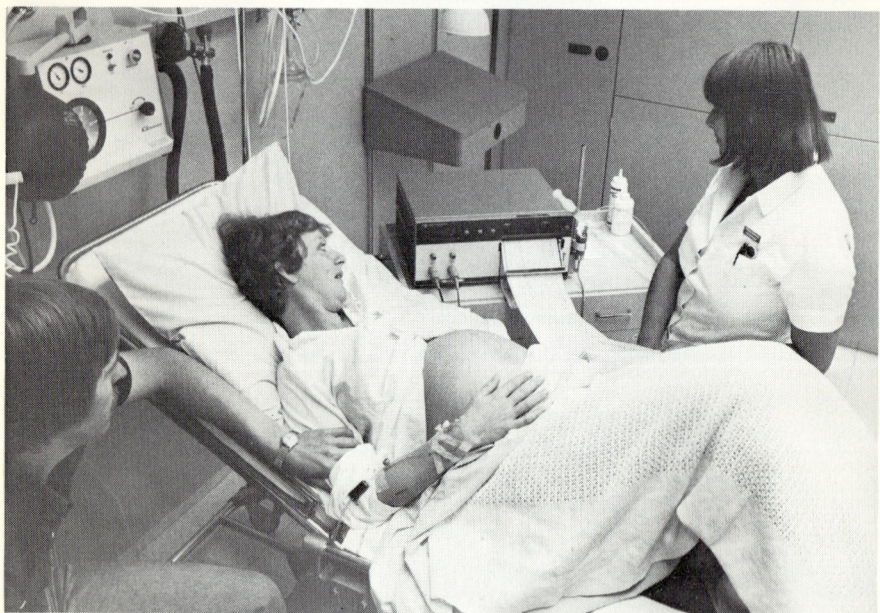

More than half the teachers in *folkeskoler* are women, but only 4 per cent school principals. (Photo: Jørgen Jørgensen).

Occupations such as nursing, midwifery etc. are still characteristically regarded as women's occupations – will men penetrate these sectors in the name of equality?
It is becoming increasingly common for fathers to be present at childbirths. (Nordfoto).

observed likewise that it was on the initiative of this committee that studycircle material was prepared with a view to getting women interested in local politics.

There are about 44,000 members affiliated to the committee, which employs 27 advisers. The Danish Family Farmers Association has a periodical called "The Farming Magazine", which like the Farmers' Unions journal contains informative material angled specifically towards women.

Joint Action by Rural Housewives

The later period of the existence of the rural housewives' organisations have been marked by drastic changes in agrarian occupations. The most dramatic manifestation of this is the fact that the number of farms fell from nearly 200,000 after the Second World War to just over half that number in 1979. Working conditions for rural housewives have totally altered in character, at least on the larger farms, one reason being that *permanent* female employees are now a rarity, there being no more than about 3,000, of whom about half are relatives and very young girls.

In 1939 there were about 104,000 women permanently employed in agriculture. At the same time the number of male employees has dwindled sharply from about 203,000 in 1939 to about 15,700 in 1976. Of course, this phenomenon is bound up with the process of mechanisation and rationalisation that has been going on, and for a large number of housewives it has meant that they have increasingly had to lend a hand both with actual farmwork and in other ways. It may be observed that most recently some increase has taken place in the numbers of employees in agriculture. But as a whole agriculture presents an exceedingly chequered picture. Many farms are now without cattle; some lease land to a neighbour; others get a tractor station to attend to some of the more laborious tasks; small farms are run as part-time enterprises with both husband and wife sometimes working on a neighbouring factory or having jobs outside agriculture altogether.

In the light of these profound changes it is not surprising that rural housekeeping itself has changed character, so that it has become more common than it used to be for part- or fully-processed foodstuffs to be bought in the same way as in urban households. Some differences between town and country still remain, however, and in any case there are not many rural households without a kitchen garden from which soft fruit can be made into jam or preserved in some other fashion.

Incidentally, it was the rural housewife who pioneered deep-freezing. Although the first deep-frozen foods appeared in the shops in the late 1940s, it was another ten years before the volume of consumption sufficed to make it profitable to deal in these new commodities. But rural housewives took up the freezing technique and banded together to establish cooperative freezers in which they could freeze and preserve both meat products and suitable garden products: cooperative freezing has now been supplanted by the home freezer, which is in very widespread use in town and country alike.

What is remarkable, however, is that the rural housewives' organisations are still so large, having about 125,000 members, though admittedly about half of these probably have no direct connection with farming but merely reside in the country. One important explanation is certainly to be found in the fact that the members can obtain help and advice from their organisations with regard both to rationalisation and mechanisation of the daily household routine and to consumer problems in the broader sense. The three organisations and their advisers have largely lived up to the requirements of the new age, and they cooperate with each other in a number of fields.

Thus, they jointly form a committee under the Ministry of Agriculture. Two representatives from each organisation are appointed by the Minister of Agriculture, who nominates one of the six to act as chairman. This committee has existed since 1955 under the name *Landbrugsministeriets Produktivitetsudvalgs Husholdningsudvalg* (Home Economics Committee under the Productivity Committee of the Ministry of Agriculture), with the aim of assisting the Ministry of Agriculture by promoting productivity in the household. Each year the Committee draws up a scheme of work and a budget for approval by the Productivity Committee, which grants the necessary funds from the sums available through the Ministry of Agriculture from *Danmarks Erhvervsfond* (the Danish Trade Fund). As well as running courses for home economics advisers, procuring teaching materials, establishing demonstration showrooms and assisting with the purchase of office supplies, the Committee has carried out a number of studies and issued reports on them. The kinds of topic covered are illustrated by the titles: "An Economic Enquiry into Laundry and Laundrywork", "Rationalisation", "New Dietary Habits – But How?", "Working Conditions of the Rural Housewife", "Agricultural Housing".

The organisations also work together on a national committee which considers current questions of a consumer character and sometimes makes representations to official authorities. In this committee plans are concerted with chairmen and advisers for such activities as courses for various categories of member such as branch chairmen or young country housewives with children, and representatives are sent from the committee to the many societies and institutions with which it collaborates. The national committee is also involved in work at the Nordic and international levels. Alle three organisations are affiliated to *Nordens Landbokvinder* (Nordic Country Women) and A.C.W.W. (Association of Country World Women). *De Danske Husmoderforeninger* (The

Federation of Danish Housewives' Society) are also affiliated to A.C.W.W.

In recent years the four housewives' organisations have co-operated in establishing information offices in towns all over Denmark, to which anyone can apply for advice on consumer questions. It is the advisers who actually do the work, which is proceeding for the time being under local experimental arrangements and was established in conjunction with the Royal Commission on Consumers Questions (see page 174) to gain experience with a view to gauging the need for consumer information over the country as a whole.

In 1978–79 there were 11 offices opening for about two hours a week. The financing of the offices varies from one place to another, depending on opportunities for getting grants from local and county authorities. At the present time it would appear that urban dwellers as well are showing interest in calling at these offices with requests for assistance with various problems and complaints.

The Federation of Danish Housewives' Society

The first organisation for urban housewives was formed in 1917 for a purpose quite different from that of improving their skills. Its moving spirit was *Thit Jensen* (1876–1957), an authoress and a person for whom the step from thought to action was but a short one. She was unhappy over the fact that housemaids had organised themselves for the purpose of obtaining fair wages and working conditions, so she formed the Copenhagen Housewives' Society as an employers' organisation. She found a president for it, but the latter had to retire after a couple of months on grounds of ill-health and was succeeded by *Carla Meyer* (1877–1954). The organisation of urban housewives then got properly under way, led by an extremely energetic, enterprising and far-sighted woman. The aim was at once changed to comprise the dissemination of domestic expertise in the widest sense, the strengthening of the home and the fostering of the training of all women in household tasks.

Only two months after being elected Carla Meyer arranged a thrift exhibition, at which over a period of two weeks about 2,000 housewives a day were taught to cushion the effect of high wartime prices by adjusting their consumption-patterns and making adroit use of such commodities as were obtainable in order to secure the highest possible nutritional value for the smallest possible outlay of money. In the same year the Society held a large housing congress and a number of practical demonstrations of such arts as jam-making and preserving. Foundations were rapidly laid on which all subsequent housewives' societies have built.

Carla Meyer was invited in 1919 to attend the national conference of the Norwegian *Hjemmenes Vel* (Welfare at Home) organisation, and she returned home full of enthusiasm and determined to set up more societies and get them linked together in a national alliance. In Norway, in fact, the idea of a Nordic Housewives' Confederation had been floated, and it was decided to try to translate it into reality at a meeting in Copenhagen the following year.

Thus it was in May 1920 the Copenhagen Housewives' Society issued invitations to a conference at which the founding of *De danske Husmoderforeninger* (The Federation of Danish Housewives' Society) was on the agenda. The invitations were sent to housewives known to be interested in the project, and in those towns where there were no contacts they were addressed to the mayors' wives. It was desired to establish cooperation with women in rural areas as well, so the Society also invited Magdalene Lauridsen, who was working to establish home economics associations, and Rebekka la Cour Madsen of the Malt District Home Economics Association. Carla Meyer saw clearly that a united front of town and country would be an exceedingly effective instrument for achieving the expansion of training in household tasks and for making representations on any other matters to the government or to Parliament.

Representatives of 30 towns and villages attended the conference, and some of these were already in the process of setting up societies. Carla Meyer got three ground-rules adopted for any housewives' society. The name was to be that of the town followed by *husmoderforening* (Housewives' Society); it was to be run by a housewife, and it was to be non-political. The latter did not constitute a ban on all political concerns, but private political views were not to be propounded and party sides were not to be taken. Stress was also laid on the importance of a national organisation able to take its place in a Nordic coalition.

The president of the *Kvindeligt Arbejderforbund* (General Union of Women Workers) was in attendance, and she explained that working women had established *Arbejdernes Husmoderforening* (Labour Housewives' Society) during the war because they had believed that the Copenhagen Housewives' Society consisted of upper-class ladies. But during the Spanish flu they had seen the love and devotion with which the Society had organised services to succour the homes afflicted regardless of class or status, and so they had now affiliated to the Copenhagen Housewives' Society.

Everyone except Magdalene Lauridsen and Rebekka la Cour Madsen was now in agreement on forming the Federation of Danish Housewives' Society and on the principle of Nordic collaboration. Carla Meyer became president of the Federation of Danish Housewives' Society and *Karen Braae* (1882–1962) vice-president. (In 1935 the latter became president of the Danish Government Home Economics Council). Carla Meyer still remained president of the Copenhagen Housewives' Society until 1922 and went on for many years after that editing its journal "The Housewife", founded in

1918 and then as now the national organisation's official organ.

Busy years followed, with exhibitions, demonstrations of food and other commodities, cooperation on commodity-testing etc. with various colleges and schools and with the Institute of Technology. A little later a testing station was opened and an arrangement made whereby manufacturers could submit various articles for approval and have them stamped "Approved by the Federation of Danish Housewives".

The resourcefulness of the age – or rather of Carla Meyer – manifested itself in the organising of baby shows, for example, where infants were exhibited and the best nursed and cared-for was awarded a prize by a noted children's doctor. Carla Meyer retired from the presidency for health reasons in 1931.

The work has continued ever since along the broad lines then laid down and supplemented by current ideas. One enterprise of particular note was the establishment of the *Marthaforbund* (League of Martha), which is still in existence. This was formed in the 1930s, its aim being to give young girls the opportunity of a basic domestic training by means of a three-year course leading to an examination. The Federation of Danish Housewives' Society ran two home economics and continuation schools for some years but eventually had to give them up.

The first home economics adviser was appointed in 1923, and another was added in 1934, but the Federation of Danish Housewives' Society has not set as much by the appointment of advisers as have the rural housewives, and in any case it has had less economic scope for this. The advisers have had to travel all over Denmark, although for a time there was one specifically for the Jutland region. The Federation of Danish Housewives' Society has two advisers at the present time.

The organisation had over 25,000 members at the time of its silver jubilee, and by the 1960s the figure had almost

167

doubled, but in recent years, as with almost all similar bodies, membership has dropped heavily to about 27,000 in 1978, with particularly severe losses in Greater Copenhagen, where the figure is under 2,000 after having been twice as high. The very latest reports are of increasing enrolments however.

The Federation of Danish Housewives' Society has always kept well abreast of developments in other organisations and in the home economics field, arranging conferences on these issues; they have also organised conferences on cultural and social questions, and outings to factories and museums have figured on the agenda as well. Extensive programmes of courses, including not only home economics subjects but also languages, sewing, gymnastics etc., have been arranged with support from public funds.

The annual national conference, attended by about 300–400 delegates, often addresses statements or resolutions to the government, e. g. on taxation matters, social problems and consumer questions.

Over the years a fair number of the Danish Housewives' Societies' members have become interested in and received training for political work, both at local level, on education committees, local councils and so forth, and in the national sphere.

The Danish Government Home Economics Council

The housewives' organisations raised the demand for establishment of a national testing and advisory institution to aid and support the home in home economics matters. As we have already noted, they themselves had endeavoured to carry out testing and examining functions, but what was lacking was a central organ capable of coordinating their individual efforts, processing their data and undertaking major projects. The organisations believed that this ought to be the function of the state, and they succeeded in getting the Ministry for Home Affairs to set up a committee to look into the question. The committee formulated proposals for establishing a Government Home Economics Council, and during the deliberations on the relevant Bill the Minister laid particular stress on the national economic significance of the individual housewives' skill and knowledge with regard both to nutrition and to the quality of household articles and appliances. The Bill was adopted and came into effect in 1935, Denmark being the first country in the world to have an institution of this character. The governing body of the Council consisted of representatives of organisations and institutions including the four home economics organisations and *Arbejdernes Oplysningsforbund* (the Workers' Educational Association) as well as institutions such as the *Sundhedsstyrelse* (Board of Health) and others. Day-to-day management of the Council was placed in the hands of its president, appointed by the Minister for Home Affairs.

After the end of the war there were many matters needing attention in the sphere of nutritional problems and a little later on also, most notably, the entire development of new machines and materials that now got under way. The Council's premises and financial grants were quite inadequate for it to meet all these tasks satisfactorily. Even so a gradual expansion of activities was achieved and premises were built furnished with laboratories, lecture- and conference-halls, offices and so forth. A substantial grant-in-aid towards the fitting-out was received from the American Benzon-Moody Foundation, and the Council took over its new building in 1956.

An amendment to the statutes in 1960 broadened the aim to the effect that the Council's activities were to be conducted in the interests of both home and society at large. The post of director and executive manager was created at the same time. The powers of the board were thus reduced and the organisation was able to develop into an efficient modern government consumer institute. The board's most important task now is the drafting of schemes of work so that the researches and other tasks undertaken by the organisations are directed towards questions that are of interest and importance to broad groups of consumers. The 18 members of the Council include representatives of the organisations already mentioned plus the Danish Women's National Council, the Danish Women's Society, the Consumers' Council, teachers and home economics teachers. There are also representatives of six ministries and government bodies including the Ministry for Industry, under whose jurisdiction the Danish Government Home Economics Council now falls, the Ministry of Education, the Ministry of the Environment and the Board of Health.

The Danish Government Home Economics Council publishes "Advice and Findings" eight times a year, a journal with about 56,000 subscribers and a printing of 70,000–75,000 copies. It reports the findings from tests and investigations carried out either at the institution's own laboratories or elsewhere if special equipment is required. It also contains diverse items of a consumer-information character. A companion bulletin called "Technical Information" is published as well and provides detailed and specified results of tests, experiments etc. for the benefit of specialists. This can be had by special supplementary subscription and is taken by about 16,000 people.

In addition, the Council publishes four new leaflets every year each covering a single topic in easily-understood form. These are distributed partly through special subscriptions (about 36,000) and partly through direct sales. A first impression of about 60,000 copies is generally produced, followed by reprints of 20,000–30,000 copies a time. They are kept up to date in new editions, and a number of them have achieved sales of over a million copies. The subjects covered are very diverse, including for example nutritional topics such as

170

"Children's Diet", "Good Dietary Habits", "Food and Hygiene", topics to do with house furnishings and fittings such as "Lights and Lighting", and food-preserving, tools, working movements, consumer information, family law and energy conservation. There are always about 40 up-to-date leaflets available and their annual aggregate distribution is over one million copies, including permanent subscribers. About 25 % of the leaflets are used for teaching purposes.

Every year the Danish Government Home Economics Council produces new material, including sets of colour slides, posters and flipover and overhead projector material, specifically intended to be used for instructional purposes in children's schools and schools of home economics and by Association advisers.

At least one press release is issued every week either dealing with some subject directly of a home economics nature or giving information on general consumer questions. These press releases, edited as required, are reproduced by a large number of newspapers, weekly magazines etc. Periodical checks have shown that the total edition of the publications thus involved in disseminating information originating from the Home Economics Council amounts to about one million copies.

The public at large can obtain guidance directly on application by telephone, in writing or in person either to the Home Economics Council or to the special information office in Copenhagen. About 100,000 persons avail themselves of this service annually, and of these about half receive help in the form of either a leaflet or a copy of "Advice and Findings" while the remainder are given individual advice.

In addition the Home Economics Council maintains close liaison with the housewives' organisations' advisers, one form of this being annual conferences of advisers held in the Council's premises, at which new test findings and other current topics are discussed while the advisers are able to raise matters about which they feel concerned or in which they are having problems.

Other informational activities include participation in exhibitions, e. g. at cattle-shows or in schools, where officials of the Council answer questions and visitors can buy the Council's various publications. Special mini-exhibitions mounted in workplaces have also evoked much interest. Finally, the officials of the Home Economics Council and its information office often act as lecturers or teachers at meetings and courses arranged by societies or institutions, e. g. pensioners' clubs, parents' associations, at health weeks in schools, and the people for whom they provide instruction on nutritional questions include day-nurses, institutional catering personnel and day-nursery staff.

Just over 13 million *kroner* were allotted under the Finance Act for the work of the Home Economics Council in 1980 to supplement its self-generated income of about two million, and this sets close limits on the tasks which can be undertaken, no matter how important. The institution employs the equivalent of 66 full-time staff, including seven engineers, two lawyers, one economist and one sociologist, along with a large number of home economics teachers, office staff and so forth.

The Consumers' Council

When the *Danske Husmødres Forbrugerråd* (Danish Housewives' Consumers' Council) began functioning in 1947, its aim was to watch over the interests of consumers in the postwar period of shortages and poor-quality products. Today it has a different character, being a consumers' political organisation seeking to represent the interests of consumers *vis-à-vis* business and industry as well as society at large. It takes a very broad view and is concerned with the interests of the consumer in the modern affluent society, including the problems of pollution and the environment.

With the exception of the Home Economics Committee of the Danish Family Farmers Associations, all the organisations that nominate members to the Danish Government Home Economics Council are represented on the Consumers' Council, and as well as these there are others such as the *Akademikernes Centralorganisation* (Central Organisation of University Graduates), *Fællesrådet for danske Tjenestemands- og Funktionærorganisationer* (the Federation of Danish Civil Servants' and Salaried Employees' Organisations), *Lejernes Landsorganisation* (the National Tenants' Organisation), Folkepensionisternes og Invalideorganisationernes Kontaktudvalg (the Old Age Pensioners' and Invalid Organisations' Contact Committee) and *Danske Studerendes Fællesråd* (the Danish Students' Joint Council). Thus it is no longer a women's organisation, but up to now it has always had a woman president. As well as the nationwide organisations there are about ten local consumers' groups represented on the Council. These groups are grass-roots organisations that have sprung up spontaneously all over the country and many of them have functioned at local level in a manner at once resourceful and unconventional. For example they have managed to get unsuitable bus schedules changed, carried out price-studies and raised the question of waiting-times in doctors' surgeries. In addition, they perform consumer information tasks and assist consumers with complaints about goods, tradesmen's bills and so forth. There are about 40–50 such groups with an aggregate membership of about 7,500. The groups are not all equally stable, and the Consumers' Council is endeavouring to support them in various ways – though there is no scope for furnishing economic assistance. The Consumers' Council has some hundreds more individual members, who are represented on the Board.

The Council attempts to safeguard the interests of consumers by submitting statements to government authorities and others. It represents consumers' interests on a number of commissions, councils and boards, and collaborates with organisations and institutions working to foster research, standardisation and the informative labelling of goods.

The Council carries out informational work by such means as distribution of the bulletin *TÆNK* (THINK), which has about 20,000 subscribers but is printed in larger numbers. This journal publishes such items as studies of goods, services and prices, and it also provides general information on consumer questions. The editorial policy is largely one of stimulating debate.

The organisations which are members of the Council, along with foundations and private institutions, finance a modest share of its activities, the remaining 85 % or so of the cost being defrayed by the government by means of an annual grant-in-aid of about four million *kroner*. The Council has a staff equivalent to 25 full-time employees, but a fair amount of unpaid work is done by interested members. The Consumers' Council functions with adroitness and energy in many fields, and its external activities are watched with great interest by the mass media.

New Activities Designed for Protection of the Consumer

Between 1969 and 1977 a royal commission delved deeply into the entire consumer field with a view to establishing a basis for an up-to-date consumer policy. The commission was charged with the duty of evaluating the coordination and division of labour between activities in the testing and informational field, particularly those for which the Danish Government Home Economics Council and the Consumers' Council were responsible. One of the tasks imposed on the commission was the drafting of proposals for changes in the law. It was able to reach agreement on many matters, e. g. on the desirability of an increase in the supply of consumer in-

174

formation, especially on radio and television and in schools, and on the setting-up of a consumer ombudsman and a consumers' complaints board. But with regard to the two Council publications – especially the question of amalgamation of THINK and "Advice and Findings" – disagreement was so strong that the commission abandoned any attempt to formulate proposals on the point. The issue of the future organisation of the two institutions, one purely governmental and the other private but mainly government-financed, was tackled in a proposal which a majority of the commission's members were able to sign, but both minority and individual reports were submitted as well. No legislative proposals have yet been mooted, but like Sweden and Norway, Denmark has now a consumers' ombudsman and a consumers' complaints board. In addition, a law has been passed to enforce the compulsory display of signs and price-labelling of almost all goods and services.

It may be added that the consumers' ombudsman set up a work group to study the question of "Sex Discrimination in Advertising". The group included representatives of the Equal Status Council, the Danish Association of Advertising Agencies, the Consumers' Council, the Danish Women's Society, and the Århus School of Commerce, and it examined how women are portrayed in today's advertising. The resulting reports showed that both women and men are represented by advertisers in grossly distorted fashion. In the case of women, however, the image portrayed is particularly out of key with reality. Discrimination against women takes place constantly in practically all fields and relates to age, occupation, leisure-time, social role, appearance, behaviour, dress, and places they frequent. Further, the majority of the group members found that one third of the advertisements illustrating persons were unacceptable from the equality standpoint.

The question of how to eliminate inequalities associated

175

with advertising was of course discussed, and the Equal Status Council suggested that a court case would be a useful device for defining the limits of the existing Marketing Act. The work group report was published at the beginning of 1979, but so far nothing has been done to implement its recommendations.

Above and below: Class of leavers, Suhr's School of Home Economics then (1906) and now; male home economics teachers are now trained there as well. (Photos courtesy of Suhr).

The pioneering Magdalene Lauridsen (1873–1957), who launched the home economics associations and was co-founder of the Home Economics Teachers' Association. She trained the first teachers of home economics at Ankerhus, Sorø, in 1902. (Photo courtesy of Ankerhus, from the 1950s).

The impressive Copenhagen premises of the Danish Government Home Economics Council, headquarters of a comprehensive range of services including information and advice, the testing of household appliances and equipment, collaboration with other organisations and the publication of articles, a regular journal and other material. (Photos courtesy of the Home Economics Council).

A variety of new activities designed for protection of the consumer have been launched in recent years, and a law has been passed enforcing the compulsory display of signs and price-labelling of almost all goods and services. (Photo: Jørgen Jørgensen).

The consumers' ombudsman has established a working party to study sex discrimination in advertising. There is still much display of the female form to attract attention in advertising and the press. (Photo: Politiken).

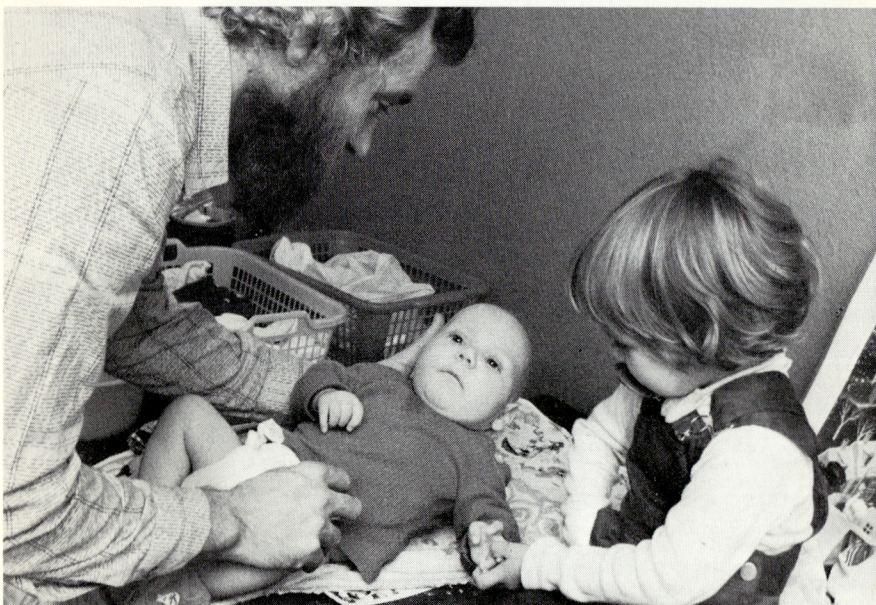

Strong feelings have often been aroused by the joint taxation of husband and wife. Two members of the taxation committee of the Danish Women's Society, Nathalie Lind (subsequently a government minister) and Jytte Christensen (chairman of the committee) bundling up lists of signatures of protest against joint taxation for delivery to the Minister of Finance. Photo 1963.
The untaxed work of the housewife. (Photo: Jørgen Jørgensen).

Below: The Danish Equal Status Council works for equality of the sexes in all spheres of life. (Nordfoto).

Sexual Liberation

Contraception

If women are to achieve anything more than merely formal equality it is a prerequisite that they themselves should be able to decide how many children they want to have and when to have them.

Contraception by means of mechanical preventive devices such as sheaths and pessaries began to be developed towards the end of the last century and swiftly became popular, especially among the better-off classes, despite strong resistance of a religious and moral character. The subject aroused passionate controversy, having been hedged about by embarrassment, prudery and concealment of truth. Yet scarcely anyone can have foreseen how events would unfold. The situation in Denmark today can hardly be regarded as a happy one, when despite sex education in schools, despite the birth control pill (which itself is not without problems) and despite far greater openness than before about sex matters, there were still about 23,500 legal abortions in 1979.

In earlier ages numbers were kept down by child mortality. As late as about 1900 something like 13 % of all children died in their first year, whereas the figure now is about 2 %. This can be attributed to the better living conditions of the population at large, better hygiene, better understanding of infant care (e. g. through guidance by health visitors), more skilful doctors, midwives and so on.

The person who managed to raise a commotion, indeed a furore, over the question of birth control was the authoress *Thit Jensen*, who stumped the country in the 1920s, preaching in crowded halls the message of family limitation through her celebrated and oft-denounced lecture on "Voluntary

Motherhood". She was both loved and hated. She had seen her own mother's health broken giving birth to eleven children, and her struggle was based on the idea of protecting motherhood by making it manageable both physically and economically. Abortion was a question that Thit Jensen did not touch upon.

The first women to bring up the question of sex education in schools – and in teacher training colleges – were working women, especially those of the General Union of Women Workers under the leadership of *Marie Nielsen*, a former teacher and a socialist. They had formed the *Arbejderkvindernes Oplysningsforening* (Working Women's Educational Association) which among its other activities gave instruction in birth control. The Association also demanded abolition of the crime of feticide and availability of abortion under medical control (1928). At the same time it stated plainly that abortion must be regarded as an evil, but in many cases a lesser evil than allowing a child to come into the world.

The Danish Women's Society scarcely dared to speak about such questions. *Gyrithe Lemche*, who was the mother of nine children, was strongly opposed to family limitation and in her novel *Tempeltjenere* (Servants of the Temple) called it "improving the breed", but the organisation did nevertheless arrange lectures on sexual hygiene during the 1920s. At first these gave no information about birth control, and it was not until the mid-1930s that this was included. When a youth section of the Danish Women's Society was established in Copenhagen in 1933 one of the points of its programme was the advocacy of sex education in schools, and shortly after the section was formed it got *Sofus Franck*, a headmaster and one of the pioneers in this field, to address it on the subject. Another well-attended meeting was on the topic of "Birth Control Viewed from a Social Standpoint". These meetings aroused considerable notice and were vigorously commented on in the press.

A colossal uproar was provoked at that time when a teacher employed by the local authority of Frederiksberg (Copenhagen) started giving his pupils lessons on sex: the affair ended in his dismissal. Opponents of the subject's being treated in schools said that it was a matter for the parents; but it was exceptional for parents to give their children instruction about this aspect of life, and more and more people gradually came round to the view that schools must include sex education in their curriculum. Copenhagen schools did so in 1946, and many local authorities followed this example. The Primary Schools Act of 1958 made provision for sex education, but only if the parents wanted it.

However, the number of illegal abortions was rising sharply. The hospitals could make their own observations, but it was in the nature of the case that only unreliable estimates of the total could be made. Some people believed that there were about 30,000 a year, and in the light of this figure the Danish Women's National Council and the Mothers' Aid organisation (see pp. 187 ff.) appealed to the government in 1961, so that a committee was established to investigate the need for education and advice in sex matters.

The result was that the Primary Schools Act was amended in 1970 to bring sex education into the school curriculum for all children. This does not mean that it has been introduced as a specific subject with an established number of hours in the timetable but that teachers, and most especially form teachers, are to deal with sex matters wherever appropriate in the context of the material being taught. Parental consent is no longer required for children to receive sex instruction, which is mandatory for both schools and pupils. Neither can teachers be excused from taking part in sex education, and lastly, it is laid down that in the final-year classes of primary schools comprehensive sex instruction, including information on birth control, *must* be given. When this statute came into effect in 1971 it provoked considerable controversy and triggered off a variety of protest actions in religious quarters and elsewhere. Thus, three married couples (though not acting from religious motives) brought the matter before the Human Rights Commission of the European Parliament, whence it was referred to the court in Strasbourg. The latter delivered a long and complex verdict in 1976 (by which time the children in question had long since left school). A debate took place in the Danish Parliament, but there was no majority for changing the law and since then peace, or at any rate quietness, has prevailed over the issue of the role of schools in this field.

After the change in social legislation that came about in 1976, one of whose effects was that the work of the Mothers' Aid organisation was handed over to new social welfare officers, the counties were charged with the duty of establishing sex clinics, whose functions were to include offering guidance in birth control. By the spring of 1979 such clinics were to be found all over the country except for a single county, furnishing free advice on birth control and, in special cases, providing contraceptive devices free of charge. Many general practitioners are involved in the publicity work, and some of them have been heard to express regret that birth control pills and other forms of contraception are not distributed free. A number of counties have, in fact, begun to supply contraceptives, and the former Minister for Social Affairs did in fact prepare a Parliamentary Bill in 1978 whereby birth control would have been gratis for all, but the economic situation halted the plan for the time being.

Simultaneously with public authorities' activities in this field, a great deal has been done on a private basis by the Family Planning Association. As well as running two sex clinics in Copenhagen, this organisation does publicity work including lectures and film shows in schools for example, and it arranges courses for nurses, publishes leaflets and so forth.

Abortion Legislation

In 1932 one of the hospital superintendents at the Frederiksberg hospital wrote an article in the newspaper *Politiken* in which he remarked, "Our hospitals are swamped with abortions and nearly all of them are criminal: it is only right to say at once that we regard abortion cases as so serious that hospitals accept these patients immediately as being in imperative need of swift and skilled help." The women he was referring to had almost all tried to induce an abortion either themselves or with the aid of a quack and were often very enfeebled from heavy bleeding. Unskilled attempts at abortion could lead to death, but even in the fairly numerous instances where success was achieved it was very often followed by inflammation of the internal female sexual organs and/or sterility.

A considerable modification of the criminal law was made in 1930 when the punishment for a woman terminating her pregnancy was reduced from eight to two years' imprisonment, but no provision was made for legal abortions. The reason for the more lenient rules is to be found in the fact that in a number of abortion cases tried by jury the women concerned had been acquitted and the quacks had received only light sentences, so it was obvious that the old statute of 1866 was out of step with contemporary conceptions of justice.

Even after these changes, however, the problems were far from being solved, and as early as 1932 the first Commission on Pregnancy was established following representations from the Medico-Legal Council. Its terms of reference were to investigate whether terminations of pregnancy carried out by doctors ought to be permitted and if so to what extent, and whether the state should support or initiate publicity designed to avoid unwanted pregnancies. After five years of deliberations a report was issued that was very free-thinking for those days. The majority recommendation was for a Parliamentary Bill to legalise termination of pregnancy on medical grounds (danger to the life and health of the woman), on ethical grounds (e. g. rape), on eugenic grounds and finally on social grounds. The latter were formulated in such a way as to permit abortion to be carried out when the pregnancy or birth would entail the risk of a permanent and significant diminution of the woman's personal, family or social position and no other means of avoiding the risk was available. The government agreed only to the first three indications and rejected the social one.

The Act as finally drafted in 1937 did not say anything about social grounds for legal abortion, nor did it contain any reference to the question of birth control counselling, although that had in fact been the intention. Instead, special Mothers' Aid institutions were statutorily established, among their numerous functions being some of those which the proposed sex clinics would have had. Thus a woman wanting her pregnancy terminated could apply to a Mothers' Aid institution, which would endeavour to dissuade her from taking any over-hasty steps, inform her about the possible forms of assistance available to her, and advise on the dangers involved in terminating a pregnancy. The Mothers' Aid organisation would also furnish assistance to unmarried pregnant women in determining the paternity of their children so as to secure an appropriate financial contribution from the father.

But nothing came of the idea of birth control counselling, one of the reasons being that doctors had no training in it and that some of them did not want to have anything to do with it. But there were still some highly idealistic members of the profession who did conduct an extensive publicity campaign which eventually led to the inclusion of birth control among the functions of the Mothers' Aid organisation.

Nevertheless the number of illegal abortions remained very high and many people began to realise that this was a matter in which there was a high degree of social lopsidedness. A lady of means could be admitted to an expensive private clinic where matters would be arranged, while a poor woman had to resort to a quack or try her hand at terminating the pregnancy herself if she felt it was impossible to go through with it.

A new commission delved into the matter yet again and in 1946 another law was enacted easing the rules for legal abortion somewhat but not going so far as to introduce true social grounds for abortion. The law placed the decision on abortion in the hands of a special joint council on which there were doctors' and Mothers' Aid representatives. Despite the fact that the commission had been unanimous in its view that termination was the worst possible solution of the question of unwanted pregnancies, only insignificant improvements were made in preventive work, and it was 1966 before statutory provision was made for all women after confinement or abortion to be offered guidance on birth control concurrently with the subsequent free health examination.

A vast growth in the number of illegal abortions was still observable, and this coincided with increasing public discussion of the right to free abortion. In 1966 the Danish Women's Society's fairly recently-etablished youth section began arranging trips to Poland and England for pregnant women wanting abortions, and this provoked a considerable debate in the press, the upshot of which was that the young people concerned left the Danish Women's Society. But at its national conference in 1969 the Society adopted a declaration in favour of abortion on demand, and the congress of the Social Democratic party backed it in the same year. Parliamentary Bills for free abortion had by that time been brought in on several occasions by the Socialist People's party, which had also demanded the appointment of a committee to look into the laws on pregnancy. This step was now taken and led to the liberalised but unsuccessful Act of 1970, one of whose provisions made it possible to obtain a legal abortion without special permission when a woman had reached the age of 38 years or had given birth to at least four children living with her and under the age of 18. Abortion was normally to be carried out before expiry of the 12th week of pregnancy and application was to be made either to Mothers' Aid or to the woman's usual doctor. As before, the Mothers' Aid organisation had to furnish information about the availability of financial and other assistance in the event of the pregnancy's being proceeded with.

The haphazard effects of the limits on the right to obtain an abortion aroused great dissatisfaction, leading in 1973 to the present law allowing abortion on demand. Operations are carried out at local authority or state hospitals before the expiry of the 12th week of pregnancy and the costs are met out of national health insurance funds. Even if the 12-week limit is exceeded, permission for termination can still be given in particular instances by a special commission of experts.

The annual number of legal abortions in the middle 1960s was about 5,000–6,000. In 1969 it was 7,000 and it rose every year after that, reaching about 13,000 in 1972. After the introduction of abortion on demand the figure increased to 16,500 and in 1974 to about 25,000, then in the following year to just under 28,000. But then a decline began, and the figure for 1979 was about 23,500.

One of the less pleasant statistics is the total of 540 abortions performed under the National Health Service during the period between the introduction of abortion on demand in October 1972 and early 1975 on girls between 13 and 15 years of age. Shortly afterwards the law relating to medical counselling of children under 15 years of age with regard to birth control was amended so that parental permission was no longer required. There are now signs that the number of abortions is falling in those counties which supply free guidance and free birth control devices to young people.

The abortion question has not been attended by quietude, and the Christian People's party opposes statutory abortion on demand. A campaign against it launched by a female Member of Parliament of this party – she is a psychiatric hospital superintendent – was defeated. The somewhat dubious and, to some, abhorrent methods she employed were largely responsible for this.

In assessing the question as a whole it ought not to be forgotten that prior to the 1973 Act a very large number of abortions were undertaken by quacks and compliant general practitioners, whereas now they take place under quite different and proper conditions in hospitals or clinics. In the nature of the case no one can say how many illegal abortions used to be performed, but various doctors and other experts have estimated the figure at about 30,000 a year.

The Fall in the Birth Rate

From the 1960s to the present time great changes have taken place in the numbers of births. In 1966 there were about 88,000, which was equivalent to 2.6 children per female, and the fall is to be regarded as resulting from a number of factors, such as easier availability of birth control devices and "the pill" as well as of legalised abortion. But a law on sterilisation introduced in 1973 also played a part. This made sterilisation available to men and women over the age of 25, and advantage is increasingly being taken of it, to the extent currently of about 15,000 sterilisations every year, more of these being men than women. It is probably people who already have the number of children they want who choose this solution. Uncertain economic conditions, the steep rise in women's employment, and the difficulties and economic burdens involved in having infants looked after discourage people from bringing children into the world. In fact it is a general phenomenon of the present age that in most highly industrialised countries birth rates are falling sharply. The latest estimated figure (from 1979) is 62,000.

The Family and the Future

Developments in the 1930s

The decline in the number of births that occurred in the 1930s gave rise to widespread debate regarding the future development of society and occasioned the introduction of new and important legislation which created essential features of present Danish policy on the family.

Sweden suffered a particularly heavy fall in the birth rate, and the issues involved were closely analysed in the book "The Population Crisis" by Alva and Gunnar Myrdal (1934). The Myrdals found that industrialism had changed the family in a number of crucial respects: the family had become small, comprising as a rule two or three children; the older generation lived apart from the younger; divorce was frequent; fathers worked away from home and children knew nothing of their work; more mothers had paid employment; children and young people were influenced not only by the school but also by magazines, films etc.; raising children had become expensive, and so forth. According to the Myrdals' theories the family needed to be strengthened if the "death of population" which they foresaw was to be averted: they aimed to do this by strengthening the family so as to make it a framework within which both children and adults would be able to thrive.

There were some countries in the 1930s which adopted such policies as rewarding large families, tightening up the rules on divorce, driving women off the labour market and hindering them from studying. But the Myrdals' ideas tended more towards the achievement of economic equality between families with and without children through the operation of tax legislation and family allowances, the availability of childminding services, assistance to lone mothers, promotion of sex education and similar measures. The Swedish government set up a commission, and a long series of proposals ensued for legislation along these lines.

Denmark too established a population commission, and by the outbreak of war it had produced reports on nursery schools, on housing subsidies for large families and on mothers' rights in connection with confinement. A law on "Mothers' Aid" was passed bringing this formerly private institution into the public sector, with branches all over the country. But the Second World War halted further developments, and many years were to pass before it became possible to carry family policy further, by which time the situation originally responsible for it – the decline in the birth rate – had faded into the background, so that family policy then became assimilated into general social policy.

New Family Structures

Towards the end of the 1960s, the debate on the subject of the family and its future was renewed, first in Sweden, then in Denmark. The occasion for this was the establishment of collective families, communal families, group families or whatever they may be termed, meaning not families in the sense generally understood, where kinship or marriage holds the members together, but families comprising a group of people who may be married couples (with or without formal documentation) or single persons, all living together and performing housework, childminding and other such functions as common tasks. The advantage of these "communes" compared with the small nuclear family consisting of father, mother and child(ren) is that they afford their members broader opportunities of fulfilling many aspects of their personalities. For the children there are playmates and ready opportunities of coming into contact with adults other than their own parents.

These communes differ widely from one another: some buy or rent a large old house; some live in apartments; others may have a farm which they work collectively; lastly there are the instances where groups of homes have established communal nursery groups, laundries, meeting-rooms and so on. There are about 10,000 communes in Denmark, with people from all levels of society, but especially from the younger age-groups. Some communes pool their finances, so that all incomes go into a common fund from which expenditures are defrayed. In other cases the members have their meals together and share the cooking, washing-up, cleaning, childminding etc. But there are wide variations in the manner in which communal dwellers order their lives.

Some communes have proved exceedingly vigorous, while others have broken up after a time, and there are some among which the members seem to move about fairly frequently. Obviously communities of this sort make heavy demands on the tolerance, consideration and maturity of their members, and even though they have the same attitude to life and may be friends when they come together, clearly conflicts can arise just as in traditional nuclear families. Possibilities of jealousy also exist of course when people live so intimately with one another, and serious conflicts can result. The press has taken a close interest in this life-style, and a good deal has been written about group sex-practices and so on. In recent years, however, these communities, which appear to be more than a mere passing fashion, have been less attended by sensationalism.

One may pose the question whether communes have solved the problem of equal rights for women in the family. The answer is quite evident: women find themselves in widely divergent situations in communes just as they do in nuclear families. Looking after the home and bringing up the children according to traditional patterns are tasks which can fall wholly or almost wholly on the female members or perhaps upon certain ones among them.

There is no legislation specially applicable to communal families. But even as early as 1968 a Bill which would have laid down financial ground-rules to be applied on dissolution of a commune or exit of one or more members was proposed by the Socialist People's party and considered by Parliament. It was rejected.

The latest developments in this field are treated in the chapter on "Documented and Undocumented Marriage".

Women and Politics

Disappointment over the Results
of Enfranchisement

There were some who believed that once women had won the right to vote in Parliamentary elections the feminist movement had no further *raison d'être*. Future work must be conducted through the medium of the political parties, which women could join and where they could advance their claims. The dissolution of the National Alliance for Women's Suffrage was a manifestation of this view.

To most of the women's organisations, however, the vote was only one of their goals. They foresaw that there would still be a need for them if women were to become equal partners in society. This turned out to be the case, even in fields that had not been anticipated at all.

In the Parliamentary election of 1918, the first in which women were able to vote, only four women were returned to the Lower House and five to the Upper out of a total of 225 members, and there was profound disappointment among adherents of the feminist cause. Gyrithe Lemche had foreseen some such result, and even before the election she was fuming in "Woman and Society" over the fact that only three of those running for election were women who had taken part in the campaign for the vote, "who *were* women of the old guard, who offered their services and were enrolled with grateful thanks in the ranks of the death battalion destined for catastrophe ..."

No great changes took place in the number of women Members of Parliament. The highest figure achieved before the Second World War in the Upper and Lower House combined was 11, in 1928. But those who did achieve election made a considerable mark and earned personal respect. The women's organisations tried to activate women towards participation in the work of political clubs and to find women willing to be nominated as candidates at elections. But undeniably it was difficult to keep spirits high. Nevertheless, the exertions of those women who had been elected gave politically-minded members of their sex an inkling of the scope women now had for influencing legislation, however few they might be. They were often used by their parties to deal with "women's questions" such as marriage, adoption, aid to children of widows and widowers, schools, maternity benefit, preventive child care and so forth; and it could happen that one of these women members might adopt an individual stance and so go against party policy on certain issues. There can be no disputing that women did bring to Parliament opinions and experience not previously available to it, but it soon became clear also that the party loyalty of women politicians ranked higher than their solidarity with the non-party feminist movement.

When *Thorvald Stauning*, a Social Democrat, formed his first government in 1924–26, he appointed *Nina Bang* (1866–1928), an historian, Minister of Education. Apart from Alexandra Kollontaj, who had been a people's commissar for a short time in the Soviet Union, there had never been a female government minister, so Nina Bang made the front pages of the world's press. She had been a member of the Upper House since 1918 and had acted with skill as spokesman of her party on a variety of trade, banking and taxation questions; she had also been a member of the Finance Committee. She felt no commitment towards the middle-class feminist cause: she was a socialist and believed socialism to be the road to the solution of women's as of other problems. She wanted clarity and order in her ministry and tried to root out obsolete traditional practices. Her thoroughness, vast erudition, skill and diligence are now beyond dispute. But unfortunately she is remembered today most notably for an episode that occurred at the Royal Theatre in connection with a performance in 1924 celebrating the 50th anniversary of the building of the Theatre. The festival play was J. L. Heiberg's *Elverhøj* (The Elf-Hill), which by tradition was introduced by the royal anthem "*Kong Christian stod* . . ." Having final authority over the Theatre, Nina Bang ordered another piece – Hartmann's "Entrance of the Gods" – to be played instead, but a counter-demonstration had been prepared, and the orchestra had scarcely finished before a student choir began singing "*Kong Christian stod* . . .", facing directly towards the royal box where the King was sitting. The public rose, but Nina Bang sat immovable in her place, while some of the other ministers present adopted a variety of extraordinary either-or postures. It was newsworthy material, especially for the humorous papers.

Nina Bang did not succeed in carrying through any major reform during her 2½ years as a minister, though she would have liked very much to have had the opportunity to change the primary schools so as to enable working-class children to be better equipped for their subsequent existence, but the scope for action by a minority government was very limited. She did issue a circular to teacher training colleges on the subject of instruction in sexual hygiene with a view to enabling teachers to provide guidance to children, and she introduced a "League of Nations Day of Peace" in schools.

Women Make Good Use of the Vote

Women participated very well in elections. Parliamentary electoral statistics do not distinguish between male and female voters, but the level of female voting in local government elections over a period of years was about 10 % below that of men. In recent years this disparity has narrowed to about 5 %, but among certain class- and age-groups women vote more sedulously than men. The City of Copenhagen Statistical Office divides up the votes by sex after every election, and the figures from Parliamentary elections tally in this respect with the information available from local elections.

The women's organisations endeavoured in various ways to make women more active politically. Towards election time they would hold four- or five-sided meetings with speakers drawn as far as possible from all political parties – preferably women, of course. The *Danske Kvinders Politiske Samråd* (Danish Women's Political Council) was established in 1936 (see page 121), and agitation to vote personally for women slowly began. Danish electoral law allows voters to put their crosses *either* against the name of a party *or* against that of a person printed on the ballot paper under the party label. This appeal to vote personally for a woman is always addressed to both sexes.

That the importance of women is understood is indicated also by the fact that several political parties eventually formed special women's sections which performed publicity functions and agitated for women to join the party but which also, in some of the parties at least, worked to promote the candidature of women in elections. Some impression of how slender an influence women had on social conditions may be gleaned from a report of 1934, according to which there were 150 government commissions, committees, councils and boards without a single female member while there were men simultaneously holding as many as about 20 public and private offices. Even commissions dealing with issues concerning women directly, such as the Maternity Commission, had a majority of men, in this case 11 men as against eight women.

Women Activated by the Shock Election of 1943

The elections to the Lower House of 1943, though a demonstration of national solidarity in face of the German occupation, were a catastrophe for feminism: only two women were

194

elected. It came as a shock both to the feminist movement and to the Social Democrats, the biggest party, who lost their only woman M.P. Many activities were started up, and it was widely and fully understood that a much more comprehensive effort would need to be made if women's participation in representative government was to be more than a formality. *Bodil Koch* (1903–72), a theologian and subsequently a Social Democratic Cabinet minister, inspired a democratic upsurge among women and launched a special movement called *Folkevirke* (People's Action). Its activities included publicity, study-groups and meetings (often in the afternoons because of the blackout and air-raid warnings), and after the war publication of the periodical *I Dag* (Today), subsequently *Folkevirke*, which still exists, and of booklets, articles and so forth. The Danish Women's Society was also immensely active, arranging for example eight simultaneous courses of lectures and discussions in different parts of Copenhagen. Among the speakers were several who later came to play very prominent roles in public life, including two prime ministers.

The first election after the German capitulation brought eight women into the Lower House, all of them new to Parliament but none of them Social Democrats. Five of these eight were elected with the help of personal votes resulting from a considerable campaign which included the distribution of handbills at polling-stations, posters, feminist election meetings and so forth, all directed towards encouraging personal voting for women. The Women's Society had been extremely active in this campaign, and many women in the various parties had worked hard and done much to produce a much larger number of women candidates than before. It now seemed fairly clear that to encourage electors to vote for women could be an effective weapon in bringing a better balance between the sexes into the elected organs of government, and this tactic has been employed ever since. It has of course been criticised as irrelevant to the real issues, but as long as women are a minority of those elected and are not given better places on the party lists, those voters of either sex who want women to be equal citizens will have to vote personally for women.

Progress now began to be made in local government elections, and in 1946 348 women got on to urban and parish councils – alongside 11,488 men. Every succeeding election showed a rise in the numbers of women elected, the figure for 1966 being 972, or just under 10 % of the total. The mergers of local authority districts in 1970 engendered considerable anxiety and uncertainty about the effect these would have on women's representation, but in the event the figure surpassed the 10 % mark and in 1974 was over 12 %.

Further Developments: No Government Without One Woman at Least

The 1947 Parliamentary elections brought 13 women into the Lower House and 12 into the Upper. There were now four women Social Democrats in the Lower House, and the newly-elected *Fanny Jensen* (1890–1969) was appointed Minister without Portfolio. She was at that time president of the *Kvindeligt Arbejderforbund* (The General Union of Women Workers), which then had about 30,000 members and she was politically experienced through her involvement in local government politics. The office allotted to Fanny Jensen was a thankless one, for she had no specific field of administration to oversee. She had to concern herself with the social and practical aspects of home, children and housekeeping, and with the interests of self-supporting women. She developed collaboration with a number of ministries on such matters as the introduction of home helps, and she also relieved the Minister of Commerce of some of the wide range of tasks imposed on him during the rationing era. She secured the permission of the Minister of Justice for the Danish Women's

196

National Council to hold an annual "flower day", when marguerites are sold for the benefit of the social and humanitarian work done by women's organisations. Fanny Jensen became a popular figure, especially among women, and she is the only working-class woman so far who has ever been a member of a Danish government. Her industry is illustrated by the fact that during her term as a minister until 1950 she spoke at 429 meetings all over Denmark. No Danish government since her day has been without at least one woman minister.

When the Social Democratic government was reconstructed after the election of 1950, *Bodil Koch* became Minister of Ecclesiastical Affairs, but the government fell after six weeks. She had been a member of the Lower House since 1947 and was a well-known figure, partly because of the countless meetings she held all over Denmark: her temperamental and highly personal utterances on foreign policy issues had attracted particular notice. She became Minister of Ecclesiastical Affairs again in 1953 and continued in office right through to 1966, when she moved to the Ministry of Cultural Affairs until 1968. The number of years she spent as a minister in charge of a department are in themselves sufficient testimony to her competence, but now and then she caused not a few prime ministers and ministerial colleagues to raise their eyebrows, for example by speaking at anti-nuclear demonstrations or criticising the attacks made by Social Democratic papers on *Aksel Larsen*, the former Communist leader, when he abandoned Communism and formed the Socialist People's party. But Bodil Koch's committed personality, familiar to the entire nation in her later years via the media of radio and television, was appreciated and even idolised to a quite unusual extent and far beyond the ranks of party politics.

When the Conservative and Liberal parties formed a government in 1950, *Helga Pedersen* (1911–80), later appointed judge of the supreme court, became Minister of

Justice. She was at that time a city court judge and president of the Danish Women's National Council, but for 13 years she had made a career in the Ministry of Justice, one of her posts being that of a minister's personal secretary, so that she was not a total stranger to the political field. Helga Pedersen displayed much independence and vigour as Minister, qualities illustrated most notably by the lenient pattern she set with regard to pardons in the post-Occupation judicial settlement. Helga Pedersen remained in the Lower House for another 11 years as a deputee of the Liberal party after her terms as a minister, making a many-faceted and distinguished contribution that included piloting a Bill establishing the National Fund for the Endowment of the Arts, of whose council she was president for ten years. Her many distinctions include that of being the first female judge on the European Court of Human Rights. Hers was a personality that inspired extraordinary esteem, marked as it was by unpretentiousness, good humour and a talent for exceedingly accurate and often very witty repartee.

The Liberal-Conservative government introduced a new constitution, and one of the changes thus brought about was female succession to the throne – though subject to the priority of sons over daughters. Another change was the abolition of the Upper House, so that Parliament now consists of the former Lower House *(Folketing)* only, with 179 members including two from the Faroes and two from Greenland. The first elections under the new system brought between 15 and 19 women into Parliament whereas the former two-chamber system had produced between 24 and 27 (out of a total of 225) in its later years.

During its final period (1950–53) the Upper House had a woman speaker, *Ingeborg Hansen* (1886–1954), a lawyer. She was the first woman in the world to be elected to the speaker's chair of a legislative assembly, and she was held in the highest regard in every quarter, not least for her outstanding skill in negotiation. She was a Social Democrat but took a stand independent of her party on a number of occasions: for example, she opposed the exclusion of juries from cases of criminal abortion and the employment of the death penalty in the post-war judicial settlement. She had been a very active force in the Danish Women's Society before becoming absorbed in politics.

When the Social Democrats came to power again in 1953 a sensation was created by the appointment as Minister of Commerce of *Lis Groes* (1910–74), 42 years of age, a graduate in political science and the mother of nine children. At the time she was president of *Danske Husmødres Forbrugerråd* (Danish Housewives' Consumers' Council) (see p. 172ff.), on which she represented the Danish Women's Society, whose vice-president she had already been and of which she was later to become president. Without any Parliamentary or administrative experience she simultaneously took over responsibility for a huge ministry and was placed in one of the most difficult posts of a minority government. She succeeded by virtue of her sound intelligence, charm and industry, and she became very popular with the general public. However, it is as the leading figure of the Danish consumer movement that Lis Groes will be specially remembered.

Women Ministers – Almost a Quarter of M.P's Now Women

At the time of writing in 1980 there are three women in the Social Democratic minority government: *Dorte Bennedsen*, a theologian, is Minister of Education after having served twice as Minister of Ecclesiastical Affairs; *Ritt Bjerregaard*, a teacher training college lecturer, is Minister of Social Affairs, having been Minister of Education on two earlier occasions; Dr *Lise Østergaard*, a professor of psychology, is Minister of Cultural Affairs after having served in 1977–79 as Minister without Portfolio with special responsibility for foreign-policy questions, particularly international development problems. There had also been three women in the previous Liberal-Social Democratic government: *Nathalie Lind*, a lawyer and a Liberal, was Minister of Justice, a post she had held previously concurrently with the Ministry of Cultural Affairs (she had also served as Minister of Social Affairs in 1968–71); the other two were Lise Østergaard and Dorte Bennedsen, who succeeded Ritt Bjerregaard as Minister of Education. The Ministry of Social Affairs had earlier been held for two periods by *Eva Gredal*, a social worker, who is now a member of the European Parliament; *Camma Larsen-Ledet*, now a mayor, was Minister of Family and Consumer Affairs; *Tove Nielsen*, a teacher, was Minister of Education in the Liberal government of 1973–75. When all are totalled it will be seen that of twelve women ministers, nine have been Social Democrats and three Liberals.

The number of women in Parliament rose only slowly, but by 1971 it had reached 30 and remained around that figure until the election of October 1979, when 42 women became M.P's – just under 23 %, almost a quarter of the total strength. This can be regarded as approaching a break-through – and personal voting contributed a great deal to the election of these women. Moreover, a number of women runners-up are standing by in readiness to move forward whenever the opportunity presents itself.

The most recent local authority elections took place in March 1978, and on that occasion portents of things to come on the political front affecting women were revealed. Of 4,759 councillors elected 842 were women, representing just under 18 % compared with just over 12 % four years previously. Although there are still some councils without a single woman – "black councils", as the Danish Women's Society has dubbed them – the number is now down to eight.

The county council elections held at the same time resulted

200

in a doubling of the proportion of women from about 8 % to about 15 % – from 28 to 54 in absolute figures. But the first and up to now only female county mayor retired after two terms of office. The ordinary local authority districts still have four women mayors all told, but there are no women at present among the six Copenhagen mayors. One of the Danish Women's Society's former presidents, a lawyer named *Edel Saunte*, was mayor for hospitals from 1962 to 1974, and *Lilly Helveg Petersen*, a teacher, was responsible for the administration of some of the city's technical services such as gas, water and heating from 1970 to 1978.

After the election of 1978 women were in a majority on the Copenhagen City Council with 28 seats as against 27 men. The presiding committee also had a female majority with a lady chairman, one man and two women.

Political Quotas for the Sexes?

After 70 years of formal equality in local government affairs and more than 60 since women first availed themselves of their rights in Parliamentary elections, and despite the latest results, women still hold less than 25 % of the seats. Little skill in divination is needed to predict that equality between the sexes in the political arena is by no means just around the corner.

Schemes have been floated in recent years for legal measures to bring about equal numerical representation of the sexes in the elective organs of state. Thus *Elin Appel*, a former M.P., suggested in *Parallel Kvindepolitik* (Parallel Feminist Politics) in 1964 that half the seats in Parliament should be reserved for women by the establishment of a special women's chamber, and in 1966 professor *Gerhard Nielsen* mooted the idea that every political party should be obliged by law to put up as many female candidates as male: in addition every voter should be given two ballot-papers and required to vote for both a woman and a man. Professor Nielsen was realistic enough to propose doubling the number of seats in order to persuade Parliament to accept the proposal, for obviously if numbers were to remain constant a considerable number of sitting members could expect to have to give way to newly-elected women, which would make adoption of the proposal a pipe-dream. Doubling the number of M.P's, however, would require an amendment of the constitution.

In their book *Ligestillingslovgivning* (Legislating for Equality) (1976), *Ruth Nielsen* and *Jytte Thorbæk*, both lawyers, favour Gerhard Nielsen's idea but consider the proposal impossible to put into practice if it is to be combined with a constitutional amendment. Neither do they believe there is any ground for linking the proposal to an increase in the number of M.P's: they consider it would suffice to amend the electoral law to read that "there shall always be elected at least 87 Members of each sex, and that all parties and others shall, for their nominations to be valid, nominate equal numbers of men and women in every county and multi-member constituency".

The prerequisite for adoption of a quota system on these lines is of course the acceptance by Parliament of the aim of "true equality", and for the rest the authors do not feel there are any valid objections to the quota principle in political elections.

At this point the question arises whether the democratic majority principle is to give way to quotas for the sexes. In consequence of personal voting, which presumably would not be abolished, an election might result in two attractive male candidates of the same party in a district being clearly preferred to the party's other candidates. Their party can select only two. Is one of them to withdraw in favour of a woman with fewer (personal and list) votes?

This example is simplified, but not much insight is required in order to grasp that the distribution of seats would occasion

202

many intractable rule-of-three problems and that many strange complications would arise if the ingeniously-constructed system of nominations, division into districts, principles of distribution of supplementary seats etc. were tampered with.

The main point at issue is whether real equality finds acceptance among the people at large – and under this proposal real equality is to be understood as being manifested when an elected assembly consists of equal numbers of men and women. Is this not a very clumsy and unrealistic conception? Are there no reactionary opponents of equal rights among women – and no progressive advocates of them among men?

Nobody so far has seriously taken up the idea of changing Denmark's Parliamentary system along the lines of the quota principles sketched out above. It seems well beyond the bounds of probability that Parliament would adopt any proposals in that direction in the foreseeable future.

Nevertheless, the quota system can easily be practised in many other spheres, e. g. by the political parties. It is not long since the Social Democratic party applied the quota principle in order to place women councillors in Copenhagen, where every fourth name on the party list was female.

The Socialist People's party introduced quotas for the sexes in 1977, so that at all party meetings at which there are elections, each sex is entitled – though not obliged – to take up 40 % of the elected places. The meaning of "not obliged" is that if there are insufficient numbers of women (or of men) willing to accept office so that the quota cannot be filled, nothing can be done about it. The 40 % rule gives flexibility, and it is only in cases where one person alone is to be elected that it cannot be applied. If there are three persons to be elected, then there must be at least one man and one woman; if four, then two of each sex must be elected; if five, then likewise at least two of each, and so on. To take an example of higher figures, if 15 are to be elected, then six places *must* go to women while the rest can go to men – and *vice versa*. Thus, ballot papers must contain votes for at least 40 % from each sex in order to be counted as valid. The Socialist People's party secured 11 seats in Parliament at the election of October 1979: the majority of these are women and a woman acts as Parliamentary party leader.

The Danish Women's Society believes that a change in the electoral law entitling women to 50 % of all Parliamentary seats is necessary as a transitional arrangement. The Society issued a discussion paper on this in 1979 which also described other possible forms of positive discrimination in favour of women (see pp. 260 ff.).

The Commission on Women

Sweden Ahead of Denmark

The term "sex roles" found its way into the Danish language in the early 1960s. This happened because sex roles and their significance had long been a subject of discussion in Sweden. Sex-role theories offered an explanation of why it was that despite the formal equality enjoyed by women, they had exceedingly little real say in any sphere of life. There were women in Parliament but what power did they have? Why did women always have on average the poorest education? Did they play any part in economic life or in important organisations? On the evidence the answer seemed to be "No: it is exceptional for women to occupy prominent positions. The rule is that they have the humblest and worst-paid work."

It was in a Swedish/Norwegian book called *Kvindens liv og arbejde* ("Women's Life and Work") (1962), edited by Edmund Dahlström, a Swedish professor of sociology, that a new analysis was offered of the situation of both men and women in the family, the economy and society. The most important explanation of the facts lay in the expectations placed by parents and others upon boys and girls respectively. Children, and indeed adults too, live up to the expectations set by the world around them. Boys and girls are orientated towards different roles by being exposed to different treatment. From the time they are very small boys are expected to be active, inquisitive, daring and strong, while girls are orientated towards passivity, caution and weakness: with some exceptions, boys and girls become what is expected of them. These theories about sex roles were new to most people at that time and they provoked widespread controversy, especially in the mass media, which debated them at length.

Attention was drawn to the way in which opinions about sex roles are reflected in advertisements, television, children's books and school books. Studies were made of school books and it was shown that women were almost ignored in them. Those few women who did find a place in them were queens and princesses or else worked at home as mothers or house-keepers, or sometimes there might be a farmer's wife. Neither women in industry nor in offices were mentioned, and altogether it could easily be seen that the male sex was dominant in school books. Boys easily found a hero or "great man" with whom to identify. Girls were afforded quite literally no opportunity of dreaming of anything else but becoming housewives, mothers and perhaps stewardesses. School books must be characterised as extremely conservative with regard to sex roles, and even readers do not reflect the society of to-day but that of yesterday.

About the same time as the Swedish controversy directly on the sex-role issue, an article by *Eva Moberg* triggered off a fierce debate on other questions closely related to it. She wrote that women would not achieve equality and liberation by obtaining completely equal rights in legislation. It would be necessary in addition to abolish every form of discrimination on the labour market and in society at large; but over and above this, if women wanted to be equal they must be gainfully occupied in the same way and to the same extent as men. She further believed that as long as marriage gave women the opportunity of being supported, women would be prevented from attaining equality and liberation. Women who stayed at home were financially and socially dependent. "But surely," she wrote, "the task of motherhood must always remain a principal role of women? The vital point is that it does not need to be. For it is the extent of that role that defines the boundaries of women's opportunities as independent individuals. Hitherto the dimensions of the mother role, both in theory and in practice, have been such as to reduce women's scope as individuals to incredibly tiny proportions compared with men's. For the biological task has been very closely linked with a number of other tasks that are always regarded as being an integral part of it. Not only the entire care of the children and the main responsibility for their upbringing but also a function as the soul of the home – in reality its slave – have been coupled with women's "natural" role ... In point of fact there is no biological connection whatsoever between the function of bearing and suckling a child and that of washing its clothes, preparing its food and bringing it up as a good and harmonious person. Not to mention such functions as scrubbing floors, cleaning windows, going errands and polishing furniture."

Eva Moberg demands what she calls "men's emancipation", viz. a complete change of men's attitudes towards home and child. Domestic chores should be divided equally between the spouses: no longer should the jaws of the kitchen-trap snap shut on the vast majority of women as soon as they rise from the bridal couch. Moberg declares that every change in the status of women must involve a change in men's.

The Danish Debate and the Commission on Women

The Swedish debate spread to Denmark, where vast numbers of meetings, articles, editorials and so forth again turned the spotlight on feminist issues. A good deal of passion was aroused, and discussions were liable to end up in unfruitful exchanges of assertion and counter-assertion about women working at home. Television took the question up as well, and early in 1964 a brilliant series of broadcasts on "Women in a Man's Society" created vigorous and widespread debate, since they demonstrated the unfair treatment meted out to women in numerous fields. They also of course illustrated the theory of sex roles in concrete terms.

A group of Social Democratic women now made representations to the Prime Minister, J. O. Krag. They had worked on a study of the juridical and practical status of Danish women for half a year but had found it impossible to get to the bottom of all the problems involved. This was partly because the group lacked sufficient expertise and partly because the scale of the task overwhelmed them. They asked the Prime Minister to set up a commission on "The Status of Women in Society", and this was done early in 1965 – about two years after *John F. Kennedy's* commission on women had concluded its work. The Danish Commission was exceedingly broadly based and very large in number. There were 48 actual members, nominated by women's, housewives' and consumers' organisations, by trade unions and by the political parties; in addition there were economic, psychological, juridical, sociological and medical experts. The chairman was *Edel Saunte*, a lawyer and an experienced politician, who had started her career as president of the Danish Women's Society and was now a Copenhagen mayor.

The Commission's terms of reference were to enquire into the position of women in society bearing in mind that "despite the fact that the two sexes have attained legal equality in almost all fields, the actual position of women in the life of the community does not fully reflect this equality". The Commission was to present suitable recommendations, possibly including legislative proposals, "with a view to creating real equality for women in all sectors of the life of the community". Lastly, it was charged to consider changes in family relationships, especially the situation of children resulting from the increasing involvement of women in economic life, the question of women's education and the use made of it, higher education and so on. Included was also specific questions such as the position of widows and single mothers.

The Commission laboured for nine years before the last of

its reports was submitted. Many issues were delved into, and it was a work of diplomacy to get the very disparate membership of the Commission to work together. Special subcommittees selected from the membership were appointed to explore the individual topics and present their conclusions for discussion in plenary session. These topics included "Women's Participation in Public Life", "The Care of Family and Children", "Women's Health", "Women's Educational Problems" and "Women and the Labour Market".

The Commission issued a main report which dealt with the broad principle of equality and recommended the setting-up of a permanent organ (a secretariat) with a watching brief over all aspects of equal rights (meaning discrimination of every kind and not merely against women). This secretariat would (1) receive complaints and possibly assist complainants with legal proceedings or with negotiations, (2) keep an eye on legislation, administrative practice, education, the mass media, advertising, contracts and agreements, and endeavour by negotiation, representations and publicity to counteract discrimination, (3) take the initiative in counteracting discriminatory tendencies, for example by urging the appointment or selection of women for jobs and political posts and by helping to publicise and to obtain educational material in other areas, and lastly to (4) encourage and collaborate in research to increase knowledge of the causes of discrimination and of means of counteracting it.

It was suggested that some kind of council on equal rights with a few members should be established to assist the secretariat. It was felt that these members should be persons who were not tied down by responsible positions in organisations or administrative bodies but who were actively involved in the field of discrimination and equality problems. Also, the members ought to be appointed for only limited periods so as to ensure frequent injections of fresh blood and thus enlarge the scope for new ideas and influences in the council.

The broad outlines of the proposal were implemented in the establishment of the Equal Status Council (see p. 211), but its terms of reference were confined to equality between the sexes and the Council itself, following tradition, was composed of representatives of organisations.

In the many years during which the Commission on Women was deliberating, nine reports were issued, recommending 84 changes of law, ministerial practice and so on. Some of these recommendations had already been put into effect even before the Commission had completed its work, and others are still being considered by the Equal Status Council. Examples of recommendations that have been implemented are the equalisation of the marrying age for both sexes at 18, compared with the previous 21 for men and 18 for women. The domestic training requirement for acceptance as trainee nurses by hospitals has been abolished in compliance with the wish of the Commission. All ballot papers in political elections now *must* contain the names of all the candidates nominated, whereas previously in some places and at certain elections the voter had to write in for himself the name of the candidate he wanted to vote for. One suggestion that has not been implemented concerns the law with regard to change of name: this would have provided that a couple proposing to marry should declare whether they wished to retain their own names or use the same name and, if so, which.

The Danish Equal Status Council

Terms of Reference and Composition

When the Royal Commission on the Status of Women completed its work in 1974 it proposed the establishment of an Equal Status Council one of whose tasks should be to tackle the problems singled out in the nine reports (see Chapter "The Commission on Women") as important to the attainment of real equality for women.

The government then decided – in 1975, designed by the United Nations as International Women's Year – to establish such a Council by administrative action, assigning to it the following tasks:

1. To scrutinise developments in society, including legislation, and to scrutinise developments on the labour market; to enquire into conditions which militate against equality; and to propose measures for changing such conditions.

2. To act as an advisory and coordinating organ for local and central authorities on equality of the sexes.

3. To submit proposals for study with regard to equality of the sexes, and to foster educational work on equal rights issues through the dissemination of publications and other means.

The Council was to consist of eight members: a president appointed by the government, one representative of the *Landsorganisation* (Federation of Danish Trade Unions), one from *Dansk Arbejdsgiverforening (the Danish Employers' Confederation)*, one from *Fællesrådet for danske Tjenestemands- og Funktionærorganisationer* (the Federation of Danish Civil Servants and Salaried Employees), three from *Danske Kvinders Nationalråd* (the Danish Women's National Council) and one from *De grønlandske Kvindeforeningers*

Sammenslutning (the Federation of Greenland Women's Associations). The president appointed was *Karen Dahlerup*, a counsellor on the staff of the Labour Market Directorate and now a Member of Parliament.

The Council's secretariat consisted at first of personnel seconded from a number of ministries, but since the Council's establishment by law in 1978 it has acquired permanent staff like other governmental institutions. It comprises one head of secretariat, four academic and four office staff. The running costs provided for in the Finance Act for 1980 amount to 1,389,000 *kroner*.

Female Membership of Councils, Boards, Commissions etc.

One of the first tasks undertaken took the form of an enquiry addressed to all ministries, departments and administrative bodies designed firstly to discover what criteria were applied in making appointments to posts on councils, committees and commissions, and secondly to elicit lists of all councils, boards, committees and commissions and their memberships.

Processing of the data thus compiled produced findings that revealed how far Danish women still have to go before they attain equality in public life. A total of 904 councils, boards and commissions had altogether 9,245 members and deputies, of whom 8,452 were men (91.4 %) and 793 women (8.6 %). In 830 cases the president or chairman was a man (91.8 %) and in 31 cases a woman (3.4 %), while 43 were not reported (4.8 %). There were 519 councils with no women members, two with no men, 215 with one woman, two with one man and 12 with more women than men.

The Council urged the Prime Minister to press authorities and organisations to work towards a more equal representation and declared its intention of following up the matter. A favourable response was received, and the Ministry for Home

Affairs also lent its weight by circulating similar recommendations to local authorities and county councils.

When a follow-up enquiry was carried out two years later changes of sex-composition had taken place. Some of the councils and other bodies no longer existed, but new ones had been created. The following summary shows what has been achieved among the councils etc. figuring in both enquiries:

	1 January 1976	*1 January 1978*
No. of members	3,654	3,735
No. and percentage of women included	300 (8.2 %)	343 (9.2 %)
No. of presidents/ chairmen	349	349
No. and percentage of women included	14 (4 %)	14 (4 %)

It might be argued that recommendation is not really an effective weapon for bringing about change in female representation on councils, boards etc., but it could be remarked in reply that of the 900 instances in which it was theoretically possible for men to be replaced by women, there were 92 in which this did in fact happen, although in a further 28 cases women were replaced by men.

Greenland Women and Home Rule

In its very first year the Council took up an issue concerning women in Greenland by requesting the Minister for Greenland Affairs to secure for women the representation they needed on the Home Rule Commission (see pp. 284ff.). Nothing came of this, however, for when the Commission was established both Danish and Greenland politicians were in agreement that it should consist exclusively of political representatives which meant in effect members of the Greenland

Provincial Council and of Parliament, and that pressure-groups such as the feminist organisations could not be represented. The Equal Status Council was dissatisfied with this reply from the Minister and protested. In fact, the Greenland Women's Associations had declared the necessity of female membership of the Commission even before the Council submitted its request. But the Council's action did yield one result inasmuch as a conference was held between the president of the Equal Status Council, the Minister for Greenland Affairs and the chairman of the Parliamentary Commission on Greenland, at which it was agreed that the Greenland Women's Associations should be invited to take part in the forthcoming meeting of the Home Rule Commission in Greenland.

Many Other Issues

Questions relating to women and the labour market have been central to the Council's tasks from the outset, and the priorities established by the Prime Minister when the Equal Status Council was created included the setting-up of a Labour Market Committee consisting of the president of the Council along with representatives of workers (from the Federation of Danish Trade Unions), of employers (from the Danish Employers' Confederation) and of salaried staffs (from the Federation of Danish Civil Servants' and Salaried Employees' Organisations). One aspect of the work done in this field by the Equal Status Council is discussed in the section on Women on the Labour Market (pp. 242ff.), and the Council has been particularly active in assisting women in various ways, such as devising proposals for remedying the high level of unemployment among women. For example, courses have been introduced for long-term unemployed women, employment counsellors have been appointed with the specific task of finding jobs for women, and success has been achieved in increasing the number of women employed under job-creation schemes etc.

In addition the Council, acting in response to requests by individuals, has taken up both issues of principle and cases of personal discrimination. A student of agricultural science, for example, enquired by telephone concerning employment as a trainee at a government experimental farm and was rejected on the ground that lodgings for women were not available and that women were not accepted as trainees as a matter of principle. The Council asked the experimental farm for a statement in the light of the Non-Discrimination Act (see page 247). The reply received being unsatisfactory the matter was submitted to the Ministry of Agriculture, and a correspondence ensued on the question of women's physical strength *inter alia*. The Council contended that it would be contrary to the Act if men were automatically given preference in jobs requiring great physical strength merely because they are stronger on average. According to the Act every individual must be judged by reference to his or her own circumstances, regardless of sex. The Ministry of Agriculture then drew the attention of the experimental farm to the fundamental principle embodied in the Non-Discrimination Act, and the Equal Status Council is to be kept informed for a year about the numbers and sex-balance of applicants and trainees at government experimental farms.

Complaints have been received of promotions being withheld, according to the complainants, because of sex discrimination. Such affairs are always complex and emotionally loaded. The cases recounted in the Council's annual reports testify to great thoroughness and tenacity on the part of the Council, but at the same time it has to be admitted that it is exceedingly difficult (and time-consuming) to bring about changes in issues of this character, where the employer (whether private or public), being in possession of all the information and having often already concluded agreements involving some third party, is in a very strong position.

The many other questions taken up by the Council have included pension and tax problems (see pp. 224f.), nationality matters, custody problems involving fathers both in dissolved and common-law marriages and complaints from fathers over having to pay a higher rate of child maintenance contribution (see pp. 263f.) than mothers. The Equal Status Council has recently considered the principle involved and has concluded that following the adoption of the Equal Pay Act in 1976 and the equalisation of men's and women's wages pursuant thereto, the contributions of father and mother ought to be the same. This opinion has been made known to the Minister for Social Affairs, who takes the view, however, that the question ought not to be decided in isolation but should be taken into account in the deliberations of the Children's Commission (see page 269) on the economic measures to be introduced for the assistance of families with children.

Publicity about the Equal Status Council and Its Work

The work of the Equal Status Council has stimulated much interest, and both the president and the members of the Council and secretariat have frequent opportunities of giving an account of its work at meetings and on courses and of answering numerous questions about it. Press, radio and television naturally follow the activities of the Council and carry interviews with the president and others, especially on issues where new ground is being broken, and radio and television also arrange discussions and other programmes about initiatives taken by the Council to foster equality of the sexes.

The Council itself endeavours to keep the public informed of its activities by means of press releases, and it also issues pamphlets dealing with particular topics in popular form.

216

For example, when the Equal Pay Act was passed by Parliament in 1976 a pamphlet entitled "Equal Pay" was published, and in the same year the Council distributed "Women in Employment", a pamphlet drafted jointly by the Danish Employers' Confederation and the Federation of Danish Trade Unions and handed over to the Council. It was subsequently updated and reprinted, and in 1978 an English-language version was issued. In the same year too a brief account was published in English of the Equal Status Council itself, its aims, composition and functioning, and in addition a folder was put out dealing with the Non-Discrimination Act under the title "Non-Discrimination at Work". Lastly, a pamphlet on sex roles in the home was brought out in 1979 entitled "Why Is It Always Me?", by means of which the Equal Status Council hopes to stimulate discussion of the division of responsibilities within the family: it is intended for use both in schools and in study circles and other groups.

Involvement in International Cooperation

Cooperation between Nordic countries on equal rights issues was established in 1974 by a decision of the *Nordic Council of Ministers*. Each of the Nordic governments has appointed a representative charged with responsibility for maintaining contact with the other countries of the group. In 1978 these representatives began meeting 4–5 times a year: as a body they constitute primarily a forum for the exchange of information, though they do also carry out a certain amount of planning and implementation of projects.

The Danish side, for example, has made a survey of current studies of the influences exercised by the mass media as it affects equal rights, and a team is working on a programme for pursuing the question further.

Another Danish research team has been examining the question of parents' and children's needs for special leave

217

during pregnancy, confinement and infancy. The report was completed in 1979 and forms part of the background material on which a Bill has been based for introducing extended maternity leave for women and paternity leave for men (see pp. 269f.).

One of the activities of the other Nordic countries meriting mention is a seminar arranged by Sweden in 1979 on the influence of social and housing policies on equality of the sexes, and a Norwegian seminar to consider a report on "Marriage and Maintenance in Nordic Countries".

The European Centre for Development and Vocational Training, an organ of the EEC, arranged a seminar in 1977 with representatives of the governments, employers and workers of the nine EEC countries on "Equality in Vocational Education". The high level of unemployment among women came in for particular discussion here, and a working party was set up to study the steps taken by member countries in the vocational guidance and vocational training fields in order to foster equality on the labour market.

The president of the Equal Status Council has represented Denmark on the United Nations Women's Commission during the period 1976–80, when one of the principal tasks undertaken was the organising of the Women's Conference held in Copenhagen in July 1980. One of the preliminaries for this event was the holding of a seminar arranged by the United Nations Economic Commission for Europe, at which the Equal Status Council was represented.

Taxation of Married Couples

Separate Assessment Still Demanded

It was as early as 1913 that the Danish Women's Society, at its annual national conference, raised the demand for separate tax assessment of married women, but no one really noticed the fact. The question was to claim an enormous amount of attention from the feminist movement – and the problems have not been solved even yet.

In 1915 the Society made representations to a committee of the Upper House which was then engaged in overhauling the system of local taxation. Modification of the following provision was requested: "A married man is assessed on the whole of his own income and that of his wife residing with him, even if she has assets of her own." In the opinion of the Society a wife ought to be taxed on her own income independently of her husband regardless of whether she had assets of her own or there was joint property of the marriage. There were three justifications for this: it was humiliating to place formerly independent (unmarried) taxpayers on a footing with children under age; a husband's failure to pay taxes would involve his wife in loss of her vote and eligibility in local elections. At this point it was claimed that the Society could cite instances where husbands had neglected to pay tax in order to prevent their wives from being elected to local councils. The third justification adduced was that under the rules prevailing taxes were often higher when the incomes were assessed jointly than they would have been if the spouses had been taxed separately. This impost on marriage was "an encouragement to cohabitation outside wedlock".

The coordination of matrimonial and taxation law was a topic dealt with, appropriately enough, in the report of the

Commission on Family Law in 1918; and of its own draft scheme for a law on the juridical effects of matrimony the Commission says that abolition of joint property under the husband's management would undermine the entire foundation of current taxation. "A rule that the husband alone is liable to tax, is the sole party responsible for correct declaration of the income of both spouses and for payment of tax, thus seems incapable of being defended. The way should accordingly be prepared for assessment of each of the spouses separately, so that each of them declares his/her own taxable income and assets and is responsible for payment of his/her tax."

In 1980 this point has still not been reached, and it looks as though even at the time the Commission on Family Law may have become frightened of the consistency of its own thinking, for it hastened to suggest the retention of the joint assessment principle with an *option* for either spouse to make an independent declaration and obtain separate assessment though without the aggregate amount of tax being affected, it being divided between the spouses in proportion to their respective income and assets. The Ministry of Justice did nothing about the tax assessment question in the Parliamentary Bill on the juridical effects of matrimony on the ground that this was a matter for tax legislation.

The Untaxed Work of Housewives

As early as 1921 there were some members of the Danish Women's Society who saw clearly one aspect of tax legislation which it has been very difficult to get politicians and others to grasp since then. At the national conference the Slagelse branch put forward a proposal that married women without incomes of their own should pay tax, for there ought to be no distinction between one woman and another in taxation matters. The demand was that married women working in the home should pay tax at least "similar in amount to what a domestic servant earns". Of course, the idea provoked discussion and protest, as also did the term "domestic servant", which at that time was in process of being replaced by "girl in the household" or "household assistant", but an application on the question was nevertheless made to the Ministry of Finance.

The underlying idea, of course, is that the work of a housewife in the home has a value which in principle, though with immense difficulty, can be quantified in monetary terms depending on the number of children, the skill of the housewife and the nature of the individual house (e. g. larger for a rural housewife – at any rate in those days – than for an urban housewife in a small apartment). The pattern that has unfolded has removed certain household tasks from the sphere of the subsistence economy and brought them into the cash economy: for example, fully and partially processed foodstuffs are bought nowadays on a scale quite different from 60 years ago; vacuum-cleaners, washing-machines, dishwashers and other appliances make housework easier; hot water is available in almost every household, and so forth.

Even so, tax legislation is still framed on the principle of giving a husband tax relief for a wife working at home. Nowadays it is called the personal allowance, and in 1979 it amounted to 14,500 *kroner*. A single person receives one personal allowance and a married couple two, whether both spouses have incomes or only one – the latter still usually being the man. It is an interesting consequence of this legislation that if a wife formerly working at home becomes gainfully occupied, the husband's tax is increased by the same income, for only one personal allowance is now deducted before assessment. Thus the tax laws are not neutral *vis-à-vis* the life-style of married women but favour women who remain at home.

Current Regulations

The Danish Women's Society has been particularly active on the taxation issue, with resolutions, submissions, articles, studies of the effects of taxation, pamphlets, meetings, radio and television discussions, petitions and so forth, all with the aim of solving the tax problems of married women. Some success has been achieved, but separate assessment has still not arrived.

When taxation at source, or "Pay As You Earn", was introduced in 1970 it quite simply became necessary for married women to be separately assessed on their incomes from wages or salaries, and at the same time it was decided that a wife who had an independent business should be separately assessed. The same principle applies to a number of other forms of income such as unemployment benefit, old age and other pensions, sick pay, sickness benefit etc. The husband is still the liable party from the tax standpoint, however, and until 1968 he was called "head of the family" in law, but in that year a group of women Members of Parliament succeeded in getting the term done away with. Joint assessment is retained on capital and on unearned income and interest payments, and losses on real property are always deducted from the husband's assessment, even when he has the lower income. On the other hand, it is now possible for married women to deduct certain contributions to pension schemes in their tax returns, but in the case of other insurances such as sickness and endowment policies and of savings accounts for children, the maximum amount deductible for both spouses together is 3,000 *kroner* a year.

A Practicable Solution

Among the numerous reports and other documents on the topic of the taxation of spouses there is one that contains a minority proposal which would solve at any rate a large part of the problem. This is to be found in a report of 1963 made by a committee established by the Minister of Finance to make a special study of the social, legal and economic effects of the taxation of married couples and to devise proposals for change with a view to the possible introduction of taxation at source. The proposal was put forward by *Jytte Christensen*, chairman of the taxation committee of the Danish Women's Society, and *Ella Jensen*, president of the Tobacco Workers' Union.

What this scheme did, in brief, was to suggest how the relations between all categories of taxpayer could be so ordered as to take reasonable account of taxable capacity in arriving at the assessment. Taxpayers would be divided into four groups: A, consisting of married couples with only one spouse in receipt of income; B, comprising married couples with both spouses in receipt of income, such as wages, income from own business or from assets; C, unmarried taxpayers; and D, meaning married couples with a "co-partner spouse", a situation commonly found in agriculture, retail trade and handicrafts. The proposal was intended to eliminate joint assessment as far as possible on both earned and unearned income. Every taxpayer in Groups A and B would be assessed separately, and the spouse with no cash income would be assessed at O. No tax would be paid on incomes below a certain limit, i. e. a basic allowance would be granted, while in Group D, which would continue to be assessed jointly, two basic allowances would be granted, to be deducted before calculation of tax on the aggregate income of the two spouses. A single scale would be used for all tax computations, so that the present breadwinner and non-breadwinner scales would be abolished, as also would the then-existing marriage allowance. The authors of the minority report took the view that "breadwinning" had to do with children and that the way to handle it was by means of increased (tax-free) child allow-

223

ances to everyone with children, especially single bread-winners.

These proposals had the additional merit of being administratively feasible in the event of taxation at source being introduced; moreover the amount of the tax yield could be determined by adjustment of the amount of basic allowance.

Of course, the proposal would lead to a certain amount of redistribution of the tax burden between the various categories of taxpayer, but these cannot be avoided if distortion and injustices in the workings of the present law are to be eliminated.

Latest Initiatives

In 1976 the Home Economics Committees of the Danish Farmers' Unions and Danish Family Farmers' Associations, the Federation of Danish Home Economics Associations, the Women in Trade and the Danish Craftsmen's Wives organisations made joint representations to the Equal Status Council (see pp. 211 ff.) complaining about the unfair tax situation of "co-partner wives", and requesting that the economic and social circumstances of this group should be considered and proposals formulated for improvement. A special working-party deliberated upon the complex issues involved and in 1978 issued a report of 178 pages with appendices.

Of vital importance to this group is the tax authorities' practice with regard to recognition of the extent to which the wife (spouse) is an active partner in the joint activity, a question which also gives rise to much anguish administratively and sometimes has to be decided by the national tax court. According to the rules in force, which were changed in 1978, a maximum of 50 % (formerly 25 %) of the business profits can be transferred as a separate income of the wife and assessed upon her for tax. The maximum amount deduc-

Important female politicians. Nina Bang (1866–1928), an historian, the first woman in the world to take office as a government minister, appointed 1924.

Ingeborg Hansen (1886–1954), a lawyer, speaker of the Upper House during the final period (1950–53) prior to its abolition.
(Photos: Royal Library).

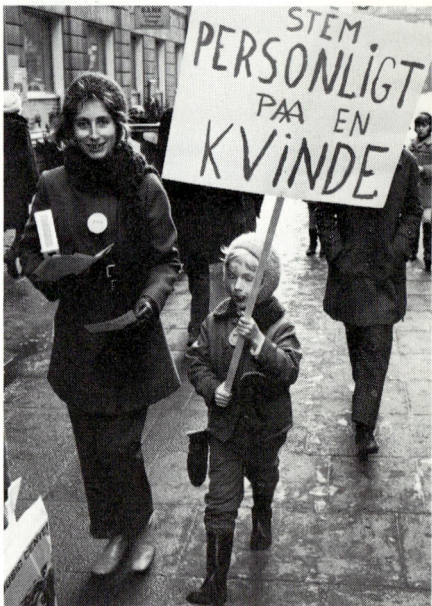

Helga Pedersen (1911–80), a supreme court judge, was appointed Minister of Justice in 1950.
Bodil Koch (1903–72), a theologian, was Minister for Ecclesiastical Affairs for many years and
Minister of Culture from 1966 to 1968.
Lis Groes (1910–74), politician and mother of nine children, a champion of the feminist and con-
sumer causes, president of the Danish Women's Society, 1957–64. (Photos: Royal Library).
The Danish Women's Society is still active in the struggle to achieve election of more women to
political bodies. The picture shows a campaigner urging voters to "Give your vote to a woman" in
the 1970 local government elections. (Photo: Politiken).

A constitutional amendment of 1953 secured female succession to the throne of Denmark. Queen Margrethe succeeded to the throne after the death of her father, King Frederik IX, in 1972. The royal family is seen here on the balcony of Amalienborg Palace on the occasion of the Queen's 40th birthday on 16 April 1980. (Nordfoto).

The ministers of the present Social Democratic minority government after an audience with the Queen in October 1979, with prime minister Anker Jørgensen in the centre. Almost a quarter of today's members of Parliament are women, a fact reflected in the numbers of ministers: three women and fifteen men. (Photo: Politiken).

The United Nations Women's Conference was held in Copenhagen in July 1980, with delegations participating from a large number of countries. (Nordfoto).

Lise Østergaard (born 1924), Minister of Culture, acted as president of the Women's Conference. Ritt Bjerregaard (born 1941), Minister of Social Affairs, has already made a name for herself in Danish politics.

tible from the husband's taxable income is 54,200 *kroner* (1979). The Equal Status Council does not regard this as meaning that discrimination against "co-partner wives" has been eliminated and feels that their situation is to be viewed as of a piece with the discriminatory treatment of other married women in taxation matters.

On top of this distortions are alleged to result from the way tax assessments influence daily sickness and unemployment benefits. In general, the report gives an account of the economic and social position of "co-partner spouses" in the legal system, which affects over 90,000 women and a number of men reckoned at the population census of 1970 at 825 – though this must be regarded as a minimum figure, for "co-partner husband" was not then a recognised designation of status, whereas "co-partner spouses" do now figure in the statute dealing with taxation at source.

The report contains proposals for four different possible models of modification of the status of "co-partner spouses" that would enable equality to be regarded as having been achieved. In addition the committee has carried out calculations of the tax consequences of the models and the consequential effects on the computation of daily sickness, maternity and unemployment benefits. Features common to all the models are their complexity and incomprehensibility to anyone who is not a lawyer and tax expert familiar with Danish law. The report has been handed to the Prime Minister with the request that it should be included in the government's legislative programme.

Since the Equal Status Council has received many other complaints regarding the discriminatory rules applying to married women generally under current taxation law, it issued a special report on the subject in 1978. This contains four drafts intended to be neutral from the standpoint of pure sex-equality. However, the purpose of these drafts is not to achieve equality between married and unmarried men and women but only between married men and married women. One of the draft proposals is based on the "splitting" system, under which all incomes of the spouses are aggregated and divided between them half and half. The effect of this is clearly to favour the spouse working in the home and to discriminate against the unmarried.

We may conclude by remarking that the debate over the taxation of spouses has not yet run its course.

Documented and Undocumented Marriage

The Statutes of 1922 and 1925

The work done by a joint Nordic commission formed in 1909 still constitutes the foundation of the Danish marriage laws. A feature of the commission unusual for those days was the representation of women on it, one from each of the three countries concerned. Finland at that time was a grand duchy under the suzerainty of Russia: nevertheless the marriage laws adopted by that country towards the end of the 1920s were likewise founded upon the same principles of equality that the other Nordic lands had attempted to formulate.

The law dealing with the legal effects of marriage provides that man and wife are to support one another and jointly attend to the needs of the family. Both are obliged to contribute to the family's sustenance according to their respective capacities, either in cash, by activity in the home or in some other manner, to an extent appropriate to the conditions of life of the spouses. Sustenance is deemed to include whatever is necessary for the household, for the children and for the spouses' expenditure, and this means that the husband has a duty to maintain his wife and children while she has an equal duty to maintain him and the children. Work in the home is regarded as economically equivalent to work outside it, but according to the law the partner who earns money must give the other cash to live on and this applies equally to the children. The law also enables a recalcitrant partner to be compelled to make his contribution as long as the marriage is in being, but such a rule is more of theoretical than of practical interest since attempts to invoke it will generally trigger off the process of separation.

The partners have an equal right to make purchases on behalf of both for daily housekeeping and the children. This means that the husband is obliged to pay for whatever the wife buys for the household and the children, but only if they are goods that are generally necessary or clothes for the children for example. The wife is under the same obligation with regard to purchases made by her husband.

The spouses have disposal of everything they own when they marry and whatever they acquire by work, inheritance, or gift subsequently during the marriage. This right of individual disposal applies even where there is total community of assets in the marriage (i.e. where there is no marriage settlement). If there is a marriage settlement with complete or partial separation of property between the spouses, this does not mean that there is any distinction between joint and separate property *during* the marriage. Community of property does not come into effect until the estate is to be divided on dissolution of the marriage by divorce or death, and each partner (or each heir) is then entitled to half of the joint assets regardless of which partner the assets belonged to. One consequence of the individual rights of control exercised by each partner is that each is liable for the debts which he or she incurs, and that the portion of the joint estate of which the partner in question has disposal must be used for defrayal of the economic responsibilities entered into. If the spouses have completely or partially separated estates, then obviously they are separately responsible for debts etc., though if they are household debts both partners are liable, and creditors can obtain judgment against them and levy distress upon the property of both.

There are exceptions to the general rule about separate disposal and separate liability so that in certain cases the spouse with right of control cannot in fact make disposals on his own. This applies to real estate on which the family lives or which it uses for business purposes, to household effects, tools and property of the children. In order to sell or pledge such assets the spouses must be in agreement. But there is free disposal over other assets, such as real estate not the dwelling-place of the family, stocks and shares, and ready cash.

Separation and Divorce

If the parties are agreed on the terms, separation and divorce can be obtained by consent on application to the appropriate authorities, meaning the county chief administrative officer in the provinces and the prefecture in Copenhagen. If the parties are not in agreement, they will have to go to the courts. The points on which there must be agreement concern who is to have parental authority over the children, whether any allowance is to be paid to one of the partners or to the children, and possibly who is to have the dwelling in which the partners have been living. Among the causes which the law recognises as constituting grounds for separation are neglect of maintenance responsibilities, intemperance, depravity and the like. If the parties are not in agreement then the injured party can go to the courts and claim separation on one of these grounds. On the other hand, for divorce it used to be insufficient for the parties to agree on wanting a divorce. Divorce required the existence of one of the conditions established by law. The most important of these were adultery, refusal of conjugal rights over a lengthy period, a prison sentence of at least two years and incurable mental illness. If the party desirous of separation or divorce was himself or herself responsible for breakdown of the marriage, it used to be very difficult to get a marriage dissolved against the other party's wishes. An "innocent"party might through malice and other such motives sometimes drag a case out for seven or eight years and take it right through to the supreme court. Separated partners in agreement on a divorce could obtain it after one and a half years at the earliest.

The New Marriage Act of 1970

During the 1960s the Nordic countries jointly worked out plans for changing these laws and bringing them more into line with the needs of the age. One of the problems here was to change the rules pertaining to dissolution of marriage so as to eliminate the scope for unreasonable and tiresome prolongation of cases. The new law accordingly contains certain clauses whose intentions appear very clear. On the subject of *separation*, for instance, it is stated that the spouses have the right to separate if they do not believe that they can continue with the marriage and are in agreement in seeking a separation. A later clause says that a spouse is entitled to a separation if the other has grossly neglected to maintain the family and committed other breaches of responsibility towards spouse and children. This latter clause can give occasion for both varying interpretations and disputes. Lastly, either spouse is entitled to separation if there are circumstances that would justify divorce.

A separated spouse is now unconditionally entitled to a divorce one year after separation, on condition of course that cohabitation has not been resumed. During the committee hearings for the Act of 1970, a majority of members took the view that in future adultery should be a ground for separation only. The reason for this was the wish to prevent overhasty actions resulting for example from isolated instances of infidelity. But the Act as it was adopted was a compromise on this point, and adultery remains a ground for divorce by the innocent party, though the court is empowered to grant separation only, for example where this is dictated by regard for the children.

In cases of cessation of marital relations without separation both partners have the right to divorce when cessation resulting from incompatibility has lasted for three years. (Previously it was four). Under the new Act a spouse cannot prevent

230

a divorce under any circumstances when marital relations have ceased for three years.

One of the other conditions that have changed is the preference formerly given to the mother in the custody of children under two years when marriages were dissolved. Provided the parents are agreed, the court will now follow their wishes in such questions unless they are against the children's interests. In such cases, or if the parents are not in agreement, the court has to decide in the light of the children's best interests which of them is to have custody.

The question of maintenance responsibilities and the amount of possible contributions is to be determined by reference to whether the applicant for an allowance is himself or herself in a position to earn something to live on and also in the light of what the other party is considered able to pay. The practice of placing a time-limit on maintenance allowances has developed, so that they may cease on conclusion of a course of education, for example, or be refused altogether in the case of young and childless wives. Under the old law there was a rule to the effect that liability to pay maintenance was generally not to be imposed on one of the partners if it was the other who by his or her manner of life had been the cause of the separation or divorce. This rule no longer exists, so that it is now possible for maintenance contributions to be ordered where it could not have been under the old law. It should be noted at this point, however, that during the Parliamentary committee stage of the 1970 Act it was laid down that when establishing liability to maintenance contribution in future it would be permissible to take account of information about the background to the separation or divorce, so that skilful lawyers are still of great importance in matrimonial cases.

The principle of equality of the sexes, as already noted, is applicable to matrimonial legislation and instances have occurred (though not very many) where women have been ordered to pay maintenance allowances to their former husbands.

One of the questions that has occasioned much difficulty in some dissolved marriages is that of visiting rights. When separations and divorces take place it is ordered that the party not awarded custody of the child or children, generally the father, shall have the right to have it or them on visits, for example at weekends or during summer holidays. If the other party tries to sabotage this right, it is always possible to enforce it with the aid of the bailiff, and this can lead to an exceedingly distasteful tug-of-war that destroys the relationship between children and parents. Under the new rules the recalcitrant party can now be punished with fines, and this sometimes helps. Moreover the new Marriage Act has a provision enabling the custody question to be determined temporarily as soon as an application for separation or divorce has been submitted. In this way the children can avoid being dragged into their parents' quarrels.

The Marriage Act of 1970 brought another change by doing away with the legal rules concerning engagements and the responsibilities entailed in a broken engagement. However, it is still not entirely impossible, for a broken engagement can still lead to the payment of damages and/or a claim for the return of gifts; as for instance if a person already married promises matrimony and accepts gifts on the understanding that it will take place. If such a gift consisted of money with which to start a business, then fraud might be involved. There are other promises of marriage that could likewise still lead to demands for compensation, e. g. if a woman gave up her job in virtue of such a promise and the marriage did not take place. Gifts for the proposed joint home can still be reclaimed but not personal gifts apart from the engagement ring.

The Marriage Laws Still Under Review

Even before the Act of 1970 had come into effect, a new Committee on Marriage had been established to consider further modifications, and in particular whether there was a need to alter the marriage laws as they concerned "certain quasi-matrimonial relationships" (common-law marriage or cohabitation outside wedlock, referred to in Danish as "undocumented marriage"). Part of the reason for this was the change in attitudes towards marriage as an institution resulting from the changed position of women in society.

This Committee has attempted to work on non-traditional lines and has successively issued a series of minor reports with a view to encouraging widespread discussion of these issues, which impinge so largely upon the life of the individual. The broad debate intended has not really materialised because so many other problems, especially economic ones, have occupied the centre of the stage in the 1970s.

In its very first report the Committee rejects the view that marriage can be contracted between persons of the same sex. The new openness about homosexuality had brought this question under considerable discussion, especially on television. The Committee argued that such marriages would not be recognised as valid in other countries and that to legalise them would probably cause foreign countries to take a very unfavourable view of Danish matrimonial law in general and of divorces granted in Denmark in particular. The same report suggested the lowering of the marrying age to 18 years for both men and women, and this was effected in 1976 simultaneously with a similar change in the age of majority. A referendum in 1978 approved the lowering of the voting age from 20 to 18 years, thus making the age rules consistent.

In its second report the Committee suggests spouses should have the right to *immediate* divorce if both parties are in agreement, whereas this is only possible at present if there are

233

special grounds for divorce such as adultery (see page 229). It is further proposed that a spouse should be able unilaterally to demand separation, and since the separation period is now one year this would mean that it would not take more than a year to obtain a divorce even in cases where the parties were not agreed. There has been no legislation on this recommendation as yet.

A third report deals with matrimonial financial relationships, and here the Committee believes that the existing arrangements, with equal shares as the main principle, should continue in force. In fact the Committee takes the view that the equal status of the sexes in marriage should be reinforced and that the spouses should be free within very wide limits to make mutual agreements about the details of their financial relationships. This question is of great importance with regard to the current tax laws.

The Committee proposes two changes with regard to decisions on the custody of children after dissolution of marriage. The first would be to establish statutorily the current practice whereby children over the age of 12 years are asked which parent they prefer to live with and the second would enable parents who are in agreement to elect to transfer custody to a third party, such as grandparents, if this would be in the interests of the child or children.

Much discussion has been devoted to the question of maintenance allowances, particularly in its bearing upon equality of the sexes. The Committee finds no possibility of abolishing maintenance allowances altogether but holds that in every case there is a need to evaluate individually the fairness of ordering such payments between former marriage partners.

The Personal Names Act

A new Personal Names Act was introduced in 1962, and the earlier rule to the effect that a child born in wedlock *must* carry its father's surname, or family name as it is called, was abolished. The situation now is that parents may decide whether their children are to have the mother's maiden name or the father's surname. But even if a child is christened or named with the father's family name, it is now entitled to change its name at any time, obtaining the right to use the mother's family name by a simple entry in the church register.

When a couple marry, it is still customary for the woman to take the man's surname, but even before the new law she had the right to continue using her maiden name provided that, *prior to marriage*, she declared her wish to do so before the ecclesiastical or civil marriage authorities. A husband now has the right to carry his wife's family name, but he must make application to the Ministry of Justice, which will grant permission.

A change affecting divorced women has been introduced by the new Personal Names Act. There was formerly a rule to the effect that a divorced woman could be deprived of the right to use her former husband's name if it was she who had been responsible for the breakdown of the marriage. This could be a great inconvenience to women such as doctors, lawyers, artists etc. known in the business world by their married names. Under the new law a divorced woman may continue to carry the name she has acquired by marriage, even if she remarries.

A child born out of wedlock generally takes the mother's maiden name but is entitled to take the name of its natural father provided paternity has been established or admitted under the appropriate rules. If the child's mother is or has been married to a man other than the child's father and takes or has taken her husband's surname, the child can acquire the same name by an entry in the church register of names.

"Undocumented Marriages"

The great and possibly insoluble problem for the Committee on Marriage is the task of formulating legal rules applicable to the increasing number of people who prefer to live together without either a civil or a church wedding. Judge *Inger Margrete Pedersen* has carried out a scrutiny of Danish legislation on behalf of the Committee in order to obtain a clearer view of the institution of marriage and at the same time to construct various models for solving the problems likely to face undocumented partners, for example when cohabitation ceases.

The difficulty here arises simply from the fact that the reason behind "undocumented" relationships is often a wish to avoid those very legal consequences entailed by marriage. Whether Parliament intends to legislate on the question has not been clarified, but when the Marriage Act of 1970 was under discussion the Socialist People's party introduced a Bill dealing with established quasi-marital relationships and their dissolution, and this was received with a certain amount of sympathy, particularly because it laid emphasis on protecting the weaker partner in the relationship. But at the same time the Bill encountered stiff opposition and was criticised as inconsistent because of the element of compulsion contained in a proposed rule whereby either partner in a quasi-marital relationship of at least three years' duration could claim acknowledgement of the relationship by the civil authorities. This would have been tantamount to introduction of a new kind of marriage – marriage by compulsion.

However, the Committee on Marriage is continuing its work on undocumented marriages and is expected to complete it sometime during 1981. At the same time the number of undocumented marriages is increasing, so that according to a study undertaken by the Danish Office of Statistics in October 1977 there were 343,000 such people, i. e. just over

236

170,000 couples, which means that about 13 % of people living together are not married.

This pattern is naturally reflected in a decline in the number of marriages being contracted, which has fallen since 1940 to just over 6 per 1,000 inhabitants annually, i. e. the lowest figure since such statistics were first compiled in 1851. At the same time the number of divorces began rising from 1968 onwards after having remained at about 6,000 to 7,000 for many years. In 1971 it increased to over 13,000 and since then has remained constant at about that level. Thus marriage has not been rated high in recent years. What the figures probably express is a tendency for life-long cohabitation to become more rare in future and to be supplanted by a pattern of successive marital partnerships of shorter or longer duration with or without formal documentation.

Why "Undocumented"?

No one has yet offered a realistic analysis of why it is in the last few years particularly that undocumented marital relationships have become so numerous, to the point where every eighth couple living together are unmarried and among the younger 20–29 year age group it is more than one couple in four.

Two basic facts have to be pointed out in this regard. The first is the dwindling influence of the traditional Christian moral view, and the second is the greater economic independence and self-reliance of women, so that the conception of marriage as the only proper and desirable means of subsistence is greatly weakened, at least among the middle classes. An enquiry undertaken by the Institute of Social Research in 1975 showed that 25 % of undocumented couples were directly opposed to marriage as an actual institution.

This enquiry suggests that 40 % of undocumented couples

regard their position as a kind of trial marriage and that many of them do in fact eventually get married because they either have a child or are going to become parents. Another reason for cohabitation outside wedlock may be that one of the partners – possibly both – is already married and for a variety of reasons (e. g. a decision as to custody of children) does not want or has not yet obtained a divorce.

The direct economic incentives to refrain from marriage which previously existed, particularly under taxation and social welfare legislation, have now been considerably reduced because the rules have been changed. Here we may particularly mention the "pillow-promise clause", as it was nicknamed, of 1973, whereby unmarried breadwinners have to sign a declaration that they are not cohabiting with someone of the opposite sex. If they are doing so, they are entitled only to ordinary child allowance and not to augmented or extra child allowance (see page 265). These changes appear not to have affected the growth in the numbers of undocumented couples. However, there are still economic advantages in cohabitation outside wedlock, for example in the case of persons enjoying unearned income, and this applies also to the tax effects of certain deduction schemes, while in the same way pensioners of various categories can avoid having their pensions reduced by not getting married.

Problems Involved in "Undocumented Marriages"

There are possibilities of disagreement in undocumented as in conventional marriages, but with the difference that matrimonial legislation has rules conferring rights (and responsibilities) on the respective parties and so attempting to regulate both the problems of daily life and, not least, the situation that arises when the parties terminate their life together. The position in which the children of undocumented marriages find themselves is that only the mother has custody and

238

she alone is their guardian. She enjoys the sole right of decision and can determine whether a child shall go to a day-nursery or nursery school, whether it shall be brought up in this way or that, and so on and so forth. Moreover it is she who is in charge of the child's finances, and she is responsible for looking after the child. The undocumented father has no kind of rights over his children even if the mother dies. It is possible in such cases, however, for the county or municipal authorities to transfer parental authority to the father on his application provided it is consistent with the child's interests.

If the parties separate, the father may now have the opportunity, following a change made in 1969 to the rules relating to visiting rights, of being together with his children. Formerly it was impossible for the father of children born out of wedlock to obtain such entitlements, and the change has been effected simply out of regard for the interests of children born of undocumented relationships. It is also possible for parents, with the assent of the county or municipal authorities, to agree upon a transfer of custody to the father alone, but they cannot have joint custody even if they want it. This question has occasioned much debate. Joint custody was introduced in Sweden by statute in 1977, but in Denmark the Commission on Marriage, at the request of the Ministry of Justice, drafted an interim proposal for resolving the matter. The idea it produced was for the courts to be given discretion to assign a child born outside wedlock to the custody of its father, even against the wishes of the mother, if this was felt to be necessary in the interests of the child. The proposal was adopted in 1978.

The parties cannot enter into binding agreements upon questions of custody as they could with regard to various other matters. Thus it is possible by agreement or by establishing a contract of cohabitation to clarify the financial conditions of the relationship and likewise to make wills in which, for example, the parties concerned name each other as sole heirs. The contract or agreement may contain elaborate rules both about the day-to-day economic and working conditions and about proprietary rights in all the furnishings and effects existing in the couple's dwelling, whether ownership is joint or separate or whether alternatively, for example, everything purchased or otherwise acquired during cohabitation shall belong to the parties jointly and in the event of cessation of cohabitation shall be divided equally. The dwelling itself, of course, constitutes an important item for such agreements, whether owned or rented, and it is possible to determine in very great detail how the mutual relations of the parties are to be arranged *vis-à-vis* the dwelling if cohabitation ceases. It has often been remarked that there are no limits to the number of documents "undocumented couples" have on one another, and indeed this is necessary if both parties are intent on securing their positions to the greatest possible extent.

But marriage offers particular advantages in certain respects. This is the case with inheritance, for example, where estate duties between spouses is very small, while between persons not of the same family as each other they reach formidable levels. If an unmarried couple have children then they become heirs and can get by with very small amounts of duty, but in such cases written wills may not have been made between the parties.

The special Danish rule enabling a spouse to retain undivided possession of the estate do not apply to an undocumented partner. Their effect is that the longest surviving partner can take over the whole of the joint estate, including fixed property, if the only children are those of the marriage and their successors. In such cases death duty becomes payable only on the decease of the longest survivor, which is generally a great financial advantage.

It is immensely difficult to make laws to fit such a complicated and individual venture as marriage and even more

One result of the Redstocking movement that manifested itself from the beginning of the 1970s was the island camps for women, which have given many women the opportunity of experiencing a new form of fellowship and solidarity between women. (Photo: Politiken, Sisse Jarner).

The traditional family pattern is being transformed, and many women have taken their fates into their own hands. (Photo: Jørgen Jørgensen).

One of the issues taken up by the Redstockings was the equal pay campaign. Demonstration outside the Court of Justice building in Copenhagen, 1970.

The Redstockings have often used untraditional and provocative forms of agitation. The first Redstocking action in Denmark took place on 8 April 1970, when a protest was made against the artificial feminine ideal promoted by the fashion industry.

One of the actions by the "Thildes" was the occupation of car parks in 1970 as a demonstration for more kindergartens. (Photos: Politiken).

Will the giddy flapper come into fashion again with her giggling and tittle-tattle? Is everything that has been gained to be lost again?
(Photo: Jørgen Jørgensen).

Job opportunities for women are limited in Greenland. Most are employed in the fishing industry. The picture shows a prawn-peeling establishment.
Only a few Greenlandic women have taken an active part in politics, although a fairly large number sit on social welfare committees, on the management boards of cooperatives etc.
Guldborg Chemnitz (born 1919) has been active in the feminist movement for many years and was recently elected president of the Greenland Women's Associations.
Elisabeth Johansen (born 1907) was the first (and so far the only) woman member of the Greenland provincial council (now the elective assembly), but retired in 1975. (Photos: Politiken).

difficult to devise fair and universal rules for people who wish simply to live together out of wedlock. This chapter has done no more than to glance at some of the rules in force and to touch upon certain of the problems. A whole literature on undocumented marriages is already flourishing and this may at least help to clarify where difficulties can arise so that the large numbers of people, young and old, rich and poor, who are living together without wanting to marry or are considering doing so should be aware, for example, of how they can secure their position to the best advantage and of the prudence of having a word with a lawyer.

Women on the Labour Market

Development

The great increase in numbers of women employed in industry and handicrafts towards the close of the nineteenth century (see page 104) was followed by a slight percentage decline during the first 30 years of the present century. But in the 1930s the number of such women rose from about 89,000 to about 142,000, at least partly because of the trade and currency restrictions then being imposed in order to protect Danish industries such as textile manufacturing.

During the entire period from the turn of the century onwards a fairly steady rise in female employment was going on in urban industries generally. Thus the number of women in commerce, in banking, and in the hotel and restaurant industries was about 20,000 in 1901 and about 92,000 in 1940. In the "non-material occupations" such as administration (both public and private), hospitals, teaching, art and science etc. there were about 22,000 women in 1911; this figure had grown by 1940 to about 73,000 (compared with about 75,000 men).

After the end of the Second World War the demand for female labour became very buoyant, and between 1930 and 1953 the female labour force more than doubled while the male increased by about 60 %. The rise was particularly steep in the case of married women, the numbers of whom in employment increased five- or sixfold from 1930 to 1953.

The trend in more recent years may be seen from the table, which shows stagnation even in the absolute figures for the male sector of the labour force coinciding with a massive increase in the proportion of women, especially married women after 1965, so that they now account for something like 30 % of the labour force.

However, the distinction between married and unmarried women gradually becomes less interesting (see page 236). What is interesting in this connection is that a very large number of women members of the labour force are employed for fewer hours than the normal seven or eight hours five days a week. Such part-time jobs are to be found only to a limited extent in the truly industrial sector, but they are common in many other establishments as is evidenced by the fact that in 1967 there were 249,000, in 1973 401,000, in 1975 426,300, and 1977 460,000 women in part-time employment. This form of employment can solve certain individual problems involving children and housework, but part-time work by women seems to have a perpetuating effect upon the current sex-role pattern.

Entire Labour Force (1000 persons)

	1960	1965	1970	1975	1976	1977	1978
	2064	2233	2380	2486	2531	2579	2625
Men..................	1448	1488	1462	1463	1480	1490	1501
Women..............	616	745	918	1023	1051	1089	1125
Proportion of married women included		380	589	674	690	716	
Men..................	70 %	67 %	61 %	59 %	58 %	58 %	57 %
Women..............	30 %	33 %	39 %	41 %	42 %	42 %	43 %
Proportion of married women included		17 %	25 %	27 %	27 %	28 %	

The employment of women has increased most notably in the public sector, where the figures show an increase from about 248,000 to about 466,000 between 1967 and 1976. Women in this sector are employed particularly in administration, teaching, the health service, the social field in the widest sense, cleaning and similar occupations. At the same time the number of women in the private sector during the same period declined somewhat from about 615,000 to about 585,000. The number of female industrial workers fell between 1966 and 1976 from about 94,000 to about 78,000, while female salaried employees in industry were unchanged at about 30,000. The latest figures show an increase in women workers in industry.

Women's Pay

Women's pay on the private labour market has always been inferior to that of men, having normally been in the past about two thirds of men's pay for more or less similar work. Only the very few skilled women workers were able to get the same pay as their male colleagues, and in the same way it was possible for a woman to earn as much or even more on piece-work.

The average wages of female industrial workers around 1960 were about 75 % of those of unskilled male workers; moreover women tended to be employed in low-wage industries or in other fields of work with particularly poor pay. As we have noted on pp. 90 ff., however, the tobacco workers had managed to achieve equal pay for equal work as early as the turn of the century.

The determination of wages and other conditions throughout the private sector was a matter arranged by negotiation between the employers and the workers' organisations, and only in situations of special crisis was there legislative intervention to resolve conflicts where the parties had reached an impasse. In 1960 Denmark ratified the I.L.O.'s equal pay convention of 1951, which says that "equal pay for work of the same value" is to be paid to women and men, but the convention is only of moral or psychological significance, and it was not really because of its ratification that something gradually began happening about women's wages from 1961 onwards. The reason is more to do with the shortage of female labour.

Equal pay was introduced for male and female bank officials in 1961, though only for the lower grades, and in the same year women slaughterhouse workers, whose wages at that time were three quarters of the pay of unskilled men, achieved the embodiment in their agreements of a proviso that their wages should rise by 5 % per annum until equal pay had been achieved. The business and office workers, representing an important sector of female employment, followed suit in 1965 with equal pay in the minimum-wage field. This means that where there are minimum-wage agreements the wage system is flexible, enabling the proficient and experienced to have wages above the minimum. Women employed in the private business and office sector are the only large group of women covered by this wage system.

Not until 1971 did the Federation of Danish Trade Unions give equal pay a high priority among its demands, and when it did, this was undoubtedly due to the attention drawn to the levels of women's wages by the *rødstrømper* (Redstockings see pp. 271ff.), the Danish Women's Society, the *Thilder* (see p. 279) and other female workers in concert – spurred on considerably by the mass media. Numerous different actions were launched by *Initiativgruppe for Ligeløn* (The Action Committee for Equal Pay) including a large demonstration at the Conciliation Board when the question was being discussed. However, immediate implementation of equal pay did not result although a minute was adopted to the effect that equal pay for equal work should be introduced as soon as possible. As well as this, a relatively substantial improvement of women's pay did take place at once. However, the General Union of Women Workers did not want to find itself being put off on the issue of equal pay and therefore advised its members to vote against the proposed agreement, so that only about 20 % expressed themselves in favour of it.

In the negotiations of 1973, when women in fact took action again, equal pay for equal work was formally implemented. But since it is exceptional for men and women to carry out identical tasks, wages came to depend upon job evaluation, which gave a loophole for continuing to pay lower wages to women than to men for work of literally the same character. Nevertheless, the outcome of the 1973 agreement has been an increase in the wages of unskilled women bringing their average pay up from just over 80 % of those of unskilled men in 1971 to just over 90 % in 1975.

Denmark joined the European Community in 1973, and when two years later the Council of Ministers adopted an equal pay directive to be embodied in legislation by the member countries within a maximum period of one year, the Equal Pay Act was brought before the Danish Parliament and was adopted in February 1976. One of the provisions of the Act is that for the same work or for work to which equal value is ascribed there must be no difference between men's and women's remuneration. A study of the effects of the Equal Pay Act is being made in the Equal Status Council but it will probably not be easy to distinguish between the effects of the Act and those of the guaranteed payment of 29 *kroner* per hour which was introduced in the agreements of 1977 and has benefited women particularly. By 1980 the guaranteed payment was 33.75 *kroner* per hour.

A report from the Low Incomes Commission on the trend of income distribution during the period 1970–76 gives an impression of the economic situation of women on the labour market.

In 1970 the overall league table of incomes shows that in almost all categories of job or occupation women had very low average incomes. Only women in responsible salaried positions had incomes equal to the average for all gainfully employed persons. Over the period from then until 1976 both skilled and unskilled women improved their relative income placings despite the rise in part-time employment and unemployment. But this does not make any difference to the fact that in 1976 these groups remained far below the average for the gainfully employed population as a whole. The relative income placing of lower-grade women employees in the retail trade was more or less the same in 1970 and 1976, and this may be partly explained by an increase in part-time work. The Commission says in fact that two thirds of all low-income earners are women, especially the unskilled in all trades and industries and the lower-grade salaried employees.

The Non-Discrimination Act

The Non-Discrimination Act became law in 1978, and its intention is that men and women are to be treated equally with regard to jobs, vocational training, promotion and conditions of employment. This too constitutes a Danish legislative follow-up to an EEC directive. Amendments were made at the same time to the Acts relating to salaried employees, assistants, apprentices and seamen to prevent discriminatory treatment on the ground of sex of persons in occupations covered by these Acts.

The Non-Discrimination Act contains a special clause enabling dispensations from the general principle of non-discrimination to be obtained in respect of occupations and training in which it is essential that the individuals concerned should be of a particular sex. In such cases the minister under whose jurisdiction the relevant activity falls, having obtained the views of the Minister of Labour and the Equal Status Council, may set aside the non-discrimination principle. The Minister of Labour, after having obtained the views of the Equal Status Council and the ministry under whose jurisdiction the matter belongs, is further empowered to permit measures designed to foster equal opportunities for men and women especially by remedying actual inequalities affecting admission to vocational training, employment, etc. (positive discrimination). The Act does not impede the protection of women with regard particularly to pregnancy and child-birth.

Two of the provisions of the Act have given occasion for a certain amount of discussion. The first of these concerns indirect discrimination connected with pregnancy or with matrimonial and family status, i. e. the fact *that pregnancy is no longer a legal ground for dismissal*, a feature against which employers have protested – while many others have said that in such circumstances dismissal can be effected on other grounds or else employers can evade the problem by employing men instead of women. However, the biggest fuss has been caused by a clause in the Act to the effect that advertisements for jobs, vocational training opportunities and so on may not be aimed at persons of a particular sex. What happened here was that *Danske Dagblades Forening* (the Danish Newspapers' Association), in an attempt to assist advertisers not to break the law, recommended the addition of the abbreviation "*m/k*" (*mandlig/kvindelig* = masculine/feminine) after job designations that were not sexually neutral. The Association found sex bias in 193 job advertisements out of 729 in a single Sunday newspaper. But a good deal of ridicule resulted from this *m/k* annotation, which some people used to comic effect by concocting such examples as "head sales-lady *m/k*", "lady cook *m/k*" etc. Advertisers have now to a certain degree learned to use neutral terms such as "worker" or "assistant" followed by a description of the job but some cases are being taken to court. In fact, job designations found in collective agreements, such as "seaman", can still be used, and so can designations supported by linguistic traditions, such as *bedemand* (undertaker), *oldfrue* (matron) and *kogekone* (cook), all of which carry a sex-connotation in Danish. In fact, the law applies exclusively to the labour market and it is still legal to exclude women, or men from various private clubs and associations, from public houses etc.

The Equal Status Council has been involved in a fair

number of cases under the Act. For example, shipowning companies do not show themselves particularly keen to employ trained women sailors and the Seamen's Union has taken legal action against two shipowners who refused to employ a woman sailor allotted to them. The court acquitted one company which was able to prove that the ship did not have separate toilets and bath facilities for women, while the other was ordered to pay compensation to the woman sailor involved, who by that time had been employed by a third shipowner. This raises the question whether it is conceivable that a shipowning company could be ordered to employ a woman sailor as well as having to pay compensation. Another question is whether a fairly long period of adjustment will not be required before this and similar categories of job will be free of problems. The case was taken to the Supreme Court.

The Council has had complaints from men who have been unable to get jobs as home helps. Here the Council has pointed out that the public sector has a duty to lead the way in breaking down traditional attitudes. The question of women in the police force – an old feminist demand – has also been taken up by the Council. The first woman in the police service was appointed as early as 1911 in Ålborg, but she was employed on office work. Then in 1914 in Århus a woman police officer was employed on police duties proper, and later on a very small number of women of special background were appointed in the larger towns, where they have been employed on police cases involving both civil and criminal offences, especially those concerning children and women. The 1921 Act on non-discrimination in public employment (see pp. 141ff.) was never applied to the police service, in which acceptance for training was impossible unless two prior conditions were met, viz. fulfilment of national service commitment either in the defence forces or in civil defence and a height of at least 177 cms without footwear. A job advertisement placed by the national commissioner of police led to a lengthy correspondence with the Equal Status Council in the course of which the latter enquired about the legal basis for the lack of equality, to which the police side replied that the Minister of Justice had been recommended to establish an experimental scheme for employing women on an equal footing with men, meaning that they should undergo the physically exacting experience of uniformed police service. The scheme was started in 1977: for acceptance on trial women were excused the national service requirement and the minimum height was set at 165 cms. Eighteen women were appointed and for the present the commissioner of police has stated that the general impression formed by the police training school is favourable and that the experimental scheme will be evaluated on the basis both of the experience there and of the practical training at police stations. The police have subsequently taken on a further 26 women and the Minister of Justice has granted the commissioner of police a dispensation from the Non-Discrimination Act until experience has been gained from the experimental scheme, while the Equal Status Council has stated its opposition to the dispensation. A press release from the police commissioner to the effect that it will never come about that half of the uniformed police will consist of women has given occasion for the spilling of much ink, and the Minister of Justice, following representations by the Equal Status Council, has had to defend the commissioner, explaining that he had only meant that in the foreseeable future there would be insufficient applications from women to enable as many women to be appointed to the police as men. There the matter rests for the time being.

Unemployment among Women

Despite the fact that more people are gainfully occupied than ever before in the history of Denmark there is still a great deal of unemployment, notably among women. There is a link between this and the fact, already noted, that married women of almost all age groups increasingly come on to the labour market and do not leave it, while certain industries such as textiles, clothing and footwear which have traditionally employed large numbers of women have been particularly hit by the economic depression. Women's employment has certainly also been adversely affected by the equalisation of men's and women's wages. In certain fields, where women's organisations are weak for example, there are of course employers who prefer to dismiss women and hold on to their men if they have to reduce their labour force.

Unemployment among women has been growing steadily in recent years. In 1978 the rate was 10.7 % for men and 16.1 % for women, and in 1979 the disparity has widened further, so that in the autumn of 1979 the weekly figures show almost twice as many women unemployed as men despite the considerably larger male labour force. In terms of aggregate unemployment, however, figures have turned out to be considerably lower than in 1978. A number of measures taken by the government are largely responsible for this. For example in 1979 persons between ages 60 and 66 were given the option of early retirement at reduced salary, and far more of them have done so than were expected, especially men.

A number of job-creation measures have been instituted with government assistance, as well as education and production programmes, the creation of trainee and apprentice posts in public and private establishments, offers of jobs to the long-term unemployed, courses for the long-term unemployed including especially women, special courses for young people and so forth.

The Equal Status Council has asserted that too little is being done to provide employment for women and it alleges that women are not included in job-creation measures to the extent justified by their proportion of unemployment. Another demand made by the Council is that labour market boards and employment exchanges should abide by the Non-Discrimination Act and help to counteract traditional views of what is women's work and what is men's. It is further urged that women should be given jobs in new establishments set up in connection with energy-saving measures or the development of new energy sources.

All these issues, of course, are watched over with great interest by the women's organisations, which arrange conferences, meetings etc., and keep an eye on local developments.

Daily Benefit for the Unemployed

In order to be covered by unemployment insurance a person has to be a member of an unemployment benefit society, whose main rule for acceptance is that the applicant shall have been employed for at least 30 hours each week during the previous five weeks as a wage-earner in a trade or profession covered by the society. At least 15 hours are required for part-time insurance, and not all unemployment benefit societies accept part-time workers. The right to daily benefit is conditional upon a certain period of membership, which has now been fixed at six months for wage-earners, while in the two recently-established unemployment benefit societies for the self-employed it is twelve months. The claimant must seek work at the employment exchange and maintain contact for weekly check-stamping. Because of the high level of unemployment the attendance requirement has now generally been reduced to every fourteenth day. Failure to attend involves at worst a risk of being disqualified from receiving benefit if it can be construed as refusal of work, and if a claimant fails to appear on the appointed day then daily benefit is lost until he reports again. Furthermore, entitlement to daily benefit is conditional on the claimant's having worked full-time as generally understood in the trade for at least 26 weeks during the last four years (formerly three years). Daily benefit can thus be received for up to three and a half years of unbroken unemployment.

The amount of daily benefit is as a general rule 90 % of the claimant's average weekly earnings in the last five weeks before he became unemployed. As well as this limit there is a ceiling applicable to all claimants to the effect that daily benefit cannot exceed 90 % of the average weekly wages in trade and industry one year previously. In the first half of 1980 the ceiling was 1,566 *kroner* per week (261 *kroner* per day). Part-time insured persons, who are entitled to two thirds of this amount, may receive a maximum of 1,044 *kroner* per week.

The level of daily benefit has always figured prominently in public debate, and it has been claimed that many women only join the labour market so as to qualify for daily benefit. This notion can be rejected because women are also coming on to the labour market in increasing numbers even in a large number of other countries with lower rates and different rules regarding unemployment. What seems more likely is that a change of attitude has been taking place so that a growing number of women take it more or less for granted, just as do men, that they should be gainfully employed and economically independent.

Another problem that has attracted notice is the paradox that many prospective employers who are looking for labour cannot find it through the employment exchanges. But what is probably wrong here is that the procedures of the employment exchanges are not based on sufficiently modern methods – and they may be undermanned too.

Unemployed persons have to be available for work, and it is not enough for women (or men) to state that they have small children but no means of having them minded. In such cases they used to lose daily benefit for five weeks. This has now been changed so that a claimant who can prove within those five weeks that he or she has found means of having the children minded can be released from disqualification. A special "child care circular" has been published on the subject, and some pressure may be brought to bear on local authorities to make them fulfil their obligations with regard to childminding, especially since it is single mothers who are particularly affected by this rule.

Education and Equality

Harsh Reality

An official report entitled "Sex Roles and Education" (1978), from a committee under the Danish Ministry of Education begins with some remarks to the effect that the bodies comprising the highest decision-makers in society – government, Parliament, labour-market organisations, the civil service, the leaders of private business life and so forth – show unmistakable signs that an obvious qualification for appointment to an important position is to be born a member of the male sex. Only exceptionally do such decision-makers lack a high level of education, but even though boys and girls, men and women have had the same educational rights for several generations now, there are still almost no women in the circle of people with great influence over public life. Three women in Denmark are ministers; the first woman was appointed head of a civil service department in 1953, the second in 1979; two women have been judges of the supreme court (but now there are none); one governmental institution directly under a ministry is directed by a woman; two or three women assistant secretaries are to be found among the ministries; when we look at Danish primary schools (the 6–16 age group), where more than half the teachers are women, we find only 4 % of school principals of the female sex.

At the same time the harsh face of reality shows how women dominate those sectors of the labour market that are associated with low status and where wages are kept down. In terms of education 20 % of boys leave primary school without learning any trade later on, while the corresponding figure for girls is 40 %. However, these figures have been less glaring in the last few years, when an effort has been made to

255

conform to the requirement of educational policy that educational opportunities are to be equal for boys and girls, for men and women.

The report cites proofs that formal equality is not sufficient to create educational equality. The accepted sex roles are buttressed by the more or less conscious influence of parents, teachers and the mass media (including advertising), grandparents, friends etc., and all these factors play a vital part in shaping the attitudes of children and young people. The report cites a study of 38 schools in one particular county. In the eighth school year (the 14–15 age group), where a number of subjects are optional, the figures for 1976/77 show that 97 % of those taking needlework were girls, with 67 % in home economics, 65 % in art, 61 % in music, 65 % in typing, 56 % in biology, 58 % in drama, and in one particular place where it was possible to opt for training in child care all 17 girls took it and no boys. On the other hand, 12 % of those taking woodwork were girls, the figure for motor mechanics being 3 % and for electronics 1 %, while the sex-distribution was fairly even in history, geography and photography. One notable item among the figures is that 40 % of those taking vocational guidance were girls.

The duration of schooling also shows a sex-role pattern, boys having a greater propensity than girls to leave school in order to get a job and earn money – at the time of the study the situation on the labour market was not as difficult as in 1980. Although primary school pupils are supposed to receive education up to and including their ninth school year (i.e. to age 16), more than twice as many boys as girls dropped out of school during the eighth and ninth school years from 1975–76, and there were more girls than boys who left school with the school-leaving examination after the tenth year (76 % compared with 66 %). Parental influence and the desire to keep girls in a protected environment will have played a large part in getting girls to stay at school longer.

Students

Girls taking the university entrance examination constituted 42 % of the total in 1951, and this proportion had risen to 52 % by 1977. The number of girls is increasing gradually on both the mathematics and language arts sides. The number of the two sexes taking the language arts examination were about equal around 1940, but in 1977 girls formed more than 75 % of the year's entry of language arts students; for mathematics the corresponding figures were 24 % in 1941 and 33 % in 1977.

The special Higher Preparatory Examination (HF), one of whose functions is to act as an entrance qualification to teacher training colleges and which also offers a wide range of subject-options, was introduced in 1968. It has attracted large numbers of women ever since its inception, so that more women than men go in for it and there is some tendency for it to develop into a woman's educational line. It is based upon choice of subject and combination of subjects. The pupils opt for "special subjects" on which they wish to concentrate, and their selections reveal sex-differences corresponding broadly to those found in the upper secondary school, though less pronounced. Girls show great interest in languages combined with psychology, art, music and sport, or biology, psychology, music, art and sport. Boys show preference, for example, for English, mathematics and the social sciences, or for mathematics, physics and chemistry; mathematics, physics, music, art and sport are also popular.

It is possible to take the Higher Preparatory Examination in a single subject only, and an increasing number of young people opt to do so. A study made in 1976 shows that of the 5,250 who took the single-subject option, 3,249 were women. Only sport, physics, chemistry and computer science had more male than female pupils, girls being in the majority in all other subjects including mathematics and social science, which do not exercise a great attraction for girls in the upper secondary schools. These two subjects were in fact the most popular with both sexes.

Schoolteachers

While women are in the majority among primary school teachers (about 29,600 compared with about 23,600 men) in 1976–77, the teaching body in the upper secondary schools is quite differently composed, about 35 % being women. The only subjects with more female than male teachers were English and French, while social science, physics and chemistry had very few female teachers. It may be observed, however, that about 25 % of mathematics teachers were women.

Only a few women have posts of responsibility in upper secondary schools. In 1976–77 only six principals out of 127, and 27 senior tutors out of 305, were women. A senior tutor carries out various administrative duties in addition to his ordinary teaching. The teacher training colleges which train teachers for the primary schools show a similar picture. There were 29 teacher training colleges in 1977, all with male principals. Only six out of 115 senior tutors were women, and only 561, or barely 29 %, of a total of 1,956 were lecturers.

Training for Skilled Jobs and Social Service Work

Great changes have been taking place in the training field during recent years, especially in qualifying courses for skilled jobs. The traditional apprenticeship system is decaying rapidly and is being replaced by basic occupational training, which is given partly in technical schools and partly on the job. The figures for apprentices and basic-training students in seven main sectors show that women are in a majority in two, viz. the service trades (which include large numbers of hairdressers) and business and office work, but women figure in large numbers in the total picture. Thus there were altogether 52,000 men and about 17,000 women under training in the seven main sectors in 1976.

The figures for women under training are fairly high in the social welfare and public health fields, with about 13,000 women compared with about 1,600 men in 1976. A notable feature is represented by the male penetration of the traditional nursing occupations, where there were about 400 men under training as against 5,600 women, and the 500 or so men (compared with a little over 1,700 women) in the child welfare sector of education. Nevertheless it is clear that these forms of training are not all that attractive to young men. Some development is going on, as we have noted, and this applies also to the numbers of students in nursery school and youth centre teacher training colleges (mostly the latter), where just over 18 % were men in 1977: both these forms of training used to be mainly the preserve of women.

Higher Education

The flow of people into "higher education", as it is termed, has been studied for the period 1966–75 and some evening-out of the sex-determined pattern of preferences exercised by students for the various fields can be observed. Over the period as a whole women have been in the majority in the humanistic university faculties and in teacher training. Social science shows a rise from 25 % women in 1966 to 34 % in 1975 and medicine a rise from 29 % to 41 % over the same period. The modest proportion of women taking civil engineering has grown from 2.3 % to 6.4 %, while architecture has increased from 11 % to 27 %, and the proportion of women undertaking the various courses available at the Royal Veterinary and Agricultural College has enlarged from 10 % to 39 %, while office training at the commercial colleges, a field formerly monopolised by women, had 13 %

male students in 1975. The flow of men into librarianship increased during the period as well. Detailed examination of the figures reveals that in the production af graduates the dropout rate is higher among women than among men. It may be noted that the proportion of women graduates in theology in 1974/75 was 25 %, in medicine 28 %, in science 19 %, in civil engineering 6 %, in dentistry 50 %, in architecture 11 % and in librarianship 72 %. It is impossible to compare intake and dropout rates directly because the duration of courses varies – even individually.

Forward to Equality?

As the various figures show, many more women are now going on with their education, but at the same time they still lag behind perceptibly, and an educational pattern largely influenced by sex-roles still prevails among both men and women. How are we to advance further in the direction of real equality? Formal rights or sexually neutral laws are not enough. How could positive discrimination be applied to the education system? One might stipulate, for instance, that for a transitional period 50 % of places on courses with restricted access should be reserved for girls, or that employers in receipt of government grants for establishing apprenticeships must employ equal numbers of the two sexes. Both of these are examples of sex quota systems.

Those who have deliberated upon these issues include the Ministry of Education committee already mentioned and the Danish Women's Society. Both of these have declared it important that teachers responsible for the education of both children and adults should themselves be aware of the significance of sex roles in determining the unequal status of women and men in our society. This applies equally to educational and careers counsellors, which means in practice that girls can be influenced by active vocational counselling to choose non-traditional occupations – which is thus one form of positive discrimination. Another form functions by giving direct preference to the under-represented sex on training courses or in jobs. It is obviously necessary in such cases that the individual concerned should have the qualifications otherwise required for the course or post in question.

It is probably lack of qualifications that is responsible for the fact that only 4 % of university professors in Denmark are women. The demand for sex-quotas in the filling of appointments at such levels has still not been voiced, and there would certainly be some headshaking and jeering, for example, if the Equal Status Council called for a ban on the appointment of men in certain posts until 50 % of them were filled by women. Yet one may well beg leave to doubt whether it can be true that so few women are capable of becoming professors. Some exciting light could certainly be thrown on these matters by a comparative study of the time spent by male and female university lecturers upon domestic chores and children and upon academic work respectively.

The Ministry of Education committee is palpably influenced by the fact that by approaching such problems as sex roles and equal rights it is dealing with sensitive subjects. It cites a statement by the Nordic Council of Ministers in 1974: "The general objectives of all educational policies ought to reflect some effort to achieve equality of rights and status. This means equal rights and duties and equal opportunities of contributing to the world of work, to the family and to society at large."

The committee continues by proposing that equal rights objectives should be clearly formulated in statutes and government regulations etc., while equal rights and sex-role questions are introduced as an independent theme in education and training. It goes on to remark that this will give teachers something to go on while also lending guidance to schools and school authorities in planning and adapting

261

courses of education. It must then be a matter firstly of getting the new independent theme introduced into education and training courses and secondly of getting Parliament to formulate clearly the aim of equal rights and embodying it in the law. So far there has been no sign of this happening.

The full report on "Sex Roles and Education" has been widely distributed throughout the entire education and training system, and the committee is proposing further studies. In addition, a number of working parties have already been set up, including one to deal with the group left over, i. e. young people who after having left the school system do not subsequently receive any form of systematic training, and another to deal with the instruction of parents.

The point hardly needs arguing that schools and education are of enormous importance to the further development of social equality for women. But regrettably it must likewise be recognised that economic crisis and general uncertainty about the future can stultify the initiatives already taken in this field.

Special Laws for Women and Children

The Unmarried Mother

As early as 1888 a law was enacted in Denmark providing
that a father's minimum contribution in respect of a child
born out of wedlock could be advanced from public funds
(i. e. by the local authority) and then collected from him. The
latter was not always easy, and fathers sometimes managed
to "sit it out". The rate of contribution was determined by the
national cost of placing a child in a good orphanage in the
locality in question, and this was called the "standard maintenance allowance". Since women's wages and employment
opportunities were much smaller than those of men, their
proportion of the standard maintenance allowance was set at
two fifths while the father had to pay three fifths.

The Danish Women's Society was deeply concerned during
the early years of the present century about the situation of
the unmarried mother, and one of the principles it sought to
establish was that mothers' maintenance allowances should
be determined by reference to the father's as well as the
mother's economic circumstances. The Society further proposed that the father should pay a share of the costs of confinement and of the mother's maintenance for one month before and two months after the birth, and that these sums likewise should be advanced from public funds if necessary. The
Society also wanted both the mother's and the father's name
to be declared at registration of the birth.

The Minister of Justice was deliberating upon these very
questions at the time, and the Society's proposals, except for
declaration of the father's name and the taking into account
of his economic circumstances in setting the amount of

maintenance allowance, were embodied in legislation. This was in 1908.

A new statute dealing with children born out of wedlock came into effect in 1938, and with certain exceptions it places upon the mother the duty of disclosing the father's name. If paternity is admitted or established, the child is entitled to bear the father's name and to inherit from him. At the same time, the father's financial obligations towards the child were increased, and both parents were made responsible for maintaining the child until its 18th birthday, bringing it up and educating it in a manner appropriate to its parents' station in life. The expenses involved in this are shared between the parents according to their economic circumstances, and in cases where both are without means the maintenance obligation is established at the level of the standard allowance. The latter amounted in 1980 to about 5,000 *kroner* a year for a father and about 3,300 *kroner* for a mother. The amount is price-indexed every half-year. Since it is usually the mother who has the child living with her, the father generally discharges his responsibilities by paying the allowance in cash, and he can in fact have his responsibilities widened to include school education and vocational training after the child's 18th year if it is regarded as reasonable considering his economic circumstances.

An unmarried pregnant woman can still claim for the father to be ordered to contribute to her maintenance for two months before and one month after the confinement and to expenses connected with the confinement. She herself has to state the amounts claimed, possibly claiming maintenance for the child at the same time. She can get help from the social welfare authorities in formulating her claims. In 1979 the standard maintenance contribution amounted to 445 *kroner* per month while confinement expenses were 255 *kroner* once and for all. If the father does not pay the various contributions, they can be advanced to the mother by the local health and social welfare authorities, and the local authority then takes over the claim against the father.

The Family Allowance System

When taxation at source was adopted in 1970, cash payments of tax-free family allowance were introduced at the same time: the allowance had formerly been chargeable to tax, so that one result of the charge was a reduction of tax arrears. The system is somewhat complex and there are four different kinds of allowance: (1) general family allowance, (2) augmented family allowance, (3) extra and (4) special. *General* family allowance is now paid in respect of all children under 16 years of age unless they are entitled to *augmented* allowance, which is given in respect of the children of single breadwinners. *Extra* allowance is paid as one allowance per household to single breadwinners, and like augmented allowance it has to be applied for when first granted. Lastly there is the *special* family allowance, which is given in respect of children of widows and widowers or of invalidity or old-age pensioners. When this was introduced the former "widoved family allowance" and the child supplement to social welfare pensions were withdrawn. Children for whom some contribution to maintenance (e. g. "standard maintenance allowance") is being made cannot receive augmented family allowance, which is reserved for cases where, for example, a child is born out of wedlock and its paternity has not been established.

Family allowances are normally paid to the mother and when they were introduced they were granted without reference to the breadwinner's income, but in 1977 a change was made so that except for the special allowance they are regulated according to the income of the household and are reduced when the income exceeds a certain amount. The actual amounts for the April quarter of 1980 were as follows:

General	....	495	*kroner*
Augmented	....	745	–
Extra	....	568	–
Special	....	1245	–

It is the taxable income for 1978 which determines whether the three first-mentioned are to be reduced, the limit for this being 144,000 *kroner*.

In the first few years after 1970 all children under 18 years of age were entitled to family allowance, but in 1975 the age-limit for general and augmented family allowance was reduced to 16 years. At the same time a *youth grant* was introduced for 16 and 17 year-olds undergoing courses of education. This is payable on application and its amount is determined according to need by reference to the local authority's assessment of the family's economic circumstances.

Rights of Pregnant Women

A pregnant woman is entitled to five free examinations by her usual doctor as well as a number of midwife examinations, also free. It is advisable in the interests of both woman and child to report to the doctor or the midwife as soon as pregnancy is confirmed. In most parts of Denmark it is possible also to take part in special courses of preparation for childbirth, in which guidance is given on the normal process of pregnancy and birth and instruction in relaxation exercises is provided.

If the woman concerned is a wage-earner entitled to daily benefit in periods of sickness or unemployment then she is likewise entitled to daily benefit during absence occasioned by pregnancy and confinement. Daily benefit can normally be granted for 14 weeks from a point estimated to be 8 weeks prior to confinement. It is paid by the local social welfare and health authorities.

A female salaried employee, in business or office work for example, is entitled to maternity leave on half-pay for up to five months commencing not more than three months prior to the expected date of confinement and ending not more than three months after it. The issue of employer's obligation to pay employees half-salary must be viewed in the context of the law relating to daily sickness benefit, under which a pregnant employee, like other wage-earners, is entitled to daily benefit, in this case supplementary daily benefit, for a maximum of 14 weeks. Benefit may not exceed 90 % of salary prior to pregnancy or the current maximum rate of daily sickness benefit, whichever is the lower.

The rule for civil servants, teachers in primary schools and so forth is that absence from work because of pregnancy or confinement qualifies for normal salary from eight weeks prior to confinement up to a total of 14 weeks in all.

Women with earned income other than wages, such as those with their own businesses, have a general entitlement to daily benefit for four weeks after confinement. This applies regardless of whether they have taken out any special insurance, whereas housewives are entitled to daily benefit only if they have arranged voluntary insurance themselves. Housewives in the legal sense are "persons who perform domestic work in their own homes for at least one person apart from themselves". The daily benefit which a housewife can receive amounts to one fourth or at most one half of the general maximum for daily benefit. The contribution required in the first half of 1980 to secure one fourth (391 *kroner* per week) amounted to about 130 *kroner* per quarter and twice that sum to secure a half. In adoption cases daily benefit can be paid for six weeks after acceptance of the child.

This account of the financial and other provisions relating to pregnancy and confinement gives the principal rules only, and there are numerous special regulations bearing for example upon complications and illnesses during pregnancy.

As regards the actual confinement, this is free if it takes place in hospital or in a maternity clinic affiliated to the county authority system. Doctors' and midwives' attendance is free, as are hospital board and lodging and transport by ambulance if that is necessary.

Future Reforms?

While Denmark early on was a pioneering country as far as unmarried mothers were concerned, there is less to commend in the sphere of family policy to which we now turn, and the situation of children in our industrialised society with its many working mothers has aroused unease. Although the normal working week is 40 hours, when transport is included many parents are away from home for nine or ten hours on five days of the week, and children big and small spend many hours in a separate children's world of schools, day-nurseries and so on. Interaction between parents and children can be rather a rushed affair on weekdays, while weekends are often taken up by the many jobs left undone during the week. Of course there are those who believe that women ought to give up working, but it does not seem as though very many women themselves are willing to forgo their right to earn money themselves and so lose their economic independence. Marriage in our day is not a stable foundation on which to build one's life. Moreover the family finances very often rest upon more than one income, and the cost of housing is particularly burdensome for many, whether living in modern apartments or in houses of their own. Likewise it is commonly a feature of the family finances that the distance between home and workplace makes a car a necessity, especially if children have to be dropped off at the day-nursery. In any assessment of the situation of children a question-mark must also be raised over the lack of scope for self-development of the somewhat older child. Even when playgrounds are built in conjunction with high-rise apartment blocks they are often quite sterile and in-

268

adequate. Moreover children often have to traverse streets and roads made dangerous by traffic, perhaps merely in order to reach some place where they can play, and a regrettably large number of accidents happen. Many children lose their lives in traffic accidents in Denmark.

It was questions like these that caused the government in 1975 to establish the *Commission on Children* which so far has issued one report dealing with maternity leave. This is the outcome of joint deliberations between the Commission and the Equal Status Council, whose interesting feature is not so much the extension proposed in the actual period of leave for mothers – vitally important though that may be – but the inclusion of fathers in the leave recommendations with a view to affording them the opportunity of developing close contact with their children at an early stage of their lives. This is tantamount to an effort to assist in breaking the traditional sex-role pattern.

Like so many other innovations in the field of family policy, this idea originates from Sweden, where it was enacted in 1974 that parents themselves could decide how the maternity leave entitlement (then amounting to six months) should be divided. It must be admitted that fathers have not shown any very intense interest in availing themselves of equal rights in this field, and the latest information indicates that about 12 % of them use part of the family leave entitlement – with daily benefit. University graduates form a high proportion of these.

The proposals of the Commission on Children centre broadly around the principle that a pregnant woman ought to be able to cease working eight weeks before the expected date of confinement. After this a convalescence of 13 weeks is recommended, followed by an early care-period of 13 weeks for mothers and a similar period for fathers. The two periods should not be transferable between the parents. In addition, a late care-period of eight weeks is recommended, divisible between the parents and to be used up to the age of nine years on occasions when the child is exposed to particularly difficult situations such as moves between institutions (e. g. from one day-nursery to another or from play-group to nursery school). It is further suggested that it should be possible for one of the parents to be at home with a sick child under nine years of age for up to ten working days a year and that if there are two or more children this should be increased to 15 days.

In the case of adoptive parents it is recommended that between the time of the child's acceptance until it reaches nine years of age they should be allowed periods of leave corresponding to the early and late care-periods, viz. $13 + 13 + 8$ weeks. Furthermore they should be able to look after the child in the event of illness in the same way as other parents.

The financial implications of the Commission's proposals are considerable and would cost five or six times as much as the 500 million *kroner* a year involved in the present arrangements. But they would also bring some savings, such as fewer and shorter stays in hospital for sick children. However, the employers' representative on the Commission dissociated himself from the recommendations at once, and when the Minister for Social Affairs was charged with the task of drafting a Parliamentary Bill it was very much scaled down on the ground that the economy of the nation could not bear such expenditures, at least not in the present situation. The Ministry for Social Affairs presented a Bill for pre- and post-confinement leave periods of eight and 14 weeks respectively. Fathers were also to have the opportunity of taking leave when the newly-born child came home and would be entitled to daily benefit for one week. The Bill also gave adoptive parents the right to daily benefit for 14 weeks. The bill has now been passed with the following modifications: the pre-confinement leave period is to be 4 weeks; fathers are not to be incorporated in the maternity leave scheme.

The New Feminist Movement

Commotion on the Left Wing

The new feminist movement first attracted the attention of the public in the spring of 1970 when a group of women, following American examples, publicly removed their brassières and suspender-belts, discarded false eyelashes, wigs and so on and flung them all together into a large rubbish bag. Beauty contests and the commercial exploitation of women's efforts to live up to the currently-advertised female ideal were the first bastion against which the new assault was launched. Other actions, imaginative or more traditional, soon followed and made it clear that the Danish feminist movement had taken on a new aspect. The mass media were deeply interested and soon found easy victims.

In principle the *Rødstrømper* (Redstockings), as they call themselves in Denmark, are not essentially different from similar movements in other western countries such as the United States, where the new feminist movement first manifested itself, the Dolle Mina movement in Holland or Women's Lib in Britain. They all have roots in the leftist movements that emerged in the late 1960s among the hippies, student rioters, anti-nuclear campaigners and the anti-Vietnam War movements. In all of them there were active girls who little by little began to rebel against merely being on hand to serve their male comrades, to hand out leaflets, duplicate documents, type out speeches for the men, but never themselves to mount the rostrum. These girls were not content simply to make tea and biscuits for the revolution.

The Redstocking movement soon spread all over Denmark and, as in Copenhagen, groups of five or ten were formed for mutual discussion of every kind of issue affecting women, in-

271

cluding such highly personal matters as their sex lives. The first objective of the movement, as in the American model, is to "raise the consciousness of its supporters", and this is best done in small groups where the participants trust one another and no men are present. Very great importance is attached to these basic discussion-groups. Through them there is created a feminist comradeship or "sisterly solidarity" to buttress the self-confidence of the individual and foster at the same time a sense of fellowship with other women. The relating of personal experiences in the groups reveals how women are oppressed both in private life and at work, and those present join together to devise means of standing firm against oppression and lend each other strength and courage to do it.

This is a movement in fact, not a society with chairmen, secretaries and treasurers. In the basic groups the various functions are shifted around, and no one is given the opportunity of sitting passively on the sidelines. Yet despite such anarchistic features, which are a source both of weakness and of strength, the groups have managed to work together and their cooperation has recently become more formalised. For example the Redstockings have united in disrupting beauty contests all over Denmark so that these are now rare sights; they have taken the initiative in establishing consumer protection groups, arranged women's camps, notably on the island of Femø where every year now women work, take holidays and hold discussions, with or without children, but always without men. They have inspired courses on feminist subjects in folk high schools, aided the establishment of a special women's folk high school, and one "Mothers' Day" they built a ramp at an underground station to make it possible to to go in and out with perambulators, and so on.

The outward-directed activities of the Redstockings were characterised by three issues in the early years: the equal pay agitation (see page 245), the campaign against Denmark's affiliation to the EEC, and the fight for free abortion on demand (see pp. 183ff.). The form of action for equal pay that attracted particular attention was occupying a bus and refusing to pay more than 80 % of the ticket price – which corresponded more or less to the proportion of female wages to male. Twenty-nine Redstockings were ejected from the bus by the police, and as the mass media had been warned of what was afoot the word went all round Denmark at once. In the debate on the EEC, the Redstockings worked in concert with the Popular Movement against Denmark's affiliation under their motto of "Women say No to the EEC".

A short time after the first actions by the Redstockings they occupied three old empty properties in Copenhagen and turned them into premises for meetings, a public house for women, a café, office for their joint activities, etc. They have had to move twice since then, and in the present building there are numerous other activities besides those already mentioned. Social counselling is available, the Joan Sisterhood gives help to battered wives and to women who have been raped, instruction in preparation for confinement is arranged for pregnant women, study circles are held, and so on.

Feminist Struggle and Class Struggle

The slogan of the Redstockings has been "No feminist struggle without class struggle: no class struggle without feminist struggle", and this fits in with their original socialist background. But it is not easy to rally the ranks of the faithful with such mottos, which try to monopolise the feminist struggle or the feminist movement for particular political ideologies and would exclude adherents of the Radical Liberals, for example. The current president of the Danish Women's Society is a young Conservative member of Parliament, who battles courageously both inside and outside her party. She advocates sex quotas, even in politics, and she and her organisation have been deeply involved in various actions and have

273

even conceived the idea of introducing a women's centre in a former almshouse. Here battered wives would be able to find shelter and help: these plans now seem certain to come to fruition. Is this woman not worthy of being called a fighter of the feminist battle? Is not the feminist struggle more than a class struggle?

The Redstocking theorists explain that the feminist struggle-class-struggle slogan signifies rejection of the concept of the feminist struggle as an isolated phenomenon unconnected with social conditions and exclusively directed against men. They further declare that their feminist struggle as an element of the class struggle shall not be waged merely on ground selected by men, and therefore that women must have their own organisation, functioning from the standpoint of women and making practical demands of current concern to women, but that a true solution of women's problems cannot be achieved within the framework of a capitalist society.

The Redstockings are attacked from the extreme leftwing of the feminist front, which accuses them of being bourgeois man-haters, but of course there is nothing new about internal conflicts or battles between new converts to a faith.

The disagreements came to public notice in connection with the International Women's Day of Struggle on 8 March 1980. Preparatory meetings with a view to assembling the various women's groups in a great joint demonstration in Copenhagen began the previous November, and about 80 groups, organisations, trade unions and so forth were invited. But it proved impossible to reach agreement on either a single slogan or several joint ones, or even on freedom of slogans. Not even freedom of slogans, based on a set of agreed minimum demands, and signs identifying the respective demonstrating groups, could gain acceptance. The result was that three events were held. Redstockings, Women over 40, the Women's Folk High School, the Women's Group for International Cooperation, the Lesbian Movement, the Anarchists and others worked in concert; the women's section of the left-wing political parties, various women trade unionists and student organisations were responsible for a second demonstration; the Women's Front arranged the third.

On the other hand, the organisation of the Festival of Women, which had been held in a large park on the outskirts of Copenhagen every August since 1974, seems to have been characterised by much greater unity. Here each of the many women's organisations has had at its disposal a territory with stalls and tents, exhibitions, slogans, books, journals and posters, as well as speechmaking and singing. In addition to this, large-scale joint events have been organised with music by women's orchestras, speeches, performances by artists, singing and so on. In the last few years attendances on the two weekend days have been as high as 40,000–50,000 women, men and children, and the general atmosphere has been one of both seriousness and festiveness. Some of the male guests have made a fuss on finding that there were some tents that would not allow them in. Similar festivals have been held in Århus in recent years with great success.

Who and How Many Became Redstockings

As in other countries, most of those who joined the new women's movement in Denmark were young women, especially university graduates, students, teachers, nursery school teachers, social workers and others of middle-class education. Only a few working-class women have been attracted to the new movement, although in certain specific situations there has been cooperation and although Redstockings have been very anxious to bring working-class women into the movement, as has been shown, for instance, by the efforts of Redstockings to help women workers by making collections during strikes, by distributing leaflets publicising sundry actions, and by taking part in demonstrations.

It is exceedingly difficult to estimate how many Redstockings there really are. One of the young graduates who herself is a member and has written about the movement estimated in 1975 that a couple of thousand had been active in the first five years. But she also writes that the feminist struggle has ramified in all directions, leading for example to the formation of new groups and activities in schools, institutions of learning, organisations and political parties, and that women are becoming increasingly active in trade unions. On the other hand, there are leading trade union women, such as the president of the General Union of Women Workers with its 90,000 or so members, who directly dissociate themselves from the Redstockings. This woman, in fact, is also chairman of the Equal Rights Committee of the Danish Federation of Trade Unions.

The Redstockings publish the journal *Kvinder* (Women), which comes out six times a year in editions of 9,500. It prints at intervals a list of the various feminist groups, about fifty in number, all over Denmark.

There is no doubt that the new feminist movement has been of much greater importance than would be suggested by the modest number of women who can be described as Redstockings. The latter have acted as a leaven or catalyst. Women in the most diverse quarters have formed small groups and large, or organisations which have taken local action when needed: in general they have worked together in ways never seen before. No one has kept watch over the scope of the manifold activities going on. There is the question of the employment of women by Danish Radio, where the entire hierarchy at head of department level and above consists of men. Studies have been published in the Danish Radio staff magazine, for example, showing how many women work in television and radio and in that way are instrumental in stabilising the current sex-role pattern. A little has been achieved: for instance news broadcasts on radio and television may now be presented by women. Exhibitions have been held at the universities on commemorative occasions such as the 50th anniversary of the foundation of Århus University. The special problems of girl students have been pinpointed. Innumerable articles and features have been written about women's revolt and women's liberation, and these frequently evoke lively exchanges of view in which men take no part at all. Films have been made such as *"Tag det som en mand, frue"* ("Wife, take it like a man!"), in which sex roles are reversed; a vast stream af books has been published both fictional and non-fictional presenting examples of women's attitudes towards their situation or giving straightforward information, e. g. about the physiological characteristics of women. At the universities, other institutions of learning and elsewhere women are being inspired to enquire into questions such as the history of women, the law relating to women, the Church's view of women, the literature of women, women's organisations in the political parties, and so forth. Bearing in mind the view that most existing scholarship has been dominated by men, efforts have been made to create a new research cross-specialisation on the topic of women. The name "feminology" has been given to it, and lecture-series have been arranged on the subject, e. g. by the University Extra-Mural Department.

In brief, the feminist question in its widest sense has involved larger and broader circles of women than ever before, and both women and men have felt themselves compelled to try to define their own position. Some men have perceived themselves as being persecuted while others have tried to live up to new roles – and a special men's movement, not directed against women, has even come into existence.

The new feminist movement in all its diversity has nurtured the self-confidence and independence of many women, and these qualities have manifested themselves in a number of unexpected ways. The high rate of divorce (see page 237) has to be viewed in the context of the fact that it is women who now increasingly want divorce. In former days countless women have put up with dictatorial husbands and perhaps even beatings, not daring to break away for fear of the financial insecurity and the harshness of existence both for themselves and for their children. Now most married women have or have had jobs, and they have gained pride. They know how matters stand, and they know also that unemployment among women is high. But with husband, children, job and home they can find themselves in a situation where it is the husband who is responsible for so much strain that it is he whom they decide to be quit of. A contributory reason for this may be the exceedingly scanty interest shown by most men in sharing the day-to-day responsibilities of house and children. This lack of solidarity can also lead women simply not to want children. Some women have turned their backs on men entirely and live in women's collectives with or without children.

The Old Women's Rights Movement and the New

Naturally the tremendous activity on the feminist front was bound to affect the Danish Women's Society, now 100 years old. In former days the Society always used to try to obtain influence when new organisations or movements emerged in its sphere of interest. In the 1940s, for example, the Society managed to place some reliable members in Bodil Koch's People's Action (see page 195) and so established useful collaboration. The same thing happened when the Danish Women's National Council was thinking of establishing local councils in provincial towns along the same lines as those of its Norwegian counterpart. This threat of competition with the local Danish Women's Society's circles was nipped in the bud. But what was going on now presented really novel and unexpected aspects. There was not even anybody to negotiate with in the early years and a certain amount of confusion prevailed among the more tradition-bound ladies.

278

Some of the very first Redstockings actually had their roots in the Danish Women's Society and came from the *Individ og Samfund* (Individual and Society organisation), an offshoot of the youth section that was formed in 1964 but cut itself off from the Danish Women's Society afterwards (see page 183). Shortly after the Redstockings appeared on the scene the group known as *Thildes børn* (Thilde's Children) was formed within the Danish Women's Society. These became known later on simply as "Thildes", being named after Mathilde Fibiger. This was a group of younger members working outwardly along the same lines as the Redstockings. The actions carried out by the Thildes attracted a high degree of public interest. Moreover, the atmosphere among some of the older Danish Women's Society members was favourable to the development of less traditional forms of activity within the organisation rather than being content with putting in appearances and submitting routine representations to the government, Parliament and other public bodies through the medium of very factual and detailed analyses of important questions concerning women. These older Society members along with some journalists formed a "basement group" with a view to modernising and rejuvenating the Society, but the group rapidly lost vigour, for the contradictions within it were too great and the loyalty of some members of the 100 year-old Society was such that when it came to the pinch they backed it up anyway.

At that time the membership of the Danish Women's Society was dwindling. It had been about 12,000 in the 1950s and fell to fewer than 10,000 in the 1960s. The organisation developed a new programme based on complete equality of the sexes. The former somewhat complicated structure of the Society was changed. The journal "Woman and Society" became full of vigorous discussion and the leadership toiled away on countless fronts. Yet, membership fell steadily.

During the Danish Women's Society's 100th anniversary

year a prize was instituted called a "Mathilde", to be awarded to women, men, organisations and so on who or which had made some significant contribution to the cause of full legal and practical equality between the sexes. The award is a jaunty little china figure with gold ringlets and a blue inscription on its tummy: naturally it was designed by a woman ceramic artist. The purpose of it is not merely to honour someone who has deserved it but also, of course, to create interest in the work of the Danish Women's Society. This venture was followed up by the Thildes who produced an anti-Mathilde – a card to be sent to persons or institutions guilty of discrimination against women or otherwise displaying lack of comprehension of the position of women. Conferment of either award is assured of good coverage in the mass media.

The first action by the Thildes took place in a Copenhagen suburb early one morning when a group of young mothers, under the slogan "Children Better than Cars", barricaded a parking place with prams and children. The mothers distributed fruit juice and biscuits to the motorists and talked to them about the shortage of nursery schools and the priority given to parking places. Various other actions followed, but the most successful and commented-on was staged in Parliament in concert with Redstockings and working women. In December 1970 a woman Member of Parliament was presenting a Private Member's Bill on equal pay, and as soon as the proposer had spoken a chanting commenced from the public gallery: "Equal pay, equal pay, we demand, we do not pray!" Banners with the slogan "Equal Pay" were unfurled from the public gallery and a rain of "equal pay cakes" – cakes with 20 % slices snipped out of them – showered down on the Members' heads. Panic ensued, and attempts were made to eject the demonstrators, but in the confusion they managed to present the proposer of the Bill with a Mathilde. An action of this kind required inventiveness and

280

considerable preparation, for among other things the banners had to be smuggled into the Parliament building hidden in the arms of cardigans and jackets, since neither bags nor outdoor coats may be taken into the public gallery.

Among the other highly successful Thilde demonstrations was the establishment of an emergency travel bureau, "*Splejs Rejs*" ("Travel-Splicers") in the main railway station. The Danish State Railways had introduced a rebate scheme whereby a traveller with an ordinary ticket could be accompanied by a partner at an additional charge of ten *kroner*. The function of *Splejs Rejs* was to "splice" travellers with partners. The scheme was a resounding success, and travellers enjoyed themselves, realising that fun was being poked at the current sex-role pattern.

The Thildes retired from the Danish Women's Society organisationally in 1978, but they still collaborate with the Society in certain fields.

Although the membership of the Danish Women's Society continued to decline, so that by the end of the 1970s it numbered about 2,000–3,000, the organisation is still vigorous and active. It keeps an eye on legislation and offers criticisms and suggestions; it does solid work on behalf of Greenland women; and it has made a considerable contribution in lending assistance and taking initiatives of its own for the benefit of women of the developing countries. Seminars for women from these lands have been held in Denmark on repeated occasions, and in general the Society has succeeded in establishing contacts with ordinary women of the developing countries.

The Future

Social conditions in the broadest sense have a crucial influence, of course, on the status of women. The old-style women's movement was a consequence of or reaction to the taking-over by industry of the tasks that formerly had fallen to women in the home. They became partially unemployed, and the unmarried daughters or sisters who previously had found enough to keep them busy in middle-class families with looking after the house and children now became a burden. It was these women most particularly who raised the demand for education and access to jobs – and who later on claimed political rights. Thus, feminism as represented by the Danish Women's Society was, appropriately enough, a middle-class movement in the same way as was the new feminist movement that emerged from the educational explosion of the 1960s and the youth revolt that followed. The changes in the conditions of production that have become known as "the second industrial revolution" demanded a vast number of people with education or training of immensely diverse kinds and at all levels. Women were needed too, and they responded in large numbers both to the educational opportunities and to the need for unskilled labour generally.

Denmark is now experiencing a time of economic crisis and of unemployment, especially among women. As in the 1930s voices can be heard demanding that women should return to the home – both married women and young girls, who could then become household helps. In this way male unemployment would be reduced. Such cries have evoked little response so far, and indeed have not really been taken seriously. Neither has the old idea, now revived, of a wage for housewives. But what do have to be treated seriously are the by no means rare instances of young girls who wager their future existence on catching a man to look after them in the old-fashioned style: one hears of 16 year-old girls becoming formally "engaged". Such tendencies are frightening and are to be regarded as the unfortunate results of large-scale unemployment among young people, caused partly by the fact that girls encounter particular difficulty in obtaining jobs as apprentices or trainees. Eighty per cent of the job opportun-

282

ities offered to long-term unemployed youth are taken up by boys, and many of these offers are in what are traditionally regarded as male occupations. They do not attract girls: so it seems that the new feminist movement and all that has been brought in its wake has not been enough to reach down to very young people. Is everything that has been gained to be lost again in the course of a few years?

Greenland

Some Figures and a Little History

Greenland and its neighbouring islands have a surface area of 2,175,600 sq.km., the vast bulk of which comprises the biggest island in the world, covered almost entirely by inland ice. Greenland's ice-free area of 341,700 sq.km. is approximately equivalent in size to East and West Germany combined, which have altogether 80 million inhabitants compared with the mere 50,000 of Greenland (1976).

The first settlements in Greenland of people from the Nordic region took place immediately prior to the year 1000, and these probably retained their links with Denmark-Norway until the beginning of the 15th century. What happened after that was that the Greenland population in the small hamlets on the west coast had contacts with European whalers and expeditions, and some attempt was also made by the Danish-Norwegian government to establish connections with these habitations because of the whaling and minor trade exchanges with Greenland, but nothing very solid or regular came out of this.

Stories of the old Norsemen's settlements lived on in the Nordic lands right through to the 18th century. *Hans Egede* (1686–1758), a Norwegian priest, was deeply interested in them and made plans to travel to Greenland in order to find the descendants of the Norsemen and convert them to Christianity. After years of toil and difficulty he succeeded in getting an expedition together, and in 1721 he and his family landed on an island off the west coast of Greenland, near the site of the present capital, Godthåb. But those few and widely-dispersed inhabitants whom Egede encountered living under conditions of exceeding grimness and severity appeared very alien to him and were certainly no descendents of the Norsemen, who had died out long ago. Despite his disappointment at not meeting any of these, however, Egede set about the work he had come to do, and supported by his sturdy wife and helpmeet Gertrud Rask, he did his best to lend what assistance he could to the native population. So began the colonisation of Greenland, which went on in the face of immense difficulties such as lack of understanding and support from the Danish side, clashes between mission and trade, and devastating epidemics caused by infection brought by the colonists. Gertrud Rask herself fell victim to smallpox and died in 1735. Although Egede battled against the Greenland exorcists – even physically – he won the trust of the people. One reason for this was that he rapidly learned to speak and understand the Eskimo tongue.

Egede's period in Greenland marked the beginning of change in the Greenland community, and firm links were now established with the kingdom of Denmark-Norway (Denmark alone after Norway attained independence in 1814). As occurs everywhere in the world where widely disparate cultures meet, many errors and injustices were committed during the colonising era and subsequently. In principle Greenland ceased to be a colony under the constitution of 1953, when it became a part of Denmark with county status. Greenland is still plagued by problems today and could not exist without a large and continuous flow of capital from Denmark. Economic opportunities are limited and quite insufficient, for the moment at least, to meet the needs of the population.

Women, Education and Employment

In Greenland of old women were not equal, and it was the menfolk who made all the important decisions. On the other hand, women were not oppressed either, and in a hunting

and food-gathering economy their contribution to the subsistence of the family was as important as that of the menfolk.
They flensed seals, processed pelts, sewed leather goods and
kamikker (sealskin top boots), and understood the art of preserving food, which included for example the collecting and
use of certain berries as preservatives. In addition, there was
the getting of water and fuel, and in some districts it was
woman's work to build the family dwelling of stone and turf.
Families generally consisted of three generations, and there
were many children. Neither boys nor girls had any possibility of receiving education apart from what was available
within the family. The first opportunity of training to become open to Greenland women was in the art of midwifery,
and in the smaller habitations where other medical personnel
were non-existent even the midwife's limited knowledge of
hygiene and health matters was often of great importance, so
that there was plenty to keep her busy. As time went by a
trickle of young women came to Denmark to obtain midwifery training and on their return occupied a particularly
important position as interpreters for doctors visiting trading
stations.

Young girls also had some opportunity of being employed
as household helps, particularly by expatriate Danes such as
managers of trading stations, and they frequently established
very close ties with these families, learned Danish and became
well-trained in domestic duties if the lady of the house was
proficient.

By degrees, as the sealing community with its subsistence
economy became modified in the direction of a fishing and
wage-earning society, new opportunities for women were
generated. They could get unskilled work in the colonies,
though it was often hard labour such as unloading ships.
When the cod fishery began to develop and fish exporting
started up it became customary for washing, salting and
packing of the cod to be done by women. The fishing industry

developed further after the last war, and many women got jobs in the fish-factories peeling shrimps and filletting fish. It now became normal for married women to have jobs outside the home.

Compulsory schooling is first mentioned in an Act of 1925, but children had attended school even before that time and Greenlanders could read and write long before 1900. It now became compulsory for children to attend school between the ages of seven and 14 years, and improvements were made in the teaching. A few years later some girls were accepted into continuation schools, which had previously been open only to boys, and in 1933 a two-year continuation school was established specifically for girls. By receiving this education girls were able to obtain apprentice situations in offices and shops or the opportunity of training as elementary schoolteachers. The school reforms of the 1950s brought the introduction of secondary schools, first in Godthåb and subsequently in some of the other towns. In the primary schools an increasing proportion of children seem to stay at school beyond the 8th, 9th, and 10th school years. Boys and girls were given equality of access to the secondary schools, in contrast to the situation prevailing in the days of the continuation schools: by the mid-1970s the school-leaving examination was being taken by 150–170 children each year, and the number is rising. After the examination there are opportunities of going on to the teacher training college in Godthåb or to teacher training colleges or upper secondary schools in Denmark. The first female student from Greenland graduated from one of the latter schools in 1959. More and more girls take the university entrance examination, and a few girls have since then completed a university education. An increasing number of the students become secondary school teachers, and several have been trained as social workers.

Opportunities of vocational training are available in the towns, where about three quarters of the population of

Greenland were living by 1976, so that young people tend to head for the urban communities, especially the larger ones, so as to avoid being faced with unemployment immediately on leaving school. About 1,100–1,200 young people were undergoing some form of long-term training by the mid-1970s, about 70 % of them in Greenland and the remainder in Denmark. About 40 % of applicants for training were women.

Women constitute just over one third of persons gainfully employed in Greenland, 60 % of these being in unskilled, often seasonal jobs, e. g. in the fish industry. Independent fields of employment for women (about half of it unskilled) are offered by schools and the health services as well as other public-sector establishments such as the Greenland Trade Department, which provides unskilled factory jobs. Only a few women hold responsible positions, which makes the picture not very different from that encountered in the rest of Denmark. The principle of equal pay for equal work is now in force, but since it is rare for men and women to have identical jobs, women generally earn less than men, just as they do elsewhere. There is a certain amount of unemployment in Greenland, and women do suffer from it even though the figures show their scope for employment to be widening.

Women in the Life of the Community

In 1862 Greenlanders were granted an exceedingly modest measure of influence over local conditions when so-called "superintendencies" (forstanderskaber) were established. A series of Acts passed during the present century has given Greenlanders more and more influence, and 1979 saw the introduction of home rule for Greenland as a result of a referendum. Until 1948 only men had the vote and were eligible for the local councils and the two provincial councils then in existence. But at a joint meeting of the provincial councils after the war one of the Greenland leaders proposed full political rights for women. The councils rejected the proposal by 15 votes to eight, but on the other hand there was a majority in favour of votes for women, whose voices otherwise went unheard. It may be remarked as a matter of curiosity that during the debates at the joint meeting the belief was voiced in a number of quarters that it would be exclusively women who would be elected to the local councils!

At the same time as the Greenlanders were continuing their deliberations over the issue, Denmark itself manifested its interest. *Bodil Begtrup*, who was then president of the Danish Women's National Council and also a member of the Danish delegation to the United Nations in New York, brought the question up, and at her prompting the Danish delegation proposed a motion to the effect that as a matter of human rights every member-state should introduce political rights for women: this was carried. On her return home Bodil Begtrup made approaches to the Greenland Administration, the Prime Minister's office and other quarters, and as the Greenlanders had already established, it proved possible to settle the matter by royal decree. By that time the Greenland provincial councils had voted by a large majority to recommend full political rights for women, and the royal decree was promulgated in 1948.

Women were able to use their vote for the first time in the local elections of 1951, when the women of Godthåb put up a woman candidate who was elected. This was *Guldborg Chemnitz*, an interpreter, who has been a consultant on feminist questions and is now director of the Greenland Educational Association. She has acted as chairman of the special Greenland Committee of the Danish Commission on the Status of Women in Society. The Committee has published three bilingual books on feminism in Greenland which are now used in connection with the educational work done

289

under her direction. Guldborg Chemnitz is a member of the Danish Equal Status Council, has been associated with social research in Greenland and among many other accomplishments has done much to foster understanding between Greenland and Denmark.

After the first local government election the number of women in local administration grew slowly: it had reached 16 by 1971 and 20 by 1975, which is equivalent to 12 % – the same proportion as was achieved by Danish women in the local elections of 1974. In addition, three of the 18 Greenland local authorities had women mayors. Thus women have done well in the local political sphere.

Developments have been less favourable in the field of provincial council elections and elections to the Danish Parliament, in which Greenland is represented by two Members under the terms of the constitutional amendment of 1953. Up to now only one woman, *Elisabeth Johansen*, a midwife, has achieved membership of the provincial council: this was in 1959 and from then until her retirement she acquitted herself with distinction, one of the issues in which she interested herself being the explosive language question. No woman has yet been a Member of Parliament, but two have acted as deputies to male Members.

There are a number of women on various committees and boards. There are no social welfare or child welfare committees without women members, and it is very common in the villages for the midwife to be a member. Women also make their mark on development committees, housing committees and local government consumers' committees. Of the committees and boards appointed by the provincial council, women are to be found for example on the appeals committee dealing with child welfare matters, the consumers' board, the social welfare board and the radio management board. Two of the district judges appointed by the high court on the recommendation of the local authorities are currently women, and there are ten female assessors in the district courts and one in the high court.

The central executive committee of GAS, the *Grønlandske arbejdersammenslutning* (Greenland Federation of Labour) had a solitary woman member for ten years, but at the present time there is none, although there are women on local executive committees of GAS sections. The Federation's section for business and office workers has many young women on its executive, and these clashed with the Federation's central executive committee in the mid-1970s when they formulated demands for higher pay and greater efficiency of the organisation. Some women in factories are foremen, and quite a few have been elected as shop stewards by their workmates.

The Greenland cooperative societies have an association managed by an executive committee of three, one of whom is a woman. The seven cooperative stores have a total of 45 members on their executive committees, including ten women.

The development of true political parties is a relatively new phenomenon in Greenland, and as far as can be judged women have not so far taken any notable part in the process. But that they are playing a prominent role in democratic growth and its representative institutions is beyond dispute.

Women's Associations

The first women's association began functioning in the same year that women received political rights. Its aims were "to bring together the women of Godthåb for mutual assistance and training in domestic matters, and to stimulate interest in public affairs". A further aim was added later: "... and to promote the ancient craft of Greenland sealskin workers". The club called itself the Housewives' Association at first, and indeed the dissemination of housekeeping skills was a matter of concern in an age when the traditional Greenland diet was being modified, especially in the urban centres, to include more and more imported items. This process had been under way for a long time but accelerated after the war simultaneously with a decline in the sealing industry that was causing a move away from a subsistence to a cash economy. Diet remains a problem of current concern in Greenland, as is testified by the poor dental standard.

The Federation of Danish Housewives' Society had close links from the outset with the Greenland women's associations and are still in close touch with them. The Society makes collections of money every year to support the work of the clubs. In recent years a substantial portion of this money has gone to the home economics and continuation school opened at Holsteinsborg in the summer of 1977. A number of local Danish societies are twinned with associations in Greenland, and it is customary for the Greenland women's clubs to be represented at the societies' annual national conference.

Another important sphere of cooperation between Greenland and Danish women's associations comprises the programme of courses begun by the Danish Women's Society in 1964. A special Greenland committee has been working in concert with the Greenland women's associations since 1960 and endeavouring to assist them in various ways, while the programme of courses is organised jointly with the Greenlanders. Selection of women to take part in the courses is done by the local women's associations and local authorities. The courses take place every other year and most of them are held in Denmark, though there are some in Greenland. The most vital aim has been to train women to play a part in community affairs, including of course political life. In addition, 17 courses have been held in Denmark for young Greenlanders receiving education in Denmark.

There are now about 60 local women's associations with about 1,600 members. They established links with one another in 1960, and they are affiliated to the Danish Women's

National Council. Their informational activities have been of great importance, but they are concerned over the fact that too few young people are involved in the work. A prominent feature of their activities has been the spreading of information concerning family planning, and this topic has been on the agenda of all the courses run in collaboration with the Danish Women's Society.

The women's associations applied to the Ministry for Greenland Affairs in 1964 for an experienced doctor to be sent to Greenland as they considered the diffusion of knowledge of family planning to be urgently needed. As a result, a woman doctor was despatched to Greenland and travelled from town to town along the coast, delivering lectures and demonstrating birth control devices. The Mothers' Aid organisation was brought into this information work as well. A couple of years later a Danish specialist in family planning visited a chief physician in Greenland and while there had meetings with the provincial council, which set up a committee of three men to submit recommendations as to measures to be taken. But this committee did not hold a single meeting during an entire four-year term of the provincial council. The subject was one on which not everyone wanted voices to be raised too loudly, and among older people there was even anger at its being mentioned at all. They considered it interference in the private life of the individual. But the women's associations were now working in concert with the provincial doctor and the local doctors, who instructed midwives and obstetricians in how to pass on the necessary knowledge to women.

A committee was formed jointly with the Danish Women's Society at the beginning of the 1970s to launch a publicity campaign all over Greenland with the specific purpose of spreading knowledge of the broader aspects of family planning. The committee, in concert with the Greenland Educational Association, arranged courses in northern, central and southern Greenland and a seminar in Godthåb, with high attendance everywhere. One topic discussed in the courses was the possibility of introducing free abortion, and many of those taking part held public meetings on the subject in their home districts afterwards. The provincial council went along with the idea, though with some misgivings, and free abortion was adopted in 1975.

The women's associations have been active in many other fields, including that of housing, on which three seminars have been held jointly with specialist organisations. They have also run a form of adult education through mothers' clubs. One particular form taken by this has been the holding of meetings in the afternoons for housewives with young children, the latter being looked after by members of the women's associations. Educational events of various kinds have been held: lectures, films, slide shows and sometimes instruction in food preparation.

The many and varied activities of the women's associations have made a positive contribution to the development of Greenland in an era when immense changes are in progress in virtually every economic and social field.

The Trend of Population – and the Uncertain Future

The population of western Greenland was counted in 1803, a figure of 6,000 being arrived at. The population has increased since that time though rather slowly during the last century, partly because of epidemics with high mortality rates, especially influenza epidemics. About 11,000 people were living in western Greenland in 1901, about 17,000 in 1941 and about 30,000 in 1962. The last of these figures includes just under 3,000 Greenlanders living at that time in northern and eastern Greenland. This population explosion, bringing about a situation where about half the people of the country were under 15 years of age, has now ended, and numbers seem to be stabilising themselves for the moment at around 40,000. There are in addition about 9,000 persons not born in Greenland, most of them from Denmark.

This sharp growth is attributable to a steep decline in mortality from 27 per 1,000 inhabitants in 1921 to 7.8 in 1960 and 7.0 in 1976, and to an increase in average life expectancy of males from 32.2 years in 1946–51 to 60.7 in 1971–75, and of females from 37.5 to 66.2 years. One reason for this is the effectiveness of countermeasures against the ravages formerly inflicted by tuberculosis. At the same time the birth rate maintained a high level until the 1960s. In 1960 itself it ran at 49 births per 1,000 population; in 1965 it was 44, in 1970 25 and in 1976 17.3. The decline is to be seen as resulting from deliberate measures to limit births, and in fact investigation has shown that almost all women who have had a child outside wedlock and who do not wish to become pregnant use birth control devices, generally the coil.

The large numbers of single mothers constitute a special problem. Childbirths outside wedlock rose rapidly in the 1950s and 1960s, and the mothers of about 70 % of first-born children are unmarried. However, a large proportion of these are living with the child's father, and marriage frequently ensues; but some of the mothers do not have any established relationship with the child's father. In former times an unmarried mother remained in her parents' home and was helped by them, while now she receives help from public funds and is entitled to a contribution from the father in connection with the birth itself and towards the maintenance of the child. She has the opportunity of an apartment of her own and of having the child looked after in an institution if she has a job. This development forms a vital point of difference between the present cultural pattern and that of the ancient seal-hunting community in which it was the family's role to meet all of its members' needs. This partial loosening of family bonds broadly mirrors the trend observable all over the industrialised world.

The profound and rapid changes that have occurred in Greenland society since the Second World War have been brought about by measures of intervention in conformity with the policy evolved by Denmark in concert with the Greenlanders themselves. It has been based mainly on the idea of encouraging the population to concentrate in the larger centres and of fostering the fishing industry, since reduced numbers of seals and a partial subsistence economy could no longer sustain the existence of the population. Even as late as 1950 the life of the people of Greenland was austere, harsh and plagued by sickness.

But life in the towns has brought its own entirely novel problems. Vandalism, children's gangs, theft and the misuse af alcohol were unknown in former days, and although the child welfare and criminal care services do what they can to patch up these consequences of the modern way of life in Greenland, their efforts meet with only moderate success. A referendum was held on the alcohol problem and resulted in the introduction on 1 April 1979 of a form of rationing. But some local authorities have found it necessary to introduce actual temporary bans on spirits in order to secure attendance at work in busy periods.

Greenland's problems are immense and numerous. Natural conditions are harsh and capricious. The fisheries are subject to unpredictable fluctuations, and few other productive occupations are available. Sealing and other forms of hunting still play a part, and a little sheep-rearing goes on in south Greenland. There is some mining and a little tourism. There may be some scope for the establishment of new small-scale industries and mines, and perhaps oil will be found off the east coast of Greenland, but nature in the Arctic is exceedingly sensitive to the brutal assaults of technology. The status of women will naturally be determined by the way in which economic life develops.

A referendum in January 1979 led to the adoption of the principle of home rule, which accordingly commenced being introduced gradually from 1 May 1979. Women were not elected to the assembly. It is to be hoped that the home rule will give the people of Greenland more real independence and a greater sense of responsibility, so that both sexes will have greater opportunities of strengthening their faith in themselves as a people capable of preserving its own identity in the future.

Index

The letters *æ*, *ø*, *å* (in that order) follow z in the Danish alphabet and entries containing these special Danish vowel signs are alphabetized accordingly; *aa* is identical with *å*.

The Index includes a great number of names of organisations, institutions, commissions, societies, etc. As a general rule, these entries are alphabetized under the principal distinguishing word of the title (which is often the more restrictive element), e. g., Country World Women, Association of; Women Artists, Society of; Danish Government Home Economics Council.

301

303

mittee of the Ministry of Agriculture (Landbrugsministeriets Produktivitetsudvalgs Husholdningsudvalg), 163

Home Economics Teachers' Association (Husholdningslærerforeningen), 124, 152

Home Guard (Hjemmeværnet), 145

Home Rule Commission, 213 f.

Hostrup, Jens Christian (1818–92) clergyman and author, 75

Human Rights Commission of the European Parliament, 180, 198

Håkon (1340–80) king of Norway, 28

IWA = International Alliance of Women, earlier known as International Women's Suffrage Alliance *(q.v.)*

Ibsen, Henrik (1828–1906) Norwegian dramatist and poet, 99

ICW – see International Council of Women

ILO – see International Labour Organisation

Independent Women's Society (Den frie kvindelige forening), 90

Individual and Society organisation (Individ og Samfund), 279

Innocent VIII's bull of 1484, pope, 32

International Council of Women (ICW), 115, 116, 117, 125

International Labour Organisation (ILO), 125, 244

International Women's Conference, Copenhagen – see United Nations

International Women's Conference, Mexico City, 123

International Women's Day of Struggle (8 March 1980), 274 f.

International Women's League for Peace and Freedom, 117, 118

International Women's Suffrage Alliance (IWSA) established in 1904; later known as the International Alliance of Women (IAW), 135

Jelling, runic stones of, 20, 23

Jensen, Ella (b. 1907) president of the Tobacco Workers' Union 1963–75, 223

Jensen, Fanny (1890–1969) Minister without Portfolio, 196 f.

Jensen, Thit (1876–1957) authoress, 41 f., 164, 177 f.

Jeppe, Karen (1876–1935) active in relief work for Armenian women and children after the First World War, 118

Joan Sisterhood, 273

Johansen, Elisabeth (b. 1907) Greenland midwife and former member of the provincial council, 290

June Constitution of 1849, 79

Jutlandic Law of 1241 (provin-

cial legal code), 18, 24, 26, 27, 40

Kalmar Union (Scandinavian union of 1397), 28 f.
Kennedy, John F., Commission on women, 208
Koch, Bodil (1903–72) theologian; was Minister of Ecclesiastical Affairs and subsequently of Cultural Affairs, 195, 197, 278
Kold, Christen (1816–70) educationist, 105
Kollontaj, Alexandra (1872–1952) Russian feminist, 192
Krag, J. O. (1914–1978) statesman, 208

Labour Housewives' Society (Arbejdernes Husmoderforening), 166
Ladelund Agricultural College, 150
Larsen, Aksel (1897–1972) Communist Party chairman 1932–58; co-founder of the Socialist People's Party, 197
Larsen-Ledet, Camma (b. 1915) mayor, 200
Laundresses and Charwomen, Union of (Foreningen for Vaske- og Rengøringskoner), 96
Lauridsen, Magdalene (1873–1957) pioneer in the field of Home Economics, 151 f., 165, 166
League of Jewish Women, 118

League of Martha (Marthaforbundet), 167
League of Nations, 118, 120
Lehmann, Orla (1810–70) politician, 85 f.
Lemche, Gyrithe (1866–1945) editor of the periodical "Woman and Society", 138 f., 178, 191
Leonora Christine (1621–98) daughter of king Christian IV, 53
Lesbian Movement, 274
Lind, Nathalie (b. 1918) lawyer and former Cabinet Minister, 200
Louise (1817–98) Danish queen, 103
Low Incomes Commission, 246 f.
Luplau, Line (1823–1891) founded the Women's Suffrage Association, 127, 128, 130, 131
Luther, Martin (1483–1546) German reformer, 31

Malt District Home Economics Association (Malt Herreds Husholdningsforening), 151, 153, 165
Margrethe (1353–1412) queen of Denmark, 28 f., 53
Marriage, Commission (1909–13) on Nordic matrimonial legislation, 227
Marriage Ordinance of 1582, 23
Mary, the Virgin, 31

305

Skåne code (provincial legal code), 27
Social Democratic Women's Union (Socialdemokratisk Kvindeforening), 140
Soroptimist International Association, 124
Sorø Folk High School, 151
Sorø School of Home Economics, 151
Sorø Teacher Training College, 152
Staël, Madame de (1766–1817) French writer, 74
Starcke, C. N. (1858–1926) politician and professor of philosophy, 98
Stauning, Thorvald (1873–1942) statesman, 192
Student's Union, 110
Svend Aggesøn (12th c.) historical writer, 20f.
Svend Estridsøn (d. ca. 1074) king of Denmark, 18f., 27
Sweyn Forkbeard (d. 1014) king of Denmark, 22
Swift, Jonathan (1667–1745) Irish satirist, 51

Tacitus, Caius Cornelius (d. ca. A.D. 120) Roman historian, 11, 13ff.
Tailoresses' Trade Union (De Kvindelige Herreskræderes Fagforening), 95, 127, 132
Tenants' Organisation, The National (Lejernes Landsorganisation), 173

Theresienstadt (concentration camp), 119
Thilde's Children (Thildes børn) named after Mathilde Fibiger, 245, 279, 280f.
Thorbæk, Jytte (b. 1939) lawyer, 202
Thott, Birgitte (1610–62) noblewoman and translator of Seneca, 50
Tobacco Workers' Union, 223
Tor (Norse deity; the rolling of his chariot was supposed to cause the thunder), 23
Tuborg Breweries, 96
Tyra, Danish queen, wife of Gorm, 20f.

United Nations (UN), 120, 125
    Commission on Women (1976–80), 120, 218
    Danish delegation, 289
    Economic Commission for Europe, 218
    Educational, Scientific, and Cultural Organisation (UNESCO), 125
    General Assembly, 120
    International Women's Year (1975), 123, 211
    Women's Conference (Copenhagen, July 1980), 218
Unity (Enigheden), the cigarmakers' trade union of 1871, 92f.
University Graduates, Central Organisation of (Akademikernes Centralorganisation), 173

What can we learn from one another?

Aim and work of the Danish Institute

Det danske Selskab, The Danish Institute is an independent non-profit institution for cultural exchange between Denmark and other countries. Abroad its aim is to inform other countries about life and culture in Denmark, particularly in the field of education, welfare services and other branches of sociology; at home to help spread knowledge of cultural affairs in other countries. Its work of information is thus based on the idea of mutuality and treated as a comparative study of cultural development at home and abroad by raising the question: What can we learn from one another? The work of the Danish Institute is done mainly in three ways:

1) By branches of the Danish Institute abroad – in Great Britain (Edinburgh), the Benelux countries (Brussels), France (Rouen), Switzerland (Zürich), Italy (Milan), West Germany (Dortmund) and its contacts in the USA and other countries. Lectures, reference work, the teaching of Danish, exhibitions, concerts, film shows, radio and television programmes as well as study tours and summer schools are an important part of the work of representatives of the Institutes that have been established abroad.

2) Summer seminars and study tours both in Denmark and abroad. Participants come from Denmark and other countries. The study tours bring foreign experts to Denmark and take Danish experts abroad. Teachers, librarians, architects and persons engaged in social welfare and local government make up a large part.

3) Publication of books and reference papers in foreign languages. Primary and Folk High Schools in Denmark, the library system, welfare services, cooperative movement, handicrafts, architecture, literature, art and music, life and work of prominent Danes are among the main subjects.

The author Martin A. Hansen called the Danish Institute a Folk High School beyond the borders: "In fact the work of the Danish Institute abroad has its roots in our finest traditions of popular education, which go right back to Grundtvig and Kold. The means and methods used are modern, the materials the very best and the approach to the work is cultural in the truest meaning of the word."

DET DANSKE SELSKAB

*The Danish Institute for Information about Denmark and
Cultural Cooperation with other Nations*

KULTORVET 2, DK-1175 COPENHAGEN, DENMARK

Publications in English:

DANISH INFORMATION HANDBOOKS

Schools and Education – The Danish Folk High Schools –
Special Education in Denmark – Public Libraries in Denmark
– Social Welfare in Denmark – Local Government in Denmark – The Danish Cooperative Movement – Women in Denmark

DENMARK IN PRINT AND PICTURES

The Danish Church – Danish Architecture – Danish Painting
and Sculpture – Danish Design – Industrial Life in Denmark
– The Story of Danish Film – Sport in Denmark – Garden
Colonies in Denmark – Copenhagen, Capital of a Democracy
– Aarhus, Meeting Place of Tradition and Progress – The
Limfjord, its Towns and People – Funen, the Heart of Denmark

DANES OF THE PRESENT AND PAST

Danish Literature – Contemporary Danish Composers – Arne
Jacobsen, by P. E. Skriver – Søren Kierkegaard, by Frithiof
Brandt – N. F. S. Grundtvig, by Kaj Thaning

DANISH REFERENCE PAPERS

The Danish Mothers' Aid Centres – Employers and Workers –
The Ombudsman – Care of the Aged in Denmark

PERIODICALS

Contact with Denmark. Published annually in English,
French, German, Italian, Netherlandish.
Musical Denmark, nos. 1–31. Published annually in English.